Supervision That Improves Teaching

Second Edition

Supervision That Improves Teaching

Second Edition

Strategies and Techniques

Susan Sullivan / Jeffrey Glanz

Foreword by Jo Blase

CORWIN PRESS
A Sage Publications Company
Thousand Oaks, California

For information:

Corwin Press
A Sage Publications Company
2455 Teller Road
Thousand Oaks, California 91320
www.corwinpress.com

Sage Publications Ltd.
1 Oliver's Yard
55 City Road
London EC1Y 1SP
United Kingdom

Sage Publications India Pvt. Ltd.
B-42, Panchsheel Enclave
Post Box 4109
New Delhi 110 017 India

Printed in the United States of America

Library of Congress Cataloging-in-Publication Data

Sullivan, Susan, 1943-
Supervision that improves teaching : strategies and techniques / by Susan Sullivan and Jeffrey Glanz.—2nd ed.
    p. cm.
Includes bibliographical references (p.   ) and index.
ISBN 0-7619-3968-7 (cloth)—ISBN 0-7619-3969-5 (pbk.)
    1. School supervision—United States. 2. Teacher effectiveness—United States.
3. Effective teaching—United States. I. Glanz, Jeffrey. II. Title.
LB2806.4.S85 2005
371.2′03—dc22   2004008122

This book is printed on acid-free paper.

05   06   07   08   10   9   8   7   6   5   4   3

Acquisitions Editor:	Robert D. Clouse
Editorial Assistant:	Jingle Vea
Production Editor:	Kristen Gibson
Copy Editor:	Jackie Tasch
Typesetter:	C&M Digitals (P) Ltd.
Indexer:	Sheila Bodell
Cover Designer:	Tracy E. Miller
Graphic Designer:	Anthony Paular

Contents

Foreword to the First Edition

When my oldest daughter was about four, she offered the following explanation of her misbehavior on a particular day: "I know what I'm supposed to do, Mommy. I just can't do it." In the jargon of educational administration, she was experiencing a dichotomy between theory and practice. This gap is, and has been, a serious concern with respect to supervisory practice.

Sullivan and Glanz maintain that "supervision is central to the renewal of classroom teaching and learning." Research supports this position. Done well, supervision can enhance teaching practice in ways that empower teachers and facilitate student learning. The supervisory literature is extensive and includes models that are conceptually sound and empirically tested: We know what works and how to do it. Unfortunately, we also know that the practice of supervision often falls far short of this goal. What we know from the research on supervision is that feedback, as the authors suggest, plays a critical role in the supervisory process. Whether or not any positive change occurs depends primarily on the quality of feedback that is provided. This aspect of the process is most important and also most neglected. Studies, for example, report that teachers want and need feedback about their work but seldom receive the type of information that enables them to strengthen or improve their own performance. Although teachers are more likely to receive "prescriptive" feedback, the type of feedback that supports personal growth and development is descriptive feedback (Osterman, 1994). Rather than judgments about their work or prescriptions on how to improve, teachers need descriptions of their practice and its effects on students. They also need the opportunity to assume personal responsibility for their performance and participate in designing modifications.

The types of strategies that Sullivan and Glanz highlight in their text are designed to improve the quality of feedback that supervisors provide. The techniques they describe are not unique, but the authors' presentation is. Not only do they provide information about various techniques that improve the quality of feedback, they also provide a learning framework based on principles of constructivism and reflective practice that facilitate understanding as well as application.

Reflective practice and constructivism share a common set of beliefs about learning (Osterman, 1999) that are reflected in the structure of this text. First is the belief that learning is an active process that requires student engagement. Learning is the ultimate responsibility of the learner, and the role of the instructor is to facilitate growth by focusing inquiry, engaging students, exploring and challenging ideas, and providing resources. The second belief is that ideas influence action. Through experience, people develop theories about how the world works, and these theories shape their behavior. Learners construct their own knowledge, building on prior experiences. Accordingly, students must have opportunities to articulate and represent their knowledge. The third important belief is that learners construct knowledge through experience, particularly problematic experience. Pedagogically, then, it is necessary to build conceptual conflict by challenging current understanding and providing opportunities to develop and test new ways of thinking and acting.

This text very admirably incorporates these principles. Each section poses problems to engage and challenge the learner. Realistic cases illustrate the relationship between beliefs and practice and describe the personal and organizational obstacles that perpetuate bureaucratic practices. Reflective activities in each section raise challenging questions, stimulate interest, and encourage the articulation and critical assessment of personal beliefs. The text also provides for development of skills through a series of progressively challenging activities. Initially, learners experiment with strategies in a supportive classroom environment. The second step involves testing the new strategy again in the work setting. Each of these activities develops skill, but, more important, the actual experimentation establishes the validity of the specific technique and builds confidence in the learner's ability to use the strategy effectively.

In constructivism and reflective practice, in contrast to more traditional educational models, the relationship between teacher and learners is that of a partnership based on common goals to improve practice rather than on hierarchical differences related to presumed differences in expertise. The structure of the text facilitates dialogue and creates a climate of openness. The language of the text is accessible. The tone is personal, warm, respectful, and collegial. The authors share responsibility for learning with the readers, presuming that the readers are intelligent, informed, and capable. If the readers don't understand Bloom's taxonomy, the authors recommend that they gain that information before proceeding. They also invite learners to supplement the text with their own suggestions and, in fact, use creative strategies suggested by their own students. These are empowering strategies that support the learning process and model the ideas about supervision that they espouse.

In contrast with the "inspection" and evaluation model that too often characterizes school supervision, the supervisory process envisioned by Sullivan and Glanz is collaborative rather than hierarchical, dialogic versus didactic, descriptive rather than judgmental, and supportive rather than punitive. This is a major shift from the more predominant inspection and evaluation model, but it is not a new paradigm, Even though it is appealing and even convincing, bringing about change in the practice of supervision is no easy task. To do so, to align action more closely with theory, involves more than simply presenting a range of feasible and effective strategies. According to Argyris and Schon (1974), ideas like these will be integrated into practice only when existing theories and patterns of behavior are identified, explored, challenged, and modified. This theoretical premise has important implications for learning. If the learning process is to be effective, its learning goals must extend beyond the mere transference of knowledge to incorporate the appropriate and effective application of knowledge.

Normally, the challenge to facilitate the application of ideas rests on the shoulders of the instructor. This text provides the information, and the instructor provides the pedagogical expertise. Here, Sullivan and Glanz have developed a text that not only provides information but more importantly engages the readers in a reflective process of observation, analysis, and experimentation designed to facilitate behavioral change. By extending well beyond the normal scope of a text and exploring dimensions of belief and practice in the context of schools and leadership, the authors provide a valuable resource. Use of this text—the learning strategies and the supervisory techniques—should support a realization of the book's stated purpose: the development of educational leaders who are able to engage in supervision designed to improve the quality of learning.

Karen F. Osterman
Hofstra University

REFERENCES

Argyris, C., & Schon, D. A. (1974). *Theory in practice: Increasing professional effectiveness.* San Francisco: Jossey-Bass.

Osterman, K. F. (1994). Feedback in school settings: No news is bad news. *Journal of Management Science, 6*(4), 28–44.

Osterman, K. F. (1999). Using constructivism and reflective practice to bridge the theory/practice gap. *Educational Leadership and Administration: Teaching and Program Development Journal, 2,* 9–20.

Foreword to the Second Edition

*Powerful Tools, Techniques, and Strategies
for Promoting Instructional Excellence*

When *Supervision That Improves Teaching* debuted, authors Susan Sullivan and Jeffrey Glanz had no foreboding of the events of 9/11, a faltering economy, or the global terrorism that would grip this nation and the world, nor could they have anticipated the disturbing effects on American education of these and other pressures—not the least of which has been the demand for standards-based reform of schools.

Lately, I've begun to fantasize about reforming the reformers. It's not that I disagree with standards and achievement; rather, I worry that related pressures have spawned undue focus on standardized tests as well as deliberate and narrow teaching to the standards. Even to an unsophisticated mind, this scarcely appears an adequate formula for school improvement. For some educators, the rhetoric of reform has evolved into a shrill and infernal nuisance. As a dizzying array of wrongheaded mandates and vehicles designed to control educators proliferates, teachers' creativity, experimentation, and participation in the democratic and professional goals of schools diminish. And, like fuel to the flame, some practitioners stubbornly persist in "pretending not to know what we know" about teaching and learning (Glickman, 1991).

Clearly, the pressure on educators for accountability for results, in concert with high stakes testing, demands an innovative form of supervision, one that spawns genuine communication, mutual support and respect, and openness to experimentation among educators. Fortunately, in this standards-based environment, and in the wake of President Bush's signing of the No Child Left Behind Act of 2001, Sullivan and Glanz have conceived of a new breed of supervisor—not an overseer, but a colleague who sits on the same side of the table with teachers, guiding, facilitating, and collaborating with them. In this second edition of *Supervision That Improves Teaching*, Sullivan and Glanz have deftly addressed accountability, flexibility, and the emphasis on proven teaching methods. No longer are hardworking teachers pitted against stressed administrators, pitted against other teachers, and pitted against constituents—difficulties that the field of supervision, originally known as inspection, has had to overcome in the nearly three hundred years since its inception. In addition, the authors sensibly dissociate observation from evaluation, and they intelligently admit the limits of observations. The core theme of the book is skillfully suggested by their apprehension about some supervision models currently being touted as effective and their dearth of research-based, empirically proven strategies and techniques.

In this new edition, Sullivan and Glanz have shrewdly adapted and simplified Glickman, Gordon, and Ross-Gordon's (2004) observation techniques. They have extended the options for observation tools well beyond, for example, the constructivist child-centered leaning and the nonverbal techniques tools presented in the first edition to a thorough but manageable set of tools for a standards-based environment (e.g., strategies for diverse learners, indicators of accountable talk in classrooms); indeed, this new section provides a heretofore unaddressed but critical update for prospective and practicing instructional leaders. The authors' bank of case studies and implementation guidelines for alternative approaches deftly supports instructional leaders to empower teachers and to encourage their critical reflection and professional growth.

In essence, Sullivan and Glanz's reflective clinical supervision model encourages and prepares educators (i.e., supervisors and teachers) to be thoughtful collaborators in the business of improving classroom instruction; in doing so, they honor the complexity of life in classrooms. Wisely, the authors recommend limiting the four-stage reflective clinical supervision cycle to one focus at a time, a principle that undoubtedly struck a chord with worried practitioners reading the first edition. Interestingly, the faintest gradations of change in our practice lend more logic to our conduct, and we hear echoes of intelligent and prudent pioneers in the field of supervision.

I sense very strongly the authors' urgency and passion; devoted in every beat of their hearts to the cause of educating our children, Sullivan and Glanz enthusiastically champion and brighten the way to developing thoughtful, reflective, dynamic conversations about learning between and among all educators. They posit and illuminate the path to respectful dialogue between and among educators—a dialogue plainly distant from the interactions we have witnessed between checklist-wielding bosses and powerless teachers—and they ask no more than to be allowed to share their thinking with us, to ignite the fires of our own passions. Finally, Sullivan and Glanz raise the question of the future of the field, urging all of us to proceed to our destination. We have a chance to put off our differences, to replace the practices we deplore, and to take on a nobler, more humanistic synergy. Certainly, what grows out of all of this is a vision of a new, transfigured era of supervision, a vision we should all have no intention of giving up.

Jo Blase
University of Georgia, Athens

REFERENCES

Glickman, C. (1991). Pretending not to know what we know. *Educational Leadership, 48*(8), 4–10.

Glickman, Gordon, & Ross-Gordon (2004). *SuperVision and instructional leadership: A developmental approach.* Boston: Allyn & Bacon.

Preface to the Second Edition

Supervision is and always will be the key to the high instructional standards of America's public schools.

Spears, 1953, p. 462

Supervision That Improves Teaching: Strategies and Techniques is intended as a practical guide to the varied and alternative approaches to supervision that aim to improve classroom instruction. We believe that supervision, as a dynamic process that facilitates dialogue to promote instructional improvement, is central to the renewal of classroom teaching and learning in the new century. Rather than merely describing and explaining varied models of supervision, this book presents the reader with research-based and empirically tested strategies and techniques.

By offering an overview of approaches for instructional improvement and some specific supervisory strategies, this volume encourages the reader to develop her or his own supervisory platform or personal principles of practice. The main feature of this text is the hands-on development of essential supervisory skills.

This text, meant for use in undergraduate and graduate courses on instructional improvement and for use by individuals in leadership positions in schools, has some unique features that set it apart from similar works. The text, designed to be user friendly, provides examples of summary sheets and observation charts as well as "crib sheets" to enhance review and actual use in the classroom. Throughout each chapter are reflective microlabs and other activities designed to reinforce new material and concepts.

Why is a book of this nature important? In an era in which supervision as a field and practice is being attacked, sometimes vociferously, those individuals who argue that supervision is vital to instructional improvement must remain vigilant to preserve the best that supervision has to offer. With the continual emphasis on student outcomes and state and national standards, supervision is, more than ever, an indispensable link that inspires good teaching and promotes student learning. We believe that when teachers are encouraged to reflect on their teaching and when individuals with supervisory responsibilities engage teachers in conversations about classroom instruction, the stage for instructional improvement is set.

This book, along with other publications, such as *The Handbook of Research on School Supervision; Educational Supervision: Perspectives, Issues, and Controversies; Handbook of Instructional Leadership: How Really Good Principals Promote Teaching and Learning; Mentoring and Supervision for Teacher Development; Differentiated Supervision; SuperVision and Instructional Leadership: A Developmental Approach; Interpersonal and Consultant Supervision Skills; Cognitive Coaching; Instructional Supervision: Applying Tools and Concepts,* and *Approaches to Clinical Supervision,* indicates the resurgence and attention given to supervision. We believe that such attention is not only warranted, but necessary so that the integrity of instructional improvement within classrooms across America and around the world will be maintained. Although scholars may busy themselves with philosophical intricacies or theoretical nuances about the viability and definition of supervision, practitioners know too well how important effective supervision is for maintaining and encouraging instructional excellence.

A number of critical assumptions about supervision underlie this work. First and foremost, although supervision as a function and a process may not have been fashionable or "pedagogically correct," we maintain that its primary aim is to assist teachers in improving instruction. As long as this purpose remains of vital importance, we believe that supervision can remain a potent force toward promoting instructional excellence in schools. Moreover, the goal of supervision is to facilitate the process of teaching and learning through a multitude of approaches that can encompass curriculum and staff development, action research, and peer, self-, and student assessment.

This text follows a logical and orderly progression, all the while encouraging the reader to understand the changing context of supervision and to develop requisite knowledge, skills, and dispositions about supervision. It culminates in the development of a personal supervisory platform and offers suggestions for a collaborative plan for supervision.

Chapter 1 provides a historical and theoretical framework for supervision. This foundation, along with an initial belief inventory **that should be completed before reading the chapter** and again at the end of the course, permits the reader to begin laying the groundwork for a personal supervisory platform.

The next chapter introduces basic interpersonal tools for initiating and providing feedback on classroom observations. The reader is introduced to "crib sheets" to practice feedback dialogue between professionals and for use on site. The theory and practice of reflection in action, a crucial tool for self-reflection and assessment, is also introduced. Chapter 3 reviews sample classroom observation tools and techniques in a way that allows readers to practice them in the college classroom and on site and to develop this essential skill. In Chapter 4, the previously learned observation tools and techniques and feedback approaches are integrated into the clinical supervision cycle framework. Opportunities for practice and simulations precede recommendations for site-based initiation.

Chapter 5 presents six alternative approaches to supervision currently in practice. Authentic case studies introduce each approach, followed by a definition and suggested steps for implementation. The final chapter, the culmination of the learning process, encourages readers to create their own personal supervisory platform, that is, a personal theory or principles of practice. In addition, this chapter includes a guide to facilitate the development of a collaborative site vision and plan for supervision.

In sum, this book reviews the supervisory strategies and techniques necessary for future educational leaders so that they can promote teaching and learning, the essence of what "good" supervision is really all about.

Acknowledgments

We thank our graduate students at the College of Staten Island and at Kean University for allowing us to develop various ideas of this book with them and for offering useful feedback.

Susan Sullivan would like to thank David Podell, the Provost and Vice President for Academic Affairs at the College of Staten Island, for his ongoing support in all of her academic endeavors. She would also like to express appreciation to the faculty and administration of Ditmas Intermediate School, in Brooklyn, New York, and, in particular, Nancy Brogan, Lynne Pagano, Elke Savoy, Madeline Castaneda, and Nasreen Farooqui for their willingness and enthusiasm in developing a peer coaching model in the International Institute at their school. Eric Nadelstern and Carmen Farina and their staffs were models not only in the development of alternatives to traditional supervision, but in their proactive open sharing of their successes and challenges. Karen Osterman of Hofstra University introduced the world of reflective practice to Susan and continues to reflect with her on teaching and intellectual endeavors.

Susan Sullivan would like to dedicate this book to her daughters, Mara, Alene, and Elena, for their supportive love and for providing the opportunity to try out all her interpersonal skills as they grew to young adulthood.

Jeffrey Glanz would like to acknowledge his colleagues in the Council of Professors of Instructional Supervision (COPIS) for stimulating, over the years, many of the ideas in this volume. Special thanks to Bert Ammerman, Principal, and Jim McDonnell, Vice Principal, of Northern Valley Regional High School District for their innovative work, which formed the basis for some of the case studies in Chapter 5.

Jeffrey Glanz would like to dedicate this volume to his father, may peace be upon him, because he taught him the value of education and urged him to achieve his potential.

About the Authors

 **Susan Sullivan** received her BA from Elmira College, her MAT from The Johns Hopkins University, and her MEd and EdD from Teachers College, Columbia University. She served as an instructor in the Department of Romance Languages of The Johns Hopkins University for 10 years and as a teacher and administrator in Baltimore, Maryland; Rome, Italy; and the New York City area. She is currently Chair of the Department of Education of the College of Staten Island, The City University of New York.
She was Coordinator of the Program in Educational Administration and continues to teach graduate courses in supervision of instruction and educational leadership. Her current research interests center on reflective practice, the role of the school district in systemic change, and of course, supervision of instruction and its alternatives. In addition to their staff development book, *Supervision in Practice,* she and Jeffrey Glanz are writing a book on learning communities for Corwin Press. She has also published in journals such as *Journal of School Leadership, Journal of Curriculum and Supervision Development, Education and Urban Society,* and *Educational Leadership and Administration: Teaching and Program Development Journal.*

 **Jeffrey Glanz** received his BA from the City University of New York and his MA and EdD from Teachers College, Columbia University. He is currently Dean of Graduate Studies and Chair of Education at Wagner College in Staten Island, New York. He formerly served as Executive Assistant to the President of Kean University in Union, New Jersey. He also served as an administrator and teacher in the New York City public schools for 20 years.
As a full professor in the Department of Education at Wagner College, he teaches graduate courses in action research, quantitative methods, and curriculum. He served for four years on the editorial board of the *Journal of Curriculum and Supervision.* He also served as editor of *Focus on Education,* the New Jersey journal for the Association for Supervision and Curriculum Development. He was Director of the Instructional Supervision Network for the Association for Supervision and Curriculum Development. Glanz is the author of *Bureaucracy and Professionalism: The Evolution of Public School Supervision,*

Action Research: An Educational Leader's Guide to School Improvement, Relax for Success: A Guide for Educators, and *Finding Your Leadership Style,* as well as the coeditor of *Educational Supervision: Perspectives, Issues, and Controversies* and *Paradigm Debates in Curriculum and Supervision: Modern and Postmodern Perspectives.* Dr. Glanz has two other books that have been published recently with Corwin: *Teaching 101: Classroom Strategies for the Beginning Teacher* and *The Assistant Principal's Handbook: Strategies for Success.*

A Brief Note
to Instructors

We are certain that this text can be used in many effective ways in your classroom or in your school. We would like to highlight some of the strategies that we have found most successful in developing supervisory and interpersonal skills. Detailed instructions for several of these strategies are provided in the text. We know that you will think of additional suggestions and hope that you will share your ideas with us.

1. *Journal writing.* Encourage students to reflect on their and others' class and site supervisory experiences in a personal journal. Reflections on supervisory practices that the students observe in their buildings and in other schools are invaluable in forming their own beliefs. The suggested *reflections* in the text also can be thought out in the journal. Students can choose to share journal entries online to solicit feedback on their ideas.

2. *Microlabs.* As explained in the Microlab Guidelines in Resource A, the Microlab permits individualized collegial sharing, while at the same time developing reflective and nonjudgmental listening skills. Groups of three to five people address two to four questions suggested in the text or inspired by students or instructor. Small group and whole class debriefing ties thoughts together, promotes more ideas, and brings closure to the process.

3. *The fishbowl.* This process can be used to discuss the ideas generated in small groups within a large-group setting. Representatives from each small group form a circle in the middle of the room and share the ideas generated in the small groups while the rest of the class listens and observes. We also use the fishbowl to allow volunteers to model feedback approaches for the rest of the class. The class learns the approach and at the same time serves as observers of the process. Directions for this approach are provided in Resource B.

4. *Videotaping or audiotaping.* We strongly encourage the use of video- and audiotapes of classroom and site practices, particularly of the planning and feedback conferences. The tapes can be used in two ways: They can

be part of the actual assignment and graded, or they can be used for the students' own learning; the knowledge that the tapes will not be shared with instructors or colleagues may increase their authenticity and acceptance.

5. *Intervisitation.* In all of our work with teachers, aspiring administrators, and practicing leaders, we have found that intervisitation within schools, between schools, and between districts plays a crucial role in creating a climate for growth. The opportunity to see the practices and models explained in a text is "worth a thousand words." Professionals see the ideas in practice, "it works," and can ask questions and debrief after the visit, reflecting on what they think might or might not work for them.

6. *E-mail and the Internet.* One of the most effective ways to involve all students in dialogue and reflection is through e-mail, Internet discussion boards, and chat rooms. These electronic sites can include some students who are more comfortable with the written than the spoken word. You can assign pairs of students to discuss *reflections* on e-mail, and you can set up a discussion board or chat room through school or college media centers. Microlabs can be assigned on the discussion board, and students can share experiences and challenges with their colleagues. The whole realm of the Internet also is available to enrich discussion and knowledge.

7. *Distance learning and the virtual classroom.* The precise descriptions and directions for site practice and the companion video facilitate the use of this book for distance learning and the virtual classroom. In the distance learning classroom, students can practice the role plays and receive feedback from their colleagues and professors. The use of videotapes or DVDs for site assignments can provide the instructor with direct knowledge of the students' practice and progress. In the virtual classroom, videos and DVDs replace the university classroom experience. In addition, all of the other technological resources—that is, e-mail, discussion board, and the Internet among others—enrich learning and discussion in the virtual classroom. See Resource C for further information.

8. *Supervision in practice.* The professional development text that we have written, *Supervision in Practice,* can also serve as an instructional aid and a tool for students to turnkey the techniques and strategies they learn. Overheads and a detailed description of cycles of workshops are useful to instructors and students.

We have included most of the preceding suggestions in more detail in the text and in the Resources. Most chapters are replete with suggestions for reflections, microlabs, and class and site practices that expand on these ideas and offer others.

1

The Changing
Context of Supervision

Democracy can provide the direction, goals, purposes, and standards of conduct that our profession and society desperately need. Clinical supervision can provide the means of translating democratic values into action, while strengthening teachers' teaching skills, conceptual understanding and moral commitment.

Pajak, 2000, p. 292

Note: *Before* you begin reading this chapter, please complete the questionnaire in Appendix 1-A, which begins on page 36.

Supervisory practice has evolved since its origins in colonial times, and its effectiveness as a means of improving instruction depends on the ability of educational leaders to remain responsive to the needs of teachers and students. An educational leader's resolve to remain adaptable also depends on an appreciation of the changing and evolving nature of supervision, especially in the new millennium. An educational leader who understands the history of supervision and how current demands are influenced by that history will be better able to confront the technological, social, political, and moral issues of the day. Educational leaders also will have to develop the requisite knowledge, skills, and dispositions that are the foundation for effective supervisory practice. This chapter explicates how supervision has evolved to its current state, how you might respond to ever-increasing supervisory needs and demands, and how your beliefs and attitudes affect how you react to daily challenges.

SUPERVISION SITUATION

Arlene Spiotta was recently appointed vice principal of Regional Valley High School, where she has worked as a teacher for three years. An affable, popular teacher, Arlene had been a teacher at Westfield High School, located in a neighboring township, for eight years. Prior to that, she was a teacher for five years in two schools in another state. She recently earned her supervisory certification and master's degree in administration and supervision at a local college.

Although Arlene received a warm welcome on the opening day of school in September, she noticed that teachers on the grade levels she supervises react much differently to her now. In one instance, she was passing the room of a former teacher-colleague, Linda Evans, who at the time was at her desk, assisting a student. When Linda noticed Arlene looking into the classroom, she stiffened in her chair and abruptly sent the pupil back to his desk. After receiving a stern and cold stare, Arlene proceeded down the hallway to her office. Arlene wondered why her colleague Linda acted so differently when she saw her now.

REFLECTION

Why do you think Linda reacted to Arlene the way she did? What factor(s) may have contributed to this situation? What dilemma is she facing in her new role?

Arlene Spiotta took for granted the fact that she was now in a position very different from that of Linda Evans. Although they were former colleagues and friends, Arlene was now a supervisor. As a supervisor, she was expected to assist and evaluate her former colleagues.

Linda Evans, on seeing Arlene apparently staring into the classroom (an assumption, we might add, that may or may not have been accurate), reacted as she had previously to other supervisors for whom she had worked. Her former supervisors were overbearing bureaucrats who looked for evidence of teacher incompetence at every turn.

Arlene, too, may have been influenced by what she considered to be behavior "expected" of a supervisor; that is, daily patrol or inspection of the hallways. After all, not only had Arlene been certified and trained as a supervisor in a state that mandates that all teachers be formally observed at least twice a year (eight times for nontenured teachers), but as an experienced teacher (of how many years? Right, 16), she had been exposed to many supervisors who had conducted themselves in very autocratic and bureaucratic ways.

REFLECTION/MICROLAB

What are some examples of how supervisors might act in "very autocratic and bureaucratic ways"? How have your former supervisors shaped your conception of what supervision is all about? How have significant ideas, events, and people influenced or informed your current practice?

SOURCE: See Resource A for microlab guidelines. Set up an Internet discussion board and/or chat room through your school or university library to exchange reflections and hold electronic microlabs. Also, choose an e-mail partner and share reflections via e-mail between classes.

Had Arlene been cognizant of how past practices of supervision can affect current relationships between teachers and supervisors, she might have tried more earnestly to establish a spirit of mutual understanding and cooperation.

REFLECTION

How might Arlene establish this "spirit of mutual understanding and cooperation"?

One of the authors recalls a time when he confronted a similar situation and the difficulty he had in circumventing expected supervisory roles. An excerpt from Jeffrey's diary is instructive:

My first appointment as an assistant principal was at P.S. "Anywhere, USA." I arrived at the school in September. My predecessor's reputation was there to greet me.

Mr. Stuart Oswald Blenheim was known as a stickler for every jot, tittle, and iota inscribed in the Board of Ed's rules and regulations. He carried a tape measure, a portable tape recorder, and a stethoscope, and considered teachers to be one of the lower forms of sapient life. The others were nonprofessional staff members and students—in "descending" order.

This supervisor made his opinions abundantly clear by word and deed. Woe to the pupil caught wandering the halls without appropriate documentation. No excuses accepted. Period. End of message.

Furthermore, the offending miscreant's pedagogue was called on the carpet; raked over the coals; strung up by the thumbs; and subjected to a wide variety of other abusive clichés.

Stuart Oswald was short; so short that it was difficult to see him among a group of eighth or ninth graders. He took full advantage of his camouflage, so that he could spy on his charges. He was known to walk up quietly to a room, place his stethoscope to the door, and gradually straighten his knees and stand on his toes so as to see through the small glass window. Teachers were constantly on the lookout for a bald head rising in their doors' windows.

Any teacher who observed this latter-day Napoleon lurking in the halls was honor-bound to pass the information on to his or her neighbors. A note referring to "Pearl Harbor," "Incoming Scud Missiles," "Sneak Attack," or "Raid's Here" was enough to raise blood pressure and churn digestive juices.

Last spring, he was appointed as principal in a school on the other side of the city.

Such was Blenheim's repute that all the teachers whom I supervised avoided my presence like the very plague. On one occasion, I passed by a room and noticed a teacher caringly assisting a pupil at her desk. Suddenly, the teacher "felt" my presence, quickly straightened her posture, and proceeded nervously to the front of the room to resume writing on the board. I walked away bewildered. However, after ascertaining that I did not suffer from halitosis, dandruff, or terminal body odor, I realized the problem. Honestly, I couldn't blame them. After all, Blenheim's initials suited him perfectly.

Thus, I was forced to overcome these habits of fear and distrust and, somehow, to win my teachers' and students' trust.

During my first meeting with my teachers, I asked rather than told them not to think of me as their supervisor. I hoped that they would consider me a colleague with perhaps more experience and responsibility in certain areas. I wanted to work with them and learn about their own expertise, knowledge, interests, and ideas. . . . I was not going to spy on them. I was not going to humiliate them. I was a real human being, just like they were, just like the children were.

They had a difficult time accepting this. They had been abused for seven years by a petty tyrant and did not believe that any AP could think differently. After all, Blenheim had been rewarded for his fine methods. This had to be the AP road to promotion.

I promised that there would be no sneak attacks. We would do our best to cooperate and learn together. I would share my experiences and readily seek their expertise and ideas so that they could be effective teachers.

It took three to six months of hard work on my part and caution on theirs, but we've finally reached the point where we smile at each other when we meet in the hall. Several of them have come to me with professional and personal problems. They were a bit surprised at some of my proposed solutions. The word got around that Blenheim was really gone.

Stuart Oswald is, of course, a caricature of an autocratic supervisor who occupied the position Jeffrey Glanz assumed many years ago. Yet, the essential message is clear: Autocratic methods in supervision still prevail, and if changes are to be made, then understanding the antecedents for such practices is necessary. To understand the changing context of supervision, a brief excursion into the history of supervision is necessary.

THE VALUE OF HISTORY

History can be understood as an attempt to study the events and ideas of the past that have shaped human experience over time; doing so informs current practice and helps us make more intelligent decisions for the future. How are prevailing practices and advocated theories connected to the past? How is what you currently do influenced, in any way, by previous practices and theories of supervision? How can an understanding of the past help us practice supervision today?

Our intention in this chapter is to indicate that past supervisory theory and practice influence what we believe about supervision and how we carry out our work with teachers and others. This chapter will help you identify your belief systems related to supervisory practice and how these beliefs are connected to the history of supervision. This identification will lay the initial foundation for the construction of a supervisory platform.

Guidelines for the creation of your own initial "personal vision statement" are a special feature of this chapter. As we indicate, what you believe about teaching and learning, for example, inevitably affects how you approach the practice of supervision. Subsequent chapters will encourage you to develop a "personal supervisory platform" that builds upon your personal vision statement.

REFLECTION/MICROLAB

Who or what in your personal or professional background influenced your present supervisory beliefs? What are some positive supervisory experiences you have encountered? What are some negative supervisory experiences you recall? Why did you feel that way? What does supervision look like in your school?

Site Practice

Activity 1. The following exercise has been adapted from Glickman, Gordon, & Ross-Gordon (1998).

1. Prepare five questions to ask two school supervisors about their beliefs and practices in relation to improvement of classroom instruction. Write a brief report including the questions and responses and your reflections on each supervisor's answers. Describe consistencies and inconsistencies in the responses and compare the supervisors' actual practices to the responses given. Do they "walk the talk"? Compare the

two supervisors' responses and reflect on the similarities and differences between their answers.

or

2. Ask two supervisors and two teachers what they consider to be the five most important tasks of instructional supervision. Write a brief report including a script of their responses. Analyze each interview. Reflect on the differences and similarities in their answers. Compare the teachers' responses with those of the supervisors and reflect on your findings. Do the supervisors "walk their talk"?

Activity 2. Shadow a supervisor of instruction for one day or on a few days when the supervisor is observing classes.

1. Provide a detailed log of the supervision of instruction that you observed. You may include *any* activities that you feel were related to supervision of instruction.

2. Describe the supervisory approaches and the process that the supervisor used.

3. What was effective in what you observed? Why? How will these effective practices improve classroom instruction? What did the teacher(s) learn?

4. Were there supervisory practices that need improvement? Why? What would you do differently?

5. What else do you think might help improve classroom instruction?

Final reflections.

THE HISTORICAL CONTEXT

Supervision has medieval Latin origins and was defined originally as "a process of perusing or scanning a text for errors or deviations from the original text" (Smyth, 1991, p. 30). Later recorded instances of the word *supervision* established the process as entailing "general management, direction, control, and oversight" (see, e.g., Grumet, 1979). An examination of early records during the colonial period indicates that the term *inspector* is referenced frequently. Note the definition of supervision in Boston in 1709:

> Be there hereby established a committee of inspectors to visit ye School from time to time, when and as oft as they shall think fit, to Enform themselves of the methodes used in teaching of ye Schollars and to Inquire of their proficiency, and be present at the performance of some of their Exercises, the Master being before Notified of their Coming, And with him to consult and Advise of further Methods for ye Advancement of Learning and the Good Government of the Schoole. (Reports of the Record Commissions of the City of Boston, 1709)

The inspectors were often ministers, selectmen, schoolmasters, and other distinguished citizens. Their methods of supervision stressed strict control and close inspection of school facilities. As Spears (1953) explained, "The early period of school supervision, from the colonization of America on down through at least the first half of the nineteenth century, was based on the idea of maintaining the existing standards of instruction, rather than on the idea of improving them" (p. 14).

American schooling, in general, during the better part of the 19th century, was rural, unbureaucratic, and in the hands of local authorities. The prototypical 19th-century school was a small one-room schoolhouse. Teachers were "young, poorly paid, and rarely educated beyond the elementary subjects"; teachers were "hired and supervised largely by local lay trustees, they were not members of a self-regulating profession" (Tyack & Hansot, 1982, p. 17). These local lay trustees (called ward boards) who supervised schools were not professionally trained or very much interested in the improvement of instruction (Button, 1961).

The tradition of lay supervision continued from the American Revolution through the middle of the 19th century or, as commonly referred to, the end of the common era. Despite the emergence during this period of a new "American system of educational thought and practice . . . the quality of supervision would not improve appreciably" (Tanner & Tanner, 1987, p. 10). With the advent of a district system of supervision and then state-controlled supervision beginning in the late 19th century, however, the character of supervision did, in fact, change dramatically.

REFLECTION

School supervision originally referred to a procedure in which someone would "examine" a teacher's classroom "looking for errors." What impact or significance, if any, does this original meaning or intention of supervision have for you as a supervisor today?

Supervision in the Late Nineteenth Century

In general, unprecedented growth precipitated by the industrial revolution characterized the second half of the 19th century. The expansion of American education, which had started in the days of Horace Mann, whom Tanner and Tanner (1987) characterized as the "first professional supervisor," continued and assumed a new dimension in the latter decades of the 19th century. The schoolmen, specifically superintendents, began shaping schools in large cities into organized networks. Organization was the rallying cry nationally and locally. There was a firm belief that highly organized and efficient schools would meet the demands of a newly born industrialized age. That hierarchically organized public schools, as social institutions, would meet the crises and challenges that lay ahead was beyond doubt (Bullough, 1974; Cronin, 1973; Hammock, 1969; Kaestle, 1973; Lazerson, 1971).

The reform movement in education in the late 19th century was reflective of the larger, more encompassing changes that were occurring in society. Although rapid economic growth characterized the 19th century, reformers realized that there were serious problems in the nation's schools. In the battle that ensued to reorganize the nation's schools, sources of authority and responsibility in education were permanently transformed (Tyack, 1974). By the end of the 19th century, reformers concerned with undermining inefficiency and corruption transformed schools into streamlined, central administrative bureaucracies with superintendents as supervisors in charge. Supervision, during this struggle, became an important tool by which the superintendent legitimized his existence in the school system (Glanz, 1991). Supervision, therefore, was a function that superintendents performed to oversee schools more efficiently.

Supervision as inspection was the dominant method for administering schools. Payne (1875), author of the first published textbook on supervision, stated emphatically that teachers must be "held responsible" for work performed in the classroom and that the supervisor, as expert inspector, would "oversee" and ensure "harmony and efficiency" (p. 521). A prominent superintendent, James M. Greenwood (1888), stated emphatically that "very much of my time is devoted to visiting schools and inspecting the work." Three years later, Greenwood (1891) again illustrated his idea of how supervision should be performed: The skilled superintendent, he said, should simply walk into the classroom and "judge from a compound sensation of the disease at work among the inmates" (p. 227). A review of the literature of the period indicates that Greenwood's supervisory methods, which relied on inspection based on intuition rather than technical or scientific knowledge, were practiced widely.

Supervisors using inspectional practices did not view favorably the competency of most teachers. For instance, Balliet (1894), a superintendent from Massachusetts, insisted that there were only two types of teachers: the efficient and the inefficient. The only way to reform the schools, thought Balliet, was to "secure a competent superintendent; second, to let him 'reform' all the teachers who are incompetent and can be 'reformed'; thirdly, to bury the dead" (pp. 437–438). Characteristic of the remedies applied to improve teaching was this suggestion: "Weak teachers should place themselves in such a position in the room that every pupil's face may be seen without turning the head" (Fitzpatrick, 1893, p. 76). Teachers, for the most part, were seen by 19th century supervisors as inept. As Bolin and Panaritis (1992) explained, "Teachers (mostly female and disenfranchised) were seen as a bedraggled troop—incompetent and backward in outlook" (p. 33).

The practice of supervision by inspection was indeed compatible with the emerging bureaucratic school system, with its assumption that expertise was concentrated in the upper echelons of the hierarchy. Many teachers perceived supervision as inspectional, rather than a helping function.

Because supervision as inspection through visitation gained wide application in schools, it is the first model that characterizes early methods in supervision (see Table 1.1, Model 1).

Our brief examination of early methods of supervision indicates that (1) amid the upheavals of late 19th-century America, supervision emerged as an important function performed by superintendents and (2) inspectional practices dominated supervision.

REFLECTION/MICROLAB

What vestiges of inspectional supervisory practices remain today? To what extent do you or others you know function as "inspectors"? How do you feel about that? Would you feel comfortable "inspecting" classrooms? Why or why not? Do certain conditions in your school/district exist that invoke an "inspectional mind-set"? Explain.

The Emergence of the Distinct Position of Supervisor

In the first two decades of the 20th century, schooling grew dramatically. As the size and complexity of schools increased, greater administrative specialization was readily apparent. Supervisors gained in stature and authority in the early 20th century. In addition to the building principal, a new cadre of administrative officers emerged to assume major responsibility for day-to-day classroom supervision. Two specific groups of supervisors commonly were found in schools in the early 20th century (see Table 1.1).

First, a *special supervisor,* most often female, was chosen by the building principal to help assist less experienced teachers in subject matter mastery. Special supervisors were relieved of some teaching responsibilities to allow time for these tasks, but no formal training was required. Larger schools, for example, had a number of special supervisors in each major subject area.

Second, a *general supervisor,* usually male, was selected to deal not only with more general subjects such as mathematics and science, but also to "assist" the principal in the more administrative, logistical operations of a school. The general supervisor, subsequently called *vice principal* or *assistant principal,* prepared attendance reports, collected data for evaluation purposes, and coordinated special school programs, among other administrative duties.

Differences in functions between special and general supervisors were reflective of prevalent 19th-century notions of male-female role relationships. William E. Chancellor (1904), a prominent 19th-century superintendent, remarked, "That men make better administrators I have already said. As a general proposition, women make the better special supervisors. They are more interested in details. They do not make as good general supervisors or assistant superintendents, however" (p. 210). Representative of the bias against women in the educational workplace were notions espoused by William H. Payne (1875): "Women cannot do man's work in the schools" (p. 49). Payne, like many of his contemporaries, believed that men were better suited for the more prestigious and lucrative job opportunities in education.

It also interesting to note that teachers readily accepted special supervisors. Special supervisors played a very useful and helpful role by assisting teachers in practical areas of spelling, penmanship, and art, for example. In addition,

Table 1.1 Timeline

	Pre-1900	1900-1919	1920s
Social/cultural markers	**1880** Edison devises first electric light; Gilbert & Sullivan's *Pirates of Penzance* **1890** Jacob Riis's *The Children of the Poor*; Vincent van Gogh dies **1892** Walt Whitman dies; Gentleman Jim Corbett beats John L. Sullivan for heavyweight boxing title	**1900** First magnetic recorded sound; Addams's Hull House; McKinley assassinated **1903** Ford Motor Company founded **1906** San Francisco Earthquake (700 killed; cost $4,000,000 in damages) **1912** Titanic sinks; Jim Thorpe (American Indian) won gold at Olympics **1914-1915** First moving assembly line **1917** Tolstoy dies; Stravinsky's *Firebird Concerto*; Dubois founds NAACP; World War I **1918** *Dewey's Democracy and Education* **1919** 19th amendment ratified; Prohibition; Red scare (Palmer Raids)	**1921-1923** President Warren G. Harding **1923** Babe Ruth sold to the NY Yankees by the Red Sox; Buber's *I & Thou* **1923-1928** President Calvin Coolidge **1924** Quotas set for immigrants in America **1925** The Roaring 20s; Chaplin's *The Gold Rush* KKK very active during this period Amelia Earhart, first woman to fly the Atlantic Ocean **1928-1932** President Herbert Hoover
Models of supervision	Supervision as inspection: Model 1 Payne–Greenwood–Balliet	Supervision as social efficiency: Model 2 Taylor–Bobbitt	Democracy in supervision: Model 3 Dewey–Hosic–Newlon

1930-1950		1960s	
1930 Grant Wood's *American Gothic*	**1945** FDR dies; Hiroshima and Nagazaki–Japan surrenders	**1960-1963** JFK President	Civil rights movement; Martin Luther King and Stokely Carmichael
1932 Roosevelt elected President	**1947** Al Capone dies; Public television	**1961** Bay of Pigs	Malcolm X
1933 Hitler appointed German Chancellor	**1948** Joe Louis retires; Truman elected President	**1962** Eleanor Roosevelt dies	Black Panthers
1934 Popular song *Brother Can You Spare a Dime?*; the Depression; Einstein's *My Philosophy*	**1948-1952** Marshall Plan	**1963** JFK assassinated by Lee Harvey Oswald	Ceasar Chavez
1935 Social Security Act; Wagner Act	**1949** U.S. tests first hydrogen bomb Computers developed	**1964** Cassius Clay—heavyweight champion; The Beatles; Civil Rights Act includes gender	American Indians begin violent protests of 50% unemployment rate and life expectancy 2/3 that of whites
1936 Carnegie's *How to Win Friends & Influence People*	**1950s-1991** Cold War	**1964-1975** Vietnam War	Hippie movement
1939 John Steinbeick's *Grapes of Wrath*; Television debut; World Fair	**1951** Alger Hiss, traitor; Color TV	**1965** Head start; Malcolm X assassinated	Marijuana sales soar
1939-1945 World War II Dust Bowl Golden age of mystery novel Roosevelt's Fireside chats	**1952** McCarthy "witch hunts"; Einstein dies; Vaccine for polio	**1967** Thurgood Marshall appointed to Supreme Court	LSD introduced
1941 Huxley's *Brave New World*; Lou Gehrig dies; Pearl Harbor; Penicillin; Rocky Graziano, Boxer of the Year	**1953** Stalin dies	**1968** RFK & Martin Luther King assassinated	Draft
1941-1944 Eisenhower commands troops in Europe	**1955** Rosa Parks	**1969** Mets—World Series Champs; Woodstock; Neil Armstrong walks on the moon	
1942-1946 Japanese sent to internment camps	**1957** Sputnik		
	1959 Alaska and Hawaii become 49th and 50th states, respectively; Fidel Castro takes over Cuba; Ian Fleming's *Goldfinger* Sen. Joseph McCarthy accuses alleged communists in army Communism		

Scientific supervision:
Model 4

Burton–Barr–Stevens

Supervision as leadership:
Model 5

Leeper

(Continued)

Table 1.1 (Continued)

1970-1980	1990s	2000-Present
1964-1975 Vietnam War	**1992, 1996** Clinton elected President	**2000** Dot com collapse; stock market crisis begins
1971 Apollo XIV launched; U.S. bombs North Vietnam	**1989-1990** Collapse of Communism	**2001** WTC and Pentagon attacks
1972 Fischer beats Spaasky	**1991** Bosnian genocide; Rodney King beating	**2002** Gary Condit scandal; sniper shootings; Enron, Worldcom, and FBI scandals
1973 Watergate; Agnew resigns; Abortion (Roe vs. Wade)	**1992** Los Angeles riots; World Wide Web born	**2003** Space shuttle Columbia explodes
1974 Nixon resigned	**1993** Terrorist bombing of WTC garage	Al Qaeda shown to the world
1976 Rozak's *Making of a Counterculture*; Carter elected President	**1994** Crises in Somalia, Bosnia, Yugoslavia	Bush popularity
1979 Noble Prize—Mother Theresa	**1995** OJ Simpson murder trial; Oklahoma City bombing— Timothy McVeigh	Focus on Iraq
1979-1981 Wayne Williams kills 23 black children	**1998** Clinton impeached	Saddam Hussein captured
1980 Reagan elected President;	**1999** School shootings	**2004** Madrid terrorist bombings
1981 Piaget dies; O'Conner—first female Supreme Court Justice; Hostages released after 444 days in Iran	Tiananmen Square	Iraq prison abuse scandal
	Rise of rap music	50th anniversary of Brown v. Board of Education
	Proliferation of the Internet and Web access	
1985 Crack introduced	Healthcare crisis	
1985-1990 Cocaine addiction up 35%	Social security reform	
1986 Challenger exploded	Gun control	
1987 Black Monday—Stock Market Crash	Booming economy	
"Just say no" campaign	Cellphones	
Clinical supervision: Model 6	Changing concepts: Model 7	Standard-based supervision: Model 8
Goldhammer—Cogan	Glickman—Sergiovanni	

12

these special supervisors did not have any independent authority and did not serve in an evaluative capacity, as did, for example, the general supervisor, who was given authority, albeit limited, to evaluate instruction in the classroom. Therefore, teachers were not likely to be threatened by the appearance of a special supervisor in the classroom. General supervisors, on the other hand, were concerned with more administrative and evaluative matters and, consequently, were viewed by the classroom teachers as more menacing. Special supervisors also probably gained more acceptance by teachers, most of whom were female, because they too were female. General supervisors were almost exclusively male and perhaps were perceived differently as a result. Frank Spaulding (1955), in his analysis of this period of time, concurred and stated that general supervisors "were quite generally looked upon, not as helpers, but as critics bent on the discovery and revelation of teachers' weaknesses and failures, . . . they were dubbed Snoopervisors" (p. 130).

The position of the special supervisor did not, however, endure for a very long period in schools. General supervisors gradually usurped their duties and responsibilities. The relative obscurity of special supervisors after the early 1920s can be attributed to discrimination based on gender. As a group comprising an overwhelming number of females, special supervisors were not perceived in the same light as were general supervisors, principals, assistant superintendents, and superintendents, who were, of course, mostly male. Gender bias and the sexual division of labor in schools go far toward explaining the disappearance of the special supervisor as such.[1] In short, general supervisors gained wider acceptance simply because they were men.

REFLECTION

How does gender affect your role and function as a supervisor today? Explain and provide an example.

Supervision as Social Efficiency

Numerous technological advances greatly influenced American education after 1900. As a result of the work of Frederick Winslow Taylor (1911), who published a book titled *The Principles of Scientific Management*, "efficiency" became the watchword of the day. Taylor's book stressed scientific management and efficiency in the workplace. The worker, according to Taylor, was merely a cog in the business machinery, and the main purpose of management was to promote the efficiency of the worker. Within a relatively short period of time, *Taylorism* and *efficiency* became household words and ultimately had a profound impact on administrative and supervisory practices in schools.

Franklin Bobbitt (1913), a professor at the University of Chicago, tried to apply the ideas that Taylor espoused to the "problems of educational management and supervision" (p. 8). Bobbitt's work, particularly his discussion of supervision, is significant because his ideas shaped the character and nature of supervision for many years. On the surface, these ideas appeared to advance professional supervision, but in reality they were the antithesis of professionalism. What Bobbitt called "scientific and professional supervisory methods" (page 9) were, in fact, scientistic and bureaucratic methods of supervision aimed not at professionalizing but at finding a legitimate and secure niche for control-oriented supervision within the school bureaucracy.

In 1913, Bobbitt published an article titled, "Some General Principles of Management Applied to the Problems of City-School Systems," which presented 11 major principles of scientific management as applied to education. Bobbitt firmly held that management, direction, and supervision of schools were necessary to achieve "organizational goals." Bobbitt maintained that supervision was an essential function "to coordinate school affairs. . . . Supervisory members must co-ordinate the labors of all, . . . find the best methods of work, and enforce the use of these methods on the part of the workers" (pp. 76, 78). The employment of scientific principles in supervision, said Bobbitt, is a necessity for the continued progress of the school system.

Many supervisors were eager to adopt Bobbitt's ideas of scientific management for use in schools. However, a few did not readily accept his views. One of the more vociferous opponents of Bobbitt's ideas was James Hosic (1924), a professor of education at Teachers College, Columbia University. Hosic contended that Bobbitt's analogy was largely false:

> Teaching cannot be "directed" in the same way as bricklaying. . . . In education, the supervisor's function is not to devise all plans and work out all standards and merely inform his co-workers as to what they are. . . . [The supervisor] should not so much give orders as hold conferences. . . . His prototype is not a captain, lieutenant, or officer of the guard in industry, but chairman of committee or consulting expert. (pp. 82-84)

Despite Hosic's criticism, schoolmen of the day readily adopted the business model, as evidenced by William McAndrew (1922), who said about his role as supervisor in the school, "I am the captain of big business" (p. 91).

The criticisms against Bobbitt's methods, nonetheless, accurately stressed a number of disturbing ideas. First and foremost was the ill-conceived notion that "education in a school" is analogous to "production in a factory." Bobbitt claimed that "education is a shaping process as much as the manufacture of steel rails." Supervisors in the early 20th century were becoming aware of the fallacy of this logic as well as realizing the negative effects of bureaucracy in education. Bobbitt's "scientific management and supervision" found justification within a school organization that was bureaucratically organized.

Still, it remains clear that the significance of Bobbitt's work was in his advocacy of scientific and professional supervisory methods. Supervisors thought that their work in schools would be more clearly defined and accepted by adopting Bobbitt's principles of scientific management. Supervisors believed, as did

Bobbitt, that "the way to eliminate the personal element from administration and supervision is to introduce impersonal methods of scientific administration and supervision" (p. 7). This was often translated into rating schemes. In a short time, supervision became synonymous with teacher rating.

In sum, just as "supervision as inspection" reflected the emergence of bureaucracy in education, so too "supervision as social efficiency" was largely influenced by scientific management in education (see Table 1.1, Model 2). Supervision as social efficiency was compatible with and a natural consequence of bureaucracy in education.

REFLECTION

How do business practices affect schools today? How might these practices influence supervision? What is the difference between efficiency and effectiveness?

The Emergence of Democratic Methods in Supervision

Bureaucratic supervision, relying on inspectional methods and seeking efficiency above all else, dominated discourse in the field from 1870-1920. This sort of supervision attracted much criticism from teachers and others (Rousmaniere, 1992). Representative of the nature of this opposition were the comments of Sallie Hill (1918), a teacher speaking before the Department of Classroom Teachers, decrying supervisory methods of rating. Hill charged:

> There is no democracy in our schools. . . . Here let me say that I do not want to give the impression that we are sensitive. No person who has remained a teacher for ten years can be sensitive. She is either dead or has gone into some other business. . . . There are too many supervisors with big salaries and undue rating powers. (p. 506)

The movement to alter supervisory theory and practice to more democratic and improvement foci, while at the same time minimizing the evaluative function, occurred in the 1920s as a direct result of growing opposition to autocratic supervisory methods (see Table 1.1, Model 3). Consequently, supervisors tried to change their image as "snoopervisors" by adopting alternate methods of supervision. The following poem, quoted in part, indicates the desired change of focus to more democratic methods in supervision:

> With keenly peering eyes and snooping nose,
> From room to room the Snoopervisor goes.
> He notes each slip, each fault with lofty frown,
> And on his rating card he writes it down;
> His duty done, when he has brought to light,
> The things the teachers do that are not right . . .

The supervisor enters quietly, "What do you need?
   How can I help today?
John, let me show you. Mary, try this way."
He aims to help, encourage and suggest,
That teachers, pupils all may do their best.

Anonymous, 1929

Influenced in large measure by Dewey's (1929) theories of democratic and scientific thinking as well as by Hosic's (1920) ideas of democratic supervision, supervisors attempted to apply scientific methods and cooperative problem-solving approaches to educational problems (Pajak, 2000). Hosic cautioned the supervisor to eschew his "autocratic past": "The fact that he is invested for the time being with a good deal of delegated authority does not justify him in playing the autocrat. . . . To do so is neither humane, wise, nor expedient" (pp. 331, 332). Continuing to build a philosophic rationale for the supervisor's involvement in "democratic pursuits," Hosic explained that it was no longer viable to apply techniques of the past. Hosic believed, as did Dewey, that it was possible to reshape a school system that had originated with the idea of bureaucratic maintenance so that it would comply with the principles of democracy.

Democratic supervision, in particular, implied that educators, including teachers, curriculum specialists, and supervisors, would cooperate to improve instruction. Efforts by prominent superintendent Jesse Newlon reinforced democracy in supervision. In an article titled "Reorganizing City School Supervision," Newlon (1923) asked, "How can the ends of supervision best be achieved?" He maintained that the school organization must be set up to "invite the participation of the teacher in the development of courses." The ends of supervision could be realized when teacher and supervisor worked in a coordinated fashion. Newlon developed the idea of setting up "supervisory councils" to offer "genuine assistance" to teachers. In this way, he continued, "the teacher will be regarded as a fellow-worker rather than a mere cog in a big machine" (pp. 547–549). Participatory school management and supervision had their origins in the work of Newlon.

REFLECTION

What other factors do you think led to the emergence of democratic supervision during this era? What does democratic supervision mean to you?

Scientific Supervision

In the 1930s and 1940s, educators believed that autocratic supervisory practices were no longer viable. They urged more scientific approaches to supervisory practice in schools. The early attempts to apply science via rating cards were now losing favor. Burton (1930), a prolific writer in supervision, explained that the use of "rating schemes from our prescientific days, . . . would be wholly inadequate today." Although Burton recognized the usefulness of rating in some instances, he believed that "it is desirable and rapidly becoming possible to have more objectively determined items by means of which to evaluate the teacher's procedure" (p. 405).

One of the foremost proponents of science in education and supervision was A. S. Barr (1931). He stated emphatically that the application of scientific principles "is a part of a general movement to place supervision on a professional basis." Barr stated in precise terms what the supervisor needed to know:

> Supervisors must have the ability to analyze teaching situations and to locate the probable causes for poor work with a certain degree of expertness; they must have the ability to use an array of data-gathering devices peculiar to the field of supervision itself; they must possess certain constructive skills for the development of new means, methods, and materials of instruction; they must know how teachers learn to teach; they must have the ability to teach teachers how to teach; and they must be able to evaluate. In short, they must possess training in both the science of instructing pupils and the science of instructing teachers. Both are included in the science of supervision. (pp. x, xi)

Barr said the supervisor should first formulate objectives, followed by measurement surveys to determine the instructional status of schools. Then, probable causes of poor work should be explored through the use of tests, rating scales, and observational instruments. The results of supervision, continued Barr, must be measured. Most important, according to Barr, the methods of science should be applied to the study and practice of supervision. More concretely, Barr (1925) asserted that a scientific analysis of teaching is a necessary part of the training of a supervisor: "How can the scientific knowledge of the teaching process be brought to bear upon the study and improvement of teaching?" Barr contended that teaching could be broken down into its component parts and that each part had to be studied scientifically. If good teaching procedures could be isolated, thought Barr, then specific standards could be established to guide the supervisor in judging the quality of instruction. He based his scientific approach to supervision "upon the success of the professional student of education in breaking up this complex mass into its innumerable elements and to study each objectively" (pp. 360, 363).

Throughout the 1930s, 1940s, and 1950s, the idea that supervision involves improving instruction based on classroom observation gained momentum. Supervision as a means of improving instruction through observation was reinforced by the use of "stenographic reports," which were the brainchild of Romiett Stevens, a professor at Teachers College, Columbia University. Stevens thought that the best way to improve instruction was to record verbatim accounts of actual lessons "without criticism or comment." Stevens's stenographic accounts were "the first major systematic study of classroom behavior" (Hoetker & Ahlbrand, 1969).

Supervisors during this era advocated a scientific approach toward their work in schools (see Table 1.1, Model 4). Scientific supervision was considered to be distinct from social efficiency and entirely compatible with democratic practices (Dewey, 1929). Burton and Brueckner (1955) claimed that "a few individuals still speak, write, and supervise as if science and democracy were antagonistic, or at least not easily combined. The truth is that each is necessary in an integrated theory and practice" (p. 82).

REFLECTION

Do you concur with Barr that teaching can be studied scientifically? How do you think stenographic reports were used? How could they be used today? How is teaching analyzed today?

Supervision as Leadership

Democratic and scientific supervision continued well into the 1950s. Democratic methods in supervision, however, clearly were expanded and clarified in the 1960s in the form of supervision as leadership (see Table 1.1, Model 5).

The political and social upheavals resulting from the urban plight, concerns for justice and equality, and antiwar sentiments dramatically affected education—and supervision, in particular. Virulent criticisms of educational practice and school bureaucracy were pervasive (e.g., Silberman's *Crisis in the Classroom*, 1970). Educators also took a serious look at supervisory practices in schools. The legacy of supervision as inspection that found justification in the production-oriented, social efficiency era was no longer viable. Bureaucratic supervision was not viable either. A new vision for the function of supervision was framed.

The work most representative of the 1960s was undoubtedly the anthology of articles that originally appeared in *Educational Leadership*, compiled by then-Editor and Associate Director of the Association for Supervision and Curriculum Development, Robert R. Leeper (1969). Leeper and the authors of this anthology maintained that supervisors must extend "democracy in their relationships with teachers" (p. 69). The way to accomplish this was to promulgate supervision as a leadership function.

Harris (1969) expressed the ideals of supervisory leadership this way:

The word *leadership* refers to showing the way and guiding the organization in definitive directions. New leadership is needed in this sense of the word. Two kinds are required:

1. Those in status positions must lead out with new boldness and find better ways of influencing the schools toward rationally planned, timed change.

2. New leadership positions must be created, and coordinated to facilitate the enormously complex job of leading instructional change. (p. 36)

Although issues of instructional leadership would not gain popularity for another 15 years, supervision as leadership essentially emerged in the 1960s.

The principal focus of supervision during this time was a concerted effort by those engaged in supervision to provide leadership in five ways: developing mutually acceptable goals, extending cooperative and democratic methods of supervision, improving classroom instruction, promoting research into educational problems, and promoting professional leadership.

REFLECTION

What does instructional leadership mean to you?

Clinical Supervision

Uncertainty plagued the field of supervision by the 1970s. Markowitz (1976) stated,

> The supervisor in the educational system is plagued by ambiguities. His or her position in the authority structure is ill-defined and quite often vulnerable. There is a lack of clarity in the definition of his or her role and a lack of agreement on the functions associated with supervision. (p. 367).

Alfonso, Firth, and Neville (1975) described this role ambiguity in terms of a "power limbo"; that is, supervisors are "neither line nor staff, neither administration nor faculty, but somewhere in between" (p. 342). Wilhelms (1969) concurred that supervision had witnessed tremendous change: "Roles are changing; staff organization is swirling; titles and functions are shifting," said Wilhelms, "but whether his [sic] title is 'principal,' 'supervisor,' 'curriculum coordinator,' or what not, the person in a position of supervisory leadership is caught in the middle" (p. x).

Lacking focus, a sound conceptual base, and purpose, supervision explored alternative notions to guide theory and practice in the field. Efforts to reform supervision were reflective of a broader attempt to seek alternatives to traditional educational practice. Clinical supervision grew out of this dissatisfaction with traditional educational practice and supervisory methods. Goldhammer (1969), one of the early proponents of clinical supervision, stated that the model for clinical supervision was "motivated, primarily, by contemporary views of weaknesses that commonly exist in educational practice" (p. 1).

The premise of clinical supervision was that teaching could be improved by a prescribed, formal process of collaboration between teacher and supervisor. The literature of clinical supervision has been replete with concepts of collegiality, collaboration, assistance, and improvement of instruction. Bolin and Panaritis (1992) explained that clinical supervision "appealed to many educators" because of its "emphasis on 'collegiality.'" The rhetoric of clinical supervision favored collaborative practice over inspectional, fault-finding supervision.

Most researchers identify Morris Cogan (1973) as the progenitor of clinical supervision (Anderson, 1993), although Pajak (1989) credits Hill (1968) with incorporating a "lesser known version of the preconference, observation, post-conference cycle" of supervision. Tanner and Tanner (1987), acknowledging Cogan's influence in developing the theory of clinical supervision, attributed the idea to Conant in 1936.

Clinical supervision, although advocated by professors and authors of textbooks, did not by any means gain wide acceptance in schools (see, e.g., Garman, 1997). Although clinical supervision received its share of criticism (e.g., Bolin & Panaritis, 1992; Tanner & Tanner, 1987), educators throughout the 1970s continued to argue that democratic methods of supervision should be extended and that vestiges of bureaucratic supervision should be excised. Supervision to improve instruction and promote pupil learning, instructional leadership, and democratic practices remained as prominent goals throughout the 1970s (see Table 1.1, Model 6).

REFLECTION

What are the chief characteristics of clinical supervision that distinguish it from other models of supervision? Have you ever used or been involved with clinical supervision? What obstacles might impede successful implementation of a clinical model in your school or district?

"Changing Concepts" Model of Supervision

During the early 1980s, public education continued to receive voluminous criticism for being bureaucratic and unresponsive to the needs of teachers, parents, and children (see, e.g., Johnson, 1990). One of the prominent proposals for disenfranchising bureaucracy was the dissolution of autocratic administrative practices where overbearing supervisors ruled by fiat. Favored was greater and more meaningful decision making at the grassroots level (Dunlap & Goldman, 1991). This idea translated into giving teachers more formal responsibility for setting school policies, thus enhancing democratic governance in schools (Glanz, 1992; Kirby, 1991). Johnson (1990) observed that "although schools have long been under the control of administrators, local districts are increasingly granting teachers more formal responsibility for setting school policies" (p. 337).

Criticism leveled at the educational bureaucracy has had consequences for school supervision (Firth & Eiken, 1982). Throughout this period, educators continued to consider alternative methods of supervision. In the early 1980s, developmental supervision, in which varied levels of teaching abilities were acknowledged, gained attention (Glickman, 1981). By the end of the decade, transformational leadership, which advocated that supervisors serve as change agents, became popular (e.g., Leithwood & Jantzi, 1990). Other writers advanced their notions of supervision as well (e.g., Bowers & Flinders, 1991).

Teacher empowerment (e.g., Darling-Hammond & Goodwin, 1993) gained attention as teachers became active participants in decision-making processes in schools. Pajak (2000) reviewed the literature on the "teacher as leader" during the previous five years. Peer supervision (e.g., Willerman, McNeely, & Koffman Cooper, 1991) appeared in the literature as an alternative to traditional supervision by "professionally trained supervisors," as did cognitive coaching (Costa & Garmston, 1997). Other collegial and democratic supervisory methods continued to receive notice (e.g., Smyth, 1991).

The publication of *Supervision in Transition* (Glickman, 1992) by the Association for Supervision and Curriculum Development marked a refinement in the changing conception of supervision as a democratic enterprise. Glickman, editor of the yearbook, clearly set the tone by stating emphatically that the very term *supervision* connoted a distasteful, even "disgusting" metaphor for school improvement. Instead of using the words *supervision* or *supervisor*, educators, or what Glickman called "risk-taking practitioners," were more comfortable with terms such as *instructional leadership* and *instructional leader*. The transition that Glickman and the authors of this comprehensive account of supervision envisioned was one that valued collegiality. Supervision, in the words of Sergiovanni (1992), was viewed as "professional and moral."

Other models and conceptions of supervision emerged in an attempt to extend democratic methods and to disassociate from bureaucratic and inspectional supervision. Clinical, developmental, and transformational supervision, among other models, had a common bond in that they emerged to counter the ill effects of supervision's bureaucratic legacy (see Table 1.1, Model 7).

REFLECTION/MICROLAB

From your experience, are collegiality and democratic supervision viable options for your school or district? Explain. Are you familiar with the implementation of any existing collegial or democratic processes? If so, which ones? How have staff and administration responded to them?

Standards-Based Supervision

Although the "changing concepts" model had an impact on supervision in the 1990s, over the last several years, especially since the turn of the new century, supervisory practice has been shaped and influenced by the general movement toward standards-based reform. Standards-based reform has affected supervision so greatly that we have identified a new and current model of supervision that has and will in all likelihood continue to impact supervision as a field of study and practice. We call that model "Standards-Based Supervision" (see Table. 1.1).

Although they are not new, standards-based teaching and learning have influenced curriculum, supervision, and teacher education in significant ways.

Supervisors and those concerned with supervision have been particularly challenged in the last several years to implement supervisory practices that ensure the technical competence of teachers. Receiving strong political backing from both state and national agencies, standards-based supervision has, in some quarters, relegated supervisors to relying on checklists to ascertain the extent to which teachers are meeting various curricular and instructional objectives embedded in core curriculum standards at various grade levels. Such supervisory practices thwart meaningful supervision aimed at fostering closer collaboration and instructional dialogue to improve teaching and learning. Pajak (2000) points to the compatibility problem of trying to use standards-based supervision with clinical supervision. He warns, "If we fail to provide empathy-based supervision, the current standards-based environment will ultimately prove stultifying for both teachers and their students" (p. 241).

To best understand standards-based supervision, some background knowledge on standards-based reform is necessary. The national movement toward standards-based education, including high-stakes testing, has served to legitimize and bolster local reform proposals that have influenced supervisory practices. Raising standards and promoting uniformity of curricular offerings to raise academic achievement has been a long established reform proposal (Seguel, 1966). Present efforts at establishing national or state standards should be viewed within a historic context. The first significant attempt to improve and "modernize" the American curriculum occurred in the 1890s. The Committee of Ten issued its report in 1892 under the leadership of Charles W. Eliot, then the president of Harvard University. The committee sought to establish new curriculum standards for high school students. Standards were established to enable all students to receive a high quality academic curriculum (Kliebard, 1987).

Notwithstanding the lofty aims of this committee, it wasn't until the establishment of the Commission on the Reorganization of Secondary Education that the school curriculum actually changed. The commission issued its report in 1918 and advocated a diversified curriculum that made allowances for a variety of curriculum "tracks" for the varied abilities of students. Known as the "Cardinal Principles of Education," the findings of this commission endorsed a differentiated curriculum that emphasized, in part, the importance of vocational training for a large segment of students (Krug, 1964).

During the first half of the twentieth century, the College Entrance Examination Board (formed in the 1890s), the Scholastic Aptitude Test (the first SAT was administered in 1926), and the American College Testing Program (established in 1959) were the guardians of standards, as applied to the academic curriculum. As a result of the Russian launch of the first artificial satellite (Sputnik) in 1957, American education was attacked vociferously. Only months after the Sputnik launching, Congress passed the National Defense Education Act (NDEA), which poured millions of dollars into mathematics, sciences, and engineering. For several years following Sputnik, the postwar baby boom increased enrollments dramatically in high schools, and achievement scores in many academic areas also improved. Academic standards, up until this time, continued to be driven by levels of student achievement and assessed by national standardized tests (Ravitch, 1995).

By the mid-sixties, however, the American school curriculum shifted from an academic orientation to a nonacademic one. Prompted by political and social reforms, educational reformers reconsidered their long-standing emphasis on academic curriculum standards. The easing of high school graduation and college entrance requirements was just one of many effects of educational reforms during this tumultuous era. Yet, by the late 1970s, criticism of nonacademic curricula focused on declining SAT scores and what was perceived as a general lowering of standards. With the election of Ronald Reagan in 1980, an era of unprecedented educational reform, focusing on a conservative political and educational agenda, was about to begin.

With the publication of the National Commission on Excellence in Education's 1983 report, A *Nation at Risk: The Imperative for Educational Reform*, attention was drawn to the assertion that schools had lowered their standards too much and that American students were not competitive with their international counterparts. The authors of this 1983 report were perturbed by the fact that American school children lagged behind students in other industrialized nations. The National Commission on Excellence in Education reported that among students from various industrialized nations, U.S. students scored lowest on 7 of 19 academic tests and failed to score first or second on any test. Similar results were reported by the Educational Testing Service (1992). Moreover, the study found that nearly 40% of U.S. 17-year-olds couldn't perform tasks requiring higher-order thinking skills.

Pressure to improve the quality of American education by articulating concrete standards for performance increased. Consequently, a spate of national and state reports continued through the 1980s, each advocating fundamental educational change. Commitment to democratic ideals and the influence of public education was reinforced once again in 1986 with the publication of the report, sponsored by the Carnegie Foundation, *A Nation Prepared: Teachers for the 21st Century* (Carnegie Forum on Education and the Economy, 1986) and the Holmes Group (1986) report. The national curriculum reform movement was catapulted into prominence and action with the Education Summit held in 1989 by then-President George Bush and state governors. A year later, in his State of the Union Address, President Bush affirmed his commitment to excellence in education by establishing six national education goals to be achieved by the year 2000. Signed into law by Congress during the Clinton administration on March 31, 1994, *Goals 2000* proclaimed, in part, that by the year 2000 "U.S. students will be first in the world in science and mathematics achievement" and "Every school will be free of drugs and violence and will offer a disciplined environment conducive to learning" (http://www.nd.edu/~rbarger/www7/goals200.html).

The adoption of national goals has been a major impetus for the increased attention to standards at the state level. In 1991, the U.S. Congress established the National Council on Educational Standards and Testing (NCEST), which encouraged educators and politicians to translate somewhat vague national goals into content curriculum standards. NCEST recommended that educators establish specific standards in specific subject areas. The National Council of Teachers of Mathematics (NCTM) led the way by publishing standards that quickly influenced textbook companies and testing agencies. These national curriculum reforms inevitably affected state educational reforms. More than 40 states have revised their curricula to reflect the standards they established.

Continuing in the tradition of standards-based education, President George W. Bush signed into law the No Child Left Behind Act of 2001, a reauthorization of the Elementary and Secondary Education Act Legislation of 1965. The purpose of the new legislation was to redefine the federal role in K–12 education and to help raise student achievement, especially for disadvantaged and minority students. Four basic principles were evident: stronger accountability for results, increased flexibility and local control, expanded options for parents, and an emphasis on teaching methods that presumably have been proven to work.

What can the history of standards-based education teach us about the practice of supervision? Pajak (2000) maintains that the "use of clinical supervision in standards-based environments is so recent that no clear consensus has yet emerged about whether this marriage is either desirable or successful" (p. 238). Our experiences and view of what is happening in the field tell us that a clear consensus is indeed apparent. The movement of standards-based education is indeed shaping supervisory practice by frequently compelling supervisors to incorporate a checklist approach to supervision. The pressure practitioners face to raise student achievement as measured on high-stakes tests is enormous. Principals and assistant principals are more accountable than ever to address prescribed core curriculum standards, promote teaching to the standards, and ensure higher student academic performance on standardized tests. Consequently, those concerned with supervision have been more inclined to incorporate supervisory practices that are a throwback to the 1930s, 1940s, and 1950s (Table 1.1, Model 4). Directive approaches of supervision find justification within a standards-based educational milieu.

UNDERSTANDING THE HISTORY OF SUPERVISION

Historically, the function and conception of supervision have changed. The earliest notions of supervision addressed the need for selectmen, committees, or clergymen to inspect the physical plant of schools and to ensure that children were receiving instruction as required by law. The legacy of inspectional supervision from the colonial period continued into the late 19th century as supervision became little more than an inspectional function local and city superintendents performed attempting to bureaucratize urban education. In the early 1900s, supervision-as-bureaucratic-inspection was reinforced and strengthened as "social efficiency" became the watchword. Influenced by social and economic forces as well as by opposition to inspectional bureaucratic methods, supervision in the 1920s and 1930s embraced democratic theory; this trend would continue throughout the century, albeit in different forms.

What can we learn from this excursion into history? For some theorists and practitioners, a lesson learned is that authoritarian supervision aimed at fault-finding and suspecting the competence of teachers should not be compatible with the modern practice of supervision. Some view the evolution of the practice of supervision as a progression from crude, unsophisticated *bureaucratic inspectional* approaches to more refined democratic participatory techniques and methodologies (see Figure 1.1).

REFLECTION

Do vestiges of bureaucratic inspectional supervisory approaches remain in your school or district? Explain. How would you characterize your supervisory approach? Use Figure 1.1 as a reference point.

Figure 1.1   Approaches to Supervision

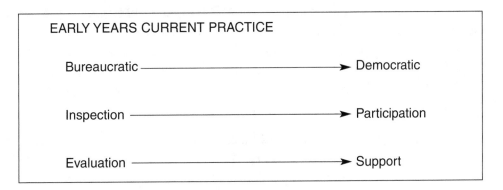

For some theorists and practitioners, the legacy of inspectional supervision lives on in the form of evaluation. Democratic supervision is viewed as helping teachers improve instruction, whereas bureaucratic supervision is associated with accountability and judgments about teachers' efficiency. This conflict between the helping and evaluative functions of supervision is long-standing. Tanner and Tanner (1987) asserted that this dilemma presents an almost insurmountable problem for supervisors: "The basic conflict between these functions is probably the most serious and, up until now, unresolved problem in the field of supervision" (p. 106).

Historically, the *evaluative* function of supervision is rooted in bureaucratic inspectional-type supervision. Maintaining an efficient and effective school organization as well as a sound instructional program mandates that teacher competency be evaluated. In other words, the evaluative aspect of the supervisory function emanates from organizational requirements to measure and assess teaching effectiveness. The origins of the *helping* or *improvement* function of supervision date back to democratic practices in the early 20th century. In other words, helping teachers improve instruction and promote pupil achievement grew out of the democratic theory of supervision.

Supervisors or people concerned with supervision, however, have faced a basic role conflict; namely, the unresolved dilemma between the necessity to evaluate (a bureaucratic function) and the desire to genuinely assist teachers in the instructional process (a democratic and professional goal).

Catherine Marshall (1992), in a comprehensive study of assistant principals, described such role conflicts:

> An assistant principal might be required to help teachers develop coordinated curricula—a "teacher support" function. But this function conflicts with the monitoring, supervising, and evaluating functions. . . . The assistant may be working with a teacher as a colleague in one meeting and, perhaps one hour later, the same assistant may be meeting to chastise the same teacher for noncompliance with the district's new homework policy. . . . When they must monitor teachers' compliance, assistants have difficulty maintaining equal collegial and professional relationships with them. (pp. 6–7)

The field of supervision has attempted to resolve this basic conflict between evaluation and improvement (e.g., Hazi, 1994; Poole, 1994; Tsui, 1995). It clearly is evident throughout the history of supervision that efforts have been made to extricate supervision from its bureaucratic heritage. Nonetheless, advances in theory are not necessarily reflected in practice. Many, if not most studies still conclude that teachers do not find supervision helpful (Zepeda & Ponticell, 1998).

REFLECTION

What experiences have you had with the dilemma of evaluation versus improvement of instruction? (Give examples.) Describe how you have attempted to resolve this dilemma.

IMPLICATIONS FOR THE PRACTICE OF SUPERVISION

Present Context and Future Necessities

For most of the 20th century, schools retained features of the factory organizational model, a legacy of 19th-century industrial society. Schools relied on hierarchical supervisory control and representative democracy. We are now, however, undergoing major societal transformations into a postindustrial era (Ambrose & Cohen, 1997) characterized "by exponential information growth, fast-paced innovation, organizational change, and participatory democracy" (p. 20). As a result of these technological, political, economic, and social changes, schools (teachers and supervisors) are "being called on today to rethink and restructure how schools operate and how teachers relate to students. . . . We sorely need new ways of thinking about educational supervision and leadership" (Pajak, 1993, p. 159).

Attempts to restructure schools, classrooms, and practices (both teaching and supervisory) abound (see, e.g., Murphy & Hallinger, 1993). Over the past several years, alternative models or approaches to school and instructional improvement and teacher evaluation have gained prominence. Among these innovative ideas are site-based management, union-sponsored peer coaching, professional partnerships, reflective practice, and teacher self-evaluation. Based on our brief discussion of the history of supervision in this chapter,[2] these innovations can be seen as ways to extend participatory democracy in supervision.

The changing context of supervision necessitates that both prospective and practicing supervisors remain responsive to unprecedented demands and opportunities. Supervisors will need specialized knowledge and skills to meet organizational challenges in the 21st century. They will need to base their practice of supervision on a foundation of dispositions and beliefs. Supervisors will have to place a premium on initiative, flexibility, tolerance for ambiguity, collaboration, and an ethical mind-set. In the future, supervisors will be expected more and more to be collaborative and assist teachers in reflecting about classroom instruction in meaningful ways.

REFLECTION

What challenges do you anticipate in your professional environment? Explain.

What Is Supervision?

Defining supervision has been a source of much debate for years (Bolin, 1987). Is supervision a function of administration, curriculum, staff development, action research, or a combination of these and other activities? Alfonso and Firth (1990) noted that the study of supervision lacks focus largely due to the "lack of research and continuing disagreement on the definition and purposes of supervision" (p. 188). In this volume, we view supervision as the center for the improvement of instruction. Supervision is the process of engaging teachers in instructional dialogue for the purpose of improving teaching and increasing student achievement. We believe that supervision for the improvement of instruction will continue to be the foremost concern of supervisors and other educational leaders well into the 21st century.

REFLECTION/MICROLAB

At this juncture, how would you define supervision? Do you believe that supervision is solely about assisting teachers in instructional improvement? If so, how can this be accomplished? Explain.

As we saw earlier in this chapter, with a firmly entrenched bureaucratic heritage, people have tried to reshape the image of supervision into a democratic enterprise aimed at instructional improvement. We maintain that your ability to facilitate teaching and learning depends as much on your belief system, because it requires knowledge and skills about instructional improvement. Much of this book is devoted to knowledge and skill development. The remainder of this chapter, however, is aimed at indicating how your beliefs might affect your response to daily instructional challenges. Are you more inclined to conceive of supervision as an inspectional, bureaucratic process, are you genuinely more concerned with developing collaborative relationships with teachers in an effort to improve instruction, or are you inclined to follow a path somewhere in the middle?

We make a bold assertion in this chapter: Bureaucratic inspectional supervision should have no place in schools in the 21st century. We must prepare supervisors who truly espouse participatory democratic values. We have found that some supervisors espouse collaboration when, in practice, they operate in rather autocratic ways. These supervisors are probably influenced very much by the traditional conceptions of supervision described earlier.

Supervision Situations

Dr. William Jones believes that teachers need close scrutiny. "Many of the new teachers," explains Jones, "are generally weak. They have just been certified and need close supervision." He continues, "In fact, even experienced teachers continually need the guidance of an expert who can provide the needed instructional and managerial assistance."

Other supervisors are genuinely interested in working with teachers collaboratively, as evidenced by Elizabeth Gonzalez, a vice principal in Elmsville Elementary School, a suburban district in the Midwest:

Elizabeth Gonzalez believes in forging collaborative relationships with teacher professionals. "I think that every teacher should develop a unique style of teaching that is right for her or him," explains Gonzalez, "As a supervisor, I am really most effective as facilitator and guide, rather than an overseer."

Why does William Jones rely only on inspectional practices, yet Elizabeth Gonzalez acts in a much more collaborative way? We believe that each of these supervisors operates from a different belief system that inevitably affects how he or she approaches supervisory responsibilities.

REFLECTION

How do you think your belief system impacts the way you view and perform supervision? Explain.

ASSESSING BELIEF SYSTEMS[3]

The bureaucratic model of schooling is based on what we believe are erroneous assumptions about how people work together most efficiently in schools. There is a growing awareness that the key to successfully shifting to a collaborative educational paradigm is dependent on the degree to which we alter our thinking patterns, belief systems, and mind-sets, or as Sergiovanni calls them, "mindscapes" (Sergiovanni, 1992, p. 41). Our belief systems are intimately connected to the language we use to articulate and communicate meanings. The needed transformation in education requires a realignment of educational phraseology with an entirely different set of definitions, meanings, and purposes. For example, a reexamination of the metaphors we use is essential. Using supervision or reflective coaching not only clearly indicates "where we're coming from," but also defines human interactions in the workplace.

Yet, a caveat about beliefs and actions or behaviors is in order. Reflective practice (see Osterman & Kottkamp, 2004) posits that our actions often are inconsistent with our intentions (or beliefs) and that new ideas do not necessarily lead to new behaviors. *Espoused theories* represent our conscious ideas, intentions, and beliefs. Following exposure to new ideas in graduate courses and workshops, we often believe that this information and the beliefs acquired through experience and formal education will guide our actions. Espoused theories, however, do not influence behavior directly. How many times have you thought after a leader's speech, "Why doesn't he or she practice what he or she preaches?" How many impressive workshops have we all attended with the best of intentions to implement our new knowledge, only to return to our old practices? How many supervisors preach active learning for all students and then conduct a postobservation conference where they tell the teacher everything he or she must do without even thinking of asking for the teacher's input?

Although we may consciously adopt new ideas, these action theories are ingrained so deeply in our consciousness that we cannot change them easily. *Theories-in-use* build and crystallize over a long period of time and become such an integral part of our beings that we are unaware of the discrepancies between our beliefs and actions or between our actions and intended outcomes. Actual change in our behaviors will take place only when we become aware of the discrepancy between a predominant theory-in-use and an unacceptable practice or outcome. Figure 1.2 shows how theories-in-use directly impact behavior. Espoused theories do not directly influence behavior and may or may not be consistent with theories-in-use.

Nonetheless we believe that it is essential to articulate our espoused theories in the form of vision statements. It is, however, through the use of reflective practice (which is presented in more detail in Chapter 2) that the new ideas we will be learning in this book and the beliefs we will develop will become theories-in-use.

Philosophy at least indirectly influences actions, which in turn affect behavior. How we think shapes the world in which we live. Our values and beliefs shape the kinds of experiences, for example, we want young children to

Figure 1.2   A Conceptual Framework Underlying Reflective Practice

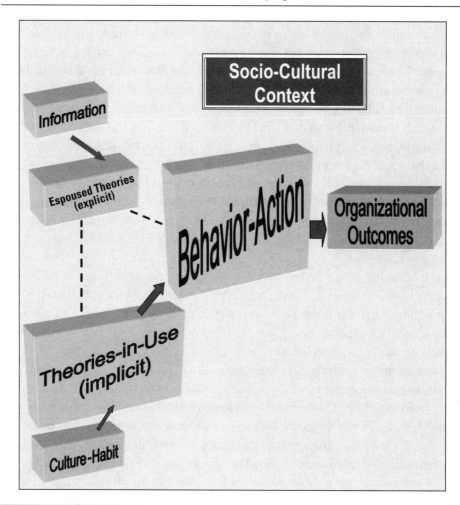

have in classrooms. They also affect what adults do in schools and define role relationships among members of a school system. If our attitudes about how best to organize large groups of people focus on hierarchical notions of differentiation and classification, then we will tend to conceptualize supervision, for example, as didactic and evaluative. Conversely, if our view of school management stresses collaboration and shared leadership, we will not be willing to construct an educational environment where disempowered individuals become spectators of, rather than participants in, their own work. This worldview will define supervision as collegial and interactive.

REFLECTION

Compose a list of your beliefs about teaching and learning, about teachers, about supervision, and about yourself. Share ideas with a colleague. How does your philosophy influence your approach to supervision with respect to engaging teachers in dialogue about instructional improvement? Explain.

Supervisory Beliefs Questionnaire

What are the qualities or dispositions we want future supervisors to possess? Are you willing and able to meet new supervisory challenges in the 21st century? The questionnaire in Appendix 1-A is designed to help you sort out your beliefs. More specifically, the survey is designed to assess your preference to function along the bureaucratic, inspectional, democratic, collegial continuum. You should have completed this questionnaire before you read this chapter. Make sure you retake the questionnaire at the end of the book to assess whether any of your beliefs have changed.

Interpreting Answers to the Questionnaire

Warning: If you have not taken the questionnaire, see Appendix 1-A.

The following responses to each statement indicate that your supervisory preferences or inclinations operate along bureaucratic, authoritarian lines:

1. T	6. T	11. F	16. T	21. T	26. F	31. F	36. F
2. T	7. T	12. T	17. F	22. F	27. T	32. F	37. T
3. F	8. T	13. F	18. T	23. T	28. F	33. T	38. F
4. F	9. T	14. T	19. F	24. F	29. T	34. F	39. F
5. T	10. F	15. T	20. F	25. F	30. F	35. T	40. T

The following responses to each statement indicate that your supervisory preferences or inclinations operate along democratic, collaborative lines:

1. F	6. F	11. T	16. F	21. F	26. T	31. T	36. T
2. F	7. F	12. F	17. T	22. T	27. F	32. T	37. F
3. T	8. F	13. T	18. F	23. F	28. T	33. F	38. T
4. T	9. F	14. F	19. T	24. T	29. F	34. T	39. T
5. F	10. T	15. F	20. T	25. T	30. T	35. F	40. F

As we stated earlier, bureaucratic inspectional supervision should have no place in schools in the 21st century. For the future, we must prepare supervisors who truly espouse and practice participatory democratic values. Supervision that assumes that supervisors are experts and superior to teachers represents vestiges of control-oriented, inspectional practices. Although these kinds of practices were prevalent in early supervision, we argue that they should no longer be accorded attention.

(In the ensuing discussion, statement numbers refer to the questionnaire in Appendix 1-A.)

Bureaucratic thought essentially suggests that

- Supervision is inspectional (Statements 1 and 14)
- Hierarchy is necessary for organizational efficiency (Statements 5 and 6)
- Supervisors are experts and teachers are not (Statements 12, 18, 27, 29, 37, and 40)
- Teachers and supervisors are not equal partners (Statement 7)
- Teachers will not improve instruction on their own (Statements 16 and 33)

That hierarchy equals expertise and supervisors know more than teachers is axiomatic according to the bureaucratic belief system.

Furthermore, the following assumptions that, at first glance, might appear unproblematic also represent bureaucratic conceptions of supervision:

- Supervision is primarily about helping teachers improve instruction (Statements 8 and 9). This belief subtly implies that teachers are deficient, need help, and could not or would not seek improvement on their own.
- Supervisors help teachers change, as if teachers are deficient and necessarily need to change (Statements 15, 23, and 35). This belief implies that something is wrong with a teacher's teaching.
- Teachers at low levels need assistance (Statement 2). This belief implies that supervisors can identify with certainty that a teacher is deficient. It also implies that supervisors should *help* teachers because they cannot improve through collaboration or self-reflection.
- Supervisors are agents of improved instruction (Statement 21). This belief implies that supervisors, not teachers, are agents of improved instruction.

The aforementioned conceptions of supervision underscore the superordinate-subordinate relationship between teachers and supervisors. Bureaucratic conceptions of supervision imply that teachers don't know as much about teaching as do supervisors and, conversely, that supervisors possess greater teaching expertise than do teachers.

REFLECTION

In your experience, is it true that teachers don't know as much about teaching as do supervisors and that supervisors possess greater teaching expertise than do teachers? Provide an example.

Democratic thought essentially suggests that

- Teaching is complex and not easily defined or understood (Statements 3 and 17)
- Individuals are more important than the organizations (Statements 4 and 32)
- Most teachers are self-directed, responsible, and competent (Statements 10, 11, 19, 20, 28, 30, 31, and 39)
- Supervision is a truly collaborative process (Statements 13, 34, 36, and 38)
- Qualitative approaches to classroom improvement are just as valid as quantitative ones (Statements 22 and 24)
- Alternative approaches to traditional supervision are viable (Statement 25)
- Supervisors function at their best when they pose questions for critical analysis by teachers (Statement 26)

The aforementioned conceptions of supervision underscore the empowering nature of supervisor-teacher relationships. Teachers and supervisors work as collaborative inquirers for the benefit of students. The telling-and-prescribing nature of traditional supervision has no place in such a paradigm for school improvement.

Developing a Personal Vision Statement

Examining your beliefs about supervision and related areas is crucial if you are to function effectively as a supervisor in the 21st century. We think that developing a personal vision statement that articulates your beliefs about teachers and supervision is critical (Osterman & Kottkamp, 1993). This section challenges you to begin this process, which will be refined continually throughout this book. Now that we understand how supervision has evolved and realize that our beliefs are influenced, in part, by that history, our challenge will be to construct a personal supervisory vision statement that supports the view that supervision remains a potent process for facilitating instructional improvement.

What are your beliefs about teaching and learning, about teachers, about supervision, and about yourselves as supervisors?

In courses that we teach, we expect our prospective supervisors to develop such a vision statement. We, of course, review the contents of this chapter with them and have them take and interpret the Beliefs About Supervision questionnaire. We also expose them to other theories and surveys that help them to uncover their often hidden assumptions about supervisory work.[4]

Although we advocate a participatory democratic orientation to supervision, we believe that traditional types of supervision such as directive informational approaches (see Chapter 2) are useful. These practices should be employed with teachers who need substantial support. Use of this form of directive informational supervision "does not necessarily mean that the supervisor acts in an authoritative or arbitrary fashion" (Daresh & Playko, 1995, p. 333). Offering some direct assistance to teachers in need is necessary only when the situation calls for it. In our questionnaire, Statement 2 is indicative of a generalization often made by supervisors without input and agreement from other parties, including perhaps lead teachers. Therefore, this book does include one traditional, directive approach that should be used judiciously.

Let's begin to develop your personal vision statement. This vision statement is a personal statement that allows you to present your views regarding education and educational administration, your philosophy, your values, your beliefs, your vision of the way schools should be, and your view about what you as a school leader would do to realize this vision. In short, the vision statement that will lead to a supervisory platform is a way for you to say what you stand for as an educational leader.

Appendix 1-B lists four areas that you will want to address in your statement and questions that may stimulate your thinking. We include questions based on the Educational Leadership Constituent Council (ELCC) standards that can also help frame your statement. Where possible,

- support your ideas with examples and theories from the literature on leadership.
- use examples that have inspired or influenced you.

Please remember that this activity is intended to help you articulate your own personal feelings and ideas. It is not a test of what you know, and there are no right answers.

Appendix 1-C presents three sample vision statements developed by our students that you can use as a guide to inspire you in developing your own. These statements vary in length and style as well as content. Two pages may suffice to elucidate one person's ideas, whereas another may require 10. These differences illustrate the idiosyncratic and essentially personal nature of visioning.

Class Practice

Bring three copies of the first draft of your vision statement to class. In groups of three, read each others' vision statements, one at a time. Provide descriptive feedback to the authors. The purpose of descriptive feedback, as differentiated from evaluative or prescriptive feedback, is to provide the reader with a deeper understanding of the ideas expressed in the vision statement (Osterman & Kottkamp, 1993). The following strategies will help avoid the prescription/evaluation trap:

- Note logical consistencies and inconsistencies among the sections of the draft
- Identify underlying assumptions
- Take notes on the writer's perspective and value orientation to clarify your own positions and values[5]

Realize, of course, that as you share your statements with others, revisions are inevitable. Incorporate your colleagues' feedback and further reflections into your revisions. We have found that we can test our vision statements through simulated role plays (Osterman & Kottkamp, 1993, pp. 95–99). In these situations, we provide students with realistic situations or case studies and have them role-play. The following section outlines three examples.

Examples of Supervisory Situations[6]

In each of the following situations, put yourself into the role of a supervisor who makes sense to you in your particular situation. It may be the role of building principal or assistant principal, department chairperson, or some other kind of district supervisor. Write down what you hope to accomplish in the role play. The class can divide into pairs, or volunteers can present each scenario. On completion of the role play, you reveal your intentions by reading your planning notes and share what you think you have achieved. The supervisee then describes how he or she felt, tells what he or she is going to do as a result of the interchange, and reflects on his or her perceptions of the supervisor's perspective.

1. You have been invited into Mrs. Sanchez's classroom to observe a high school social studies lesson on censorship in the media. You've spent 40 minutes observing the lesson and taking detailed descriptive data. At the postconference, Mrs. Sanchez feels the lesson was great. You have some reservations, however.

2. You are new to your supervisory position, and teachers are eager to find out more about you. At a grade or faculty conference, you are introduced to the faculty, at which time you make a 2-minute introductory statement. After the meeting, several teachers warmly welcome you to the school, but two teachers in particular inform you that your "lofty" ideas will fail "in our school."

3. A teacher has been late to school and to homeroom. The situation first came to your attention when you observed students standing by the classroom doorway after the last bell had rung. You questioned the students and discovered that there was a pattern to the teacher's late arrival. You have left a note in the teacher's mailbox requesting that he or she see you after school. In the current situation, the teacher has just arrived.

REFLECTION

How did you feel about the way you responded to these situations? How did your personal vision statement stand up to the feedback you received? How do you think you might revise your statement? What aspects of the statement made the most sense for you and the least sense to you? Explain.

CONCLUSION

The supervisory landscape has evolved since the early inspectional practices of supervisors in the 19th and early 20th centuries. Supervision in a postindustrial society requires a new breed of supervisor, one who advocates and affirms participatory democratic practices. Who are these supervisors? What kind of supervisors do we want to attract into the field? Are you more inclined to encourage teachers in ongoing, meaningful dialogue about instructional improvement, or do you feel more comfortable suggesting to teachers ways to improve their teaching?

We have suggested in this chapter that supervision in postindustrial times requires that supervisors develop a personal vision statement so that they begin to consciously affirm their beliefs about teaching and supervision. Such reflective practice is a powerful way to enhance professional development.

Confronted by complex and seemingly perplexing social, political, technological, and moral issues, educational supervisors, perhaps more than ever before, play a crucial role in developing sound educational programming that is both educative and meaningfully relevant. Considering these awesome and challenging responsibilities, we believe educational supervision can play a vital role in promoting excellent instruction.

APPENDIX 1-A

Questionnaire Beliefs About Supervision

Please answer *true* (T) or *false* (F) to each of the following statements. Be honest: Answer *true* if the statement generally describes a belief you once held or currently hold. If a statement represents a belief that holds true in most situations, although not in all, answer true. Answer false if the statement in no way describes a belief you once held or currently hold. If a statement represents a belief that is false in most situations, although not in all, answer false. There is no need to share your responses with anyone.

T	F	1.	When it comes down to it, supervision, as I conceive of it, is essentially about looking for errors.
T	F	2.	Guided directed approaches to supervision are most appropriate for teachers at low levels of personal and professional development.
T	F	3.	Teaching is a highly complex, context-specific, interactive activity.
T	F	4.	Organizational concerns are almost always secondary to individual needs.
T	F	5.	The supervisor's position in the hierarchy, as compared to the teachers', is unproblematic.
T	F	6.	Hierarchy of offices is necessary for organizational efficiency.
T	F	7.	I am not comfortable participating with teachers as partners.
T	F	8.	Supervision is about offering teachers specialized help in improving instruction.
T	F	9.	Supervision is about examining and analyzing classroom teaching behaviors so that recommendations can be made with regard to the course of action teachers should take instructionally.
T	F	10.	Teachers can help supervisors improve their performance.
T	F	11.	Most teachers are self-directed.
T	F	12.	Supervisors should be expert diagnosticians.
T	F	13.	Supervision is primarily a collaborative process in which teachers and supervisors talk about ways to improve instruction.
T	F	14.	Supervision is about looking for errors and then engaging teachers in dialogue so that they realize these deficiencies on their own.
T	F	15.	The focus of supervision should be about helping teachers change and improve instruction.
T	F	16.	Without assistance, teachers generally will not make changes.
T	F	17.	Reality in classrooms is essentially subjective, not objective, and teaching is a complex endeavor that requires continual study.
T	F	18.	Although supervisor-teacher collaboration is important, a supervisor's judgment must ultimately hold sway.
T	F	19.	Schools are centers of inquiry in which teachers themselves must assume responsibility for instructional excellence.
T	F	20.	Teacher self-evaluation plays a prominent role in instructional improvement.
T	F	21.	The supervisor is the agent of improved instruction.
T	F	22.	Qualitative approaches to instructional improvement are just as valid as quantitative approaches.

T   F   23.   Supervisors help teachers change.
T   F   24.   Reflective dialogue is an integral component of supervision.
T   F   25.   Instructional improvement activities include peer coaching, action research projects, and problem-solving groups, as well as more traditional development activities.
T   F   26.   Supervision is primarily about asking questions that facilitate the examination of teacher practice in the classroom.
T   F   27.   When I offer teachers constructive criticisms, I expect they will consider them carefully.
T   F   28.   Experienced, high-functioning teachers should have complete control over their professional development.
T   F   29.   The supervisor ultimately should determine what and how a teacher should teach.
T   F   30.   Teachers should be encouraged to carry out their own educational goals and curricular decisions.
T   F   31.   Teachers should be given options on how they want to teach.
T   F   32.   Teachers should disobey official regulations if they feel that they interfere with the welfare of students.
T   F   33.   Teachers don't spend enough time thinking about ways to improve instruction.
T   F   34.   Supervisors should create opportunities for teachers to make professional and personal choices, not shape their behavior.
T   F   35.   Supervisors should attentively listen to the teachers' concerns and offer critical assessment and constructive ideas for change.
T   F   36.   Schools will improve primarily when a norm of collegiality exists in which shared discussion and shared work among all staff members exist.
T   F   37.   The knowledge base of a supervisor is generally superior to that of a teacher.
T   F   38.   Supervisors actively should seek input from teachers, parents, and students about ways to improve instruction.
T   F   39.   Most teachers don't need specific instructions on what to teach and how to teach.
T   F   40.   Supervisors should have more expertise than teachers with respect to teaching and learning.

APPENDIX 1-B

My Personal Vision Statement[7]

(Note that the following questions serve as a guide. Organize your statement any way you'd like.)

- *Student outcomes*
  What are your goals or hopes for your students?
  What are the types of skills, attitudes, and feelings you want students to possess?

- *Instructional climate*
  What type of climate is needed to support the student outcomes you identified above?
  What can you do to help establish that climate?

- *Teaching and learning*
  What are your views about teaching and learning?
  How should instruction be organized and delivered to support the type of climate and student outcomes you desire?

- *Leadership and governance*
  What is your philosophy on leadership?
  What can leaders do to create effective schools?
  How will you exercise leadership in your building?
  What will the governance structure look like?
  What are your responsibilities as a leader?
  How will you work with teachers and staff, students, parents, community, and district officials?

- Concluding statement

The Educational Leadership Constituent Council (ELCC; http://www.npbea. org/ELCC/) believes that the knowledge and ability to promote the success of all students require that aspiring leaders be able to address the following questions:

1. How would you facilitate the development, articulation, implementation, and stewardship of a school vision of learning supported by the school community?

2. How would you promote a positive school culture, providing an effective instructional program, applying best practice to student learning, and designing comprehensive professional growth plans for staff?

3. How would you manage the organization, operations, and resources in a way that promotes a safe, efficient, and effective learning environment?

4. What are your ideas for collaborating with all families and other community members, responding to diverse community interests and needs, and mobilizing community resources?

5. Provide examples of how you would act with integrity, fairly, and in an ethical manner.

6. How would you seek to understand, respond to, and influence the larger political, social, economic, legal, and cultural context?

APPENDIX 1-C

Personal Vision Statements

Sample 1[8]

As we embark on our leadership careers, we are faced with the challenge of teaching our children well. To accomplish this, we must make our schools more effective. Schools must prepare students for the many challenges they will face throughout their lives by ensuring that they gain perspective and become critical, reflective thinkers well equipped to make informed decisions and value judgments. More important, our children must become self-confident, respectful, proud, compassionate, moral, and ethical human beings. To meet this monumental task as educational leaders, we must ensure that teachers are committed not only to pedagogical excellence and greater student achievement, but also to developing the whole child. To understand how I plan to achieve these goals, it is essential to examine four areas: instructional climate, instruction, student outcomes, and leadership and governance. It is in this vein that I present my personal vision statement.

Instructional climate. I have chosen to discuss instructional climate first, as it is the foundation for effective instruction and positive student outcomes. The school will be viewed as a community with its members being administrators, teachers and other school personnel, students, and parents. All members of the school community will feel welcome, comfortable, respected, safe, and secure so that all realize that they are valued by and important to the community. These feelings facilitate community members working cohesively as a team to enable all children to reach their goals and achieve success.

The atmosphere will be one in which there is understanding, acceptance, and appreciation of diversity. This fosters a climate of acceptance for all students and encourages students to appreciate the individuality and uniqueness of others, thereby enhancing the development of individuality, the pursuit of individual interests and talents, and students' tolerance of diversity.

The school must be a place where there is mutual respect, trust, and honesty among all members of the community. Teachers will be treated and will act as professionals; their ideas and opinions will be solicited, listened to, and valued. Teachers will have a voice in developing curriculum and resources, aligning assessment strategies with curriculum, evaluating student performance and school effectiveness, allocating instructional and noninstructional resources, and deciding general school policy issues and any other matters involving them or their students. Teachers will respect one another and work together on teams to develop resources, plan and evaluate lessons and assessment strategies, and monitor student progress. This will promote an atmosphere of collegiality. Teachers and other school personnel will model respect by recognizing and acknowledging our students' rights.

Similarly, students must respect faculty and one another. Students will also be encouraged to voice their opinions in an environment where they can trust that their ideas will be respected, listened to, taken seriously, and, when feasible, acted upon. Students will be encouraged to discuss their progress and any concerns they have with their teachers. All staff will have an open-door policy for students and will be willing to lend an ear if need be. Teachers will be encouraged to be sensitive to student concerns but to communicate honestly and respectfully with their students. This will create bonds of trust and loyalty between staff and students and will foster a strong sense of community throughout the school.

To further build trust, loyalty, and self-esteem, teachers will establish a comfortable, supportive classroom environment. Students will never feel rejected or humiliated by incorrect responses or limited skills. The teacher will make the classroom an amiable, encouraging, physically attractive, open, positive environment where there is tolerance of diverse views. It must be free of tension and sarcasm. Thus, students will be encouraged to take intellectual risks.

As members of the school community, parents will be warmly welcomed into the school and treated with respect. They will be recognized as partners in their children's education and development. As such, parents will be encouraged to play an active role in the education process by conferring with teachers at least four times per year, by volunteering to serve on school committees (i.e., school planning team, door patrol, parents' lounge, fund-raising committees, etc.), by voicing their opinions on educational matters that affect their children and by taking part in programs offered by the school to benefit them and their children (i.e., ESL for parents, college night, career day, family counseling, school picnic, etc.). Parents will be encouraged to collaborate with their children and their teachers to help their children reach their potential. Teachers, students, and parents will be empowered to play major roles in developing school policy and in the running of the school.

Our community's house (school building) will be warm and inviting. will showcase our students and their accomplishments. The hallways will be painted and decorated with student-created murals and collages, artwork, photography, sculptures, and crafts. Enlarged photos of students performing and working will be displayed throughout the building. Examples of positive publicity (i.e., news and magazine articles, awards, plaques, trophies, etc,) will also be showcased throughout the school. A parent lounge will be arranged so parents can meet or obtain information about issues relevant to their child's development. As an educational leader, I will organize support groups for parents of "at-risk" students so that parents can discuss their frustrations, get involved in their children's education, and become active members of the community. Furthermore, I will work to maximize parent participation through the development of community outreach and parent education programs.

Developing community and creating and maintaining a positive and productive learning environment while maximizing teaching potential and student achievement requires that teachers, administrators, and schools be continuously evolving and going through a process of self-renewal and evaluation, When this exists, members of the community can work together to build consensus. Every member of the community will realize that he or she is an integral part of the whole and that his or her ideas are welcomed and valued. Our school will have a supportive, just, and purposeful environment characterized by mutual respect for all members of the community. Through consensus, the school community will develop clear goals and high expectations for our students, as well as a synergistically created and universally shared vision and purpose. We will be a community that truly enables our students to thrive.

Instruction. There is much truth to the Sioux Indian adage: "Tell me and I'll listen; show me and I'll understand; involve me and I'll learn." Thus, teachers must work to make learning interesting and challenging by actively engaging their students in the learning process. Teachers must be trained to limit "teacher talk" and information delivery. Instead they must facilitate "student talk" through effective questioning, class discussions, and student interactions, thereby involving their students and facilitating learning.

To motivate and stimulate students and to transform their classrooms into effective laboratories for learning, teachers will employ a variety of teaching strategies including cooperative and mastery learning, class debates, panel discussions, student presentations, journals and learning logs, and interdisciplinary and inquiry-based instruction. In using these strategies and in applying an inductive approach to instruction, and recognizing that all students learn in different ways, teachers will endeavor to use a broad spectrum of source materials. These materials will help make their lessons relevant to their students' lives and present information from various perspectives and through different media. Teachers will use materials such as newspaper headlines, articles and editorials, maps, graphs, charts, cartoons, fine art, music, film and video presentations, primary source readings, literature, guest speakers, and the Internet as teaching tools. Based on their exposure to differing points of view, students will be given opportunities to draw conclusions, make decisions, form opinions, and make value judgments.

Furthermore, this variety of instructional techniques and sources will create interesting and exciting lessons that are appealing to and actively engage students. This approach will foster an atmosphere where students are stimulated and enthusiastic about learning, readily offer opinions on controversial issues, make keen observations, develop problem-solving and research skills, work cooperatively to solve problems and prepare presentations, and provide sustained responses to questions. Moreover, engaging students in these activities promotes the use of higher-order thinking skills and enables students to gain experience and perspective in decision making, critical thinking, and evaluation.

To encourage students and to build self-esteem and confidence, teachers will praise students for their efforts and participation. Teachers will encourage students to be intellectual risk takers by establishing a comfortable, supportive classroom environment. Teachers will never use rejection or humiliation as a means of instruction.

Teachers will plan and present their lessons with a careful blend of coverage and depth. Lessons will be centered on a specific problem or question for student analysis and assessment. In planning, teachers will be guided by the principle that "less is more." Thus, they will cover less factual content but will teach it with more depth, focusing on an evaluative issue or question that provokes critical and reflective thinking and sparks class discussion. The key to doing this and to achieving positive student outcomes is carefully planned lessons. Lessons will include: a clear, well-defined aim in the form of a question for student analysis and assessment; a motivation to raise the students' interest in the topic; procedures and activities for development of the lesson; source materials and thought-provoking questions to actively engage students in the learning process; a summary activity or question to provide students with the opportunity to assess and take or defend a position on the issue presented by the aim; and an application activity that connects or relates the major concepts and ideas of the lesson with a current situation in the students' world today.

The curriculum must address the needs of the whole child. It must be designed with broad goals that not only take into account the students' academic, emotional, physical, and social development, but also reinforce active thinking and reasoning and nurture students' curiosity. The curriculum must set high standards for all students in the areas of literacy (written and spoken) and in all major subject areas, music and art, physical fitness, and language. The curriculum will allow students to develop an in-depth understanding of all subjects and see their relation to one another and to their lives. This will be accomplished by using an interdisciplinary and thematic approach to teaching and by having students apply what they have learned to real-life situations. The curriculum will provide students with a wide variety of experiences to bolster and enhance their prior experiences and make connections to their everyday life experiences. Teachers will be given opportunities to team-plan and -teach so that these curriculum goals can be met.

In addition, volunteerism will be a major component of our school's curriculum. Each student will be required to do volunteer work in the form an internship. Students may intern with a local councilperson or senator, at a hospital or old-age home, in a local grammar school, at a legal aid office, or for another local charity. This program will build strong bonds and ties to the community while simultaneously giving students the opportunity to establish intergenerational ties and encouraging students to learn from elders. Moreover, it will increase students' responsibility and help to make them productive citizens. Interning will give students a "real world" experience in which they can employ many of the hands-on skills and much of the knowledge they have acquired. Furthermore, volunteerism is an important part of our country's future and the future of public education. As we restructure the public education system, we will be relying more and more on volunteers from the private sector to enrich our school community. This internship program may establish a foundation for getting members of the community to volunteer in our school.

Just as lessons will be presented using a variety of teaching strategies, so assessment of student learning will be accomplished by evaluating the whole student using a broad spectrum of assessment tools. In addition to objective and essay tests, students will develop portfolios. Portfolios provide students with an opportunity to exhibit their achievements and their progress throughout their academic careers. Moreover, they provide the teacher with a clearer, more accurate picture of the whole child and how much he or she has progressed. Teachers will also be encouraged to use student journals as an assessment tool. Journals provide students with the opportunity to express their opinions and to engage in reflective, analytical thinking. They also aid students in becoming proficient writers and provide the teacher with an opportunity to see the students' thought processes. Student journals are an excellent assessment tool. In addition, research and creative projects, individual and group presentations, learning logs, and teacher observations are valuable assessment tools that can be used for student evaluation. Assessment will focus on real-world situations and problems that require students to use higher-order thinking processes and demonstrate complex integrated performance. Assessment strategies will enable students to demonstrate what they know and what they are capable of.

Furthermore, they will provide teachers with a means to evaluate student growth and progress over a period of time using various types of evidence.

Student outcomes. All children deserve the opportunity to maximize their potential and become the best they can be. In this instructional climate and using these instructional methods, I believe each student can acquire the skills and understand the concepts required by New York State regulations, be a well-rounded person, and achieve success. Students will develop high expectations for themselves and will set high but realistic goals. As a product of this environment, students will know that if they persevere, they will successfully reach their goals.

On graduation, each child will be able to communicate effectively using the written and spoken word. In addition, they will be able to read with comprehension; perform mathematical calculations and think logically to solve problems; appreciate the fine and performing arts; realize their relationship to their environment and the global community; have an awareness of history and geography and understand their influence on people's lives and their relevance to the world today; understand the basics of science and scientific thought; be computer proficient and understand the role, the relevance, and the impact of modern technology in our world. Students will be able to make connections across the disciplines and realize the relevancy of what they have learned to their lives. Students will know how to think critically and reflectively and will have the necessary perspective to make value judgments.

Students' inquisitiveness and curiosity will not be extinguished. Rather, they will leave school with a well-developed love of learning and an appreciation for the learning process that will remain with them throughout their lives. They will be independent learners who can seek and obtain knowledge on their own. Each child will leave school with the ability to ask and seek out answers to questions, to make discoveries, and to take risks. They will learn about their heritage and the heritage of others so that they are appreciative, understanding, and tolerant of diversity. Students will develop their individuality, realize their importance as individuals, and understand the value of the contributions they can make to society. However, they will also be able to work cooperatively in groups and be able to be consensus builders. Students must also realize the power of persuasion but have the ability to compromise to benefit the needs of many.

In addition, it is vital that on graduation students have a well-developed sense of self-respect as well as respect for others and for the environment. Children will leave school feeling self-confident and secure, with a positive self-image. Students will feel that while attending school they are an integral part of the community and will realize the value of community and shared leadership and decision making. They must feel that they are respected, understood, listened to, valued, and appreciated community members. Students will go out into the world with the knowledge that they learned and performed to the best of their ability. On leaving school, children will have a sense of direction and purpose. They will leave as independent and interdependent individuals capable of availing themselves of the opportunities to participate as ethical and productive citizens in a globally interdependent society.

Leadership and governance. An effective, proactive, visionary, and interdependent principal is at the heart of a school that provides a nurturing instructional climate, effective and meaningful instruction, and positive student outcomes. The principal is instrumental in setting the tone for the school and in creating the school's unique culture.

To create and maintain a productive and positive learning environment while maximizing teaching potential and student achievement, I firmly believe that administrators, teachers, and schools must be constantly evolving by going through a process of self-renewal and evaluation. As a leader, it is incumbent on me to guarantee that this process occurs so that our school can remain effective. To establish and maintain this learning environment and to ensure that this process occurs, I will be proactive, visible, accessible, flexible, understanding and interdependent, and I will create a sense of community. As such, I will continuously be engaged in rapport building by facilitating and fostering good communication and cooperation leading to consensus and cohesiveness among administration, faculty, students, and parents. Maintaining a positive and nurturing instructional climate will be a top priority and will remain in the forefront of my vision. These characteristics and their outcomes will help to create a clear vision and mission for our school.

As principal, I envision my school running within the framework of an interdependent philosophy. To facilitate interdependence, I will work in concert with faculty and other school personnel, students, and parents to promote feelings of cohesiveness and community. In furtherance of creating a sense of community and to increase my visibility, I will initiate a school planning team. Besides me, this team will include other school leaders, at least one teacher representative from each department, and parent and student representatives. The team will collaborate to write, evaluate, and revise our school's educational plan. This plan will include a collaboratively developed vision resulting in the creation of a mission statement for our school. The team will also be concerned with such issues as ensuring that our school's mission and philosophy are carried out; creating a welcoming and orderly atmosphere for staff, students, and parents; securing and allocating instructional and noninstructional resources; developing meaningful professional activities and workshops for staff; maximizing parent participation through the development of community outreach and parent education programs; designing an organizational plan and structure; developing and using instructional materials in alignment with our instructional programs; aligning assessment strategies with curriculum; evaluating student performance and school effectiveness; and providing crisis intervention and support services. Implementation of a school planning team will foster a collaborative, consensual school community where administrators, faculty, parents, and students can regularly communicate and cooperate with one another to ensure that our school's mission is effectively carried out.

To further build and reinforce a sense of community, I will encourage intervisitation between teachers. This will promote teamwork and the sharing of ideas and materials between colleagues. Through this interaction and intervisitation, teachers will broaden their knowledge, enhance their pedagogical perspective; renew their professional spirit, commitment, and relationships; and build community. For these same reasons, I will also create educational teams within and across disciplines. Within these teams, teachers can work together to plan and evaluate lessons, develop interdisciplinary resources, and support one another.

As principal, I will act supportively and as a resource for my colleagues. I will offer guidance and training on effective teaching and questioning strategies and techniques; the development and use of primary source materials for the classroom; the creation of themes, aims, and projects in thrust with New York State's performance standards; and classroom management strategies. By working with teachers in a cooperative environment, I will facilitate community, teamwork, professional growth, and effective teaching, leading to positive student outcomes. Principals who help colleagues develop their own skills and enhance their professional performance positively impact multitudes of students. As a principal, I see myself as a catalyst who motivates and facilitates effective teaching and student learning as well as playing a significant role in the development of youngsters' attitudes, ideas, and values. Thus, it is my responsibility to ensure that my teachers are committed to enhancing their performance to achieve pedagogical excellence. Similarly, department chairs will support and intensively coach new teachers and closely watch their progress. I will also initiate a peer coaching or mentoring program whereby all teachers who are new to our school will be paired with an effective, experienced teacher for a 6-month period. The pair will observe one another and reflect on each other's lessons. Teacher pairs may also work together to plan lessons and discuss classroom management issues and procedures, and the mentor will help the newer teacher get acquainted with the school building and other personnel. The mentor will help the new teacher become a viable member of our community.

To further build community, I will work to establish strong ties to and have open lines of communication with the Superintendent's office, the surrounding community and its leaders, and the neighboring business and professional communities. This will enable our school to obtain many grants and additional resources. These contacts may also provide opportunities for professional development workshops, student internships, speakers to address parents' concerns and to speak to classes, advisers for school clubs and teams, and funding for special projects. In addition, this will increase our school's visibility and make us accessible to the community.

To ensure my own visibility and accessibility, I will maintain an open door policy for teachers, students, and parents so that they can feel free to drop in and discuss issues, problems, or concerns they have. I will also be sure to walk around the building numerous times during the day, speaking to students and staff, dropping into offices and classrooms, and observing classes. In the mornings, I will position myself at the main entrance to greet arriving staff and students. As principal, I hope to teach a class so that I never lose touch with the students and so I can better relate to teachers and their concerns.

As a leader, I will not demand anything from staff that I do not demand from myself. I will be fair, just, and even-handed and will offer praise and encouragement to my staff. I will act as their coach and treat them as members of our school's team. Hopefully, this will ensure that they become team players. I will treat them as professionals and will communicate with them openly and honestly. I will provide them with opportunities for self-evaluation and reflective thinking and will offer constructive criticism. I will never embarrass or humiliate them and will always treat them with respect. It is my hope that they will treat me the same way.

I envision a school in which the teamwork mind-set is shared by all. This team spirit will permeate the environment, and its effects will be evidenced by the quality education all students receive. Our school's philosophy revolves around the healthy development of the whole mind: socially, emotionally, and academically. By recruiting staff who understand and believe in our mission to be proactive, all will benefit from interdependency. Teachers and other staff will be empowered so that a proactive and interdependent environment can be created and maintained. Our school's priority will be to address the needs of the students and their families so that all can achieve success as independent and interdependent, productive members of society. I truly believe that with this philosophy of leadership and governance, we can have a productive, effective, nurturing school community where children receive a quality education and achieve social, emotional, and academic success.

Sample 2

Student outcomes. I believe that every student can learn. No matter what socioeconomic group students come from, they all deserve the opportunity to become the best that they can be. Students should develop high expectations for themselves and set high goals.

They should learn to read, write, and be able to use numbers in early grades. They should learn how to think critically and use higher-level thinking skills. They should learn how to obtain knowledge on their own and see that all knowledge is connected. They should develop a love of literature. They should learn about their community, their country, and the world.

I would want the students to develop responsibility for themselves, other students, adults, and their surroundings. They should be involved in many activities that raise self-esteem. They should learn about their own heritage as well as the contributions of many different groups. Children should feel good about themselves.

Every child is special in some way. Students would have the opportunity to develop talents in many different areas, such as art, music, gymnastics, chess, and so on. Perhaps a student would excel in one of these areas and that would serve to motivate him or her to come to school and to try to excel in other areas as well. Students should want to come to school.

Young children are usually excited about starting school. This enthusiasm should not be allowed to burn out. It should be nurtured.

Instructional climate. The school climate should be nurturing, supportive, and respectful. The teachers must show respect to each other, the parents, and the students, through their words and actions.

Negative comments would be kept to a minimum. Praise and positive reinforcement would be evident throughout the building. Student of the Week bulletin boards featuring projects and stories would be on display in all classrooms. Awards, such as best attendance, most improved, and so on would be given out at assembly programs. Lists of winners would be prominently displayed. Bulletin boards would show students' work and be bright and up–to-date. Students would be actively involved in decorating their rooms and hallway bulletin boards. Murals, for example, could be painted in classrooms, hallways, and lunchrooms.

School should be a place that is comfortable and safe. Parents would be welcomed as volunteers and as visitors. The community should be involved, as everyone works together to motivate the students to reach their goals.

I would want to create an atmosphere where teachers are treated as professionals and where cooperation and collegiality are the rule, not the exception.

Instruction. Grouping in this school would be heterogeneous so no child is stigmatized for being in "2-8." Children would be able to help each other. Class size would be as small as possible so the students could get as much individual attention as possible.

Teachers would be encouraged to sit at their desks as little as possible. Their desks would be off in the corner of the room. Teachers would be actively engaged with the students at all times. For group lessons, whenever possible, students would sit in a circle as close to the teacher as they can, given the size of the group. Students would sit in groups, not in rows.

Balanced literacy and an interdisciplinary approach would be used. Multicultural matters would be plentiful and a part of the curriculum. Hands-on activities would be used as much as possible, particularly in science and mathematics. Collaborative work among the students would be encouraged. Students would have opportunities to get up and move around and not be expected to sit at their desks all day. Encyclopedias, other resource materials, and computers would be available to enhance learning.

Music and art would no longer be considered extras. They would have a prominent role in the school. There would be a school band, chorus, and so on. Every class would have time to visit centers where students could further explore existing interests and develop new ones. Trips would be a part of the curriculum.

Leadership and governance. The leader sets the tone for the school and is responsible for setting the instructional climate. I would be a visible presence and would not be locked in my office. I would walk around the school at least once a day visiting every room. I would try to get to know as many students as possible. I would teach a lesson at least once a week to a different class. I would give out the awards at the Awards Assembly myself and invite the award winners to a Breakfast With the Principal.

A planning team would be initiated, which would have a chief role in the governance of the school. I would ask for volunteers and hope to get a group of teachers and other staff members who would be enthusiastic about sharing increased responsibility and willing to take on extra work. I would arrange for a common meeting time during the school day at least once a week. I would meet with them once a month or more frequently if they so desired. I would hope that we could attract parents to this committee as well. I would ask the team to look for areas in which we need improvement, but also to be on the lookout for positive things going on in the school.

I would speak about these positive things over the loudspeaker and at faculty conferences. I would encourage teachers to share projects with me as well as with other teachers. The planning team would be actively involved in preparing the agenda for these meetings. We would divide up into smaller groups and engage in staff development. The committee would decide the topics and pick the leaders.

The planning team would also be involved in establishing a school newspaper. This would encourage the sharing of ideas and special events going on throughout the building and the community. This would also help develop a sense of pride.

I would work hard to establish ties to the community school district personnel as well as the community and business community so that we could obtain as many grants as possible for the school. This would be a way of increasing our valuable resources. I would also provide as many opportunities as possible for professional development workshops and intervisitations between teachers and between our school and other schools. The team could send out groups to visit other schools in our district as well as in other areas.

The school should work closely with the parents. Workshops could be held for them on various topics of interest, and they would be invited to read to the students as volunteers and to form clubs, especially at lunchtime, such as sewing, chess, or basketball. Parents can serve as role models and show their children how important education is to them. They can also take part in special school events such as Career Day.

I would offer intense supervision to new teachers and closely watch their progress. I would set up a system of buddy teachers and set up a schedule of observations by new teachers of more experienced personnel. I would use video cameras extensively to tape lessons done by new teachers. They could then view them and analyze the lessons themselves and later with me.

An open door policy would be established. Teachers and parents would be encouraged to come to me with their questions and concerns. As a leader I would try to create a feeling of *community:* Everyone working together toward a common goal—helping our children be the best that they can be! I would encourage staff members and parents to become more involved in the school and to be willing to take on more responsibility. In this way I believe that they would develop the feeling that it is truly "our school," that these are "our children," and that while undeniably the problems we face are "our problems," the successes we realize will surely be "*our successes*"!

Sample 3

Leadership platform. A school is a community of individuals who are committed to a set of guiding principles, and who take personal responsibility for the success of each member of the community. As the educational leader of this school community, my mission is to support the development of an educational environment that addresses the intellectual and developmental needs of the middle school child, that acknowledges individual variability while maintaining a high level of expectations for all, and that provides a variety of forums for individual and collective reflection and self-assessment.

Central to the creation of a school culture that reflects my vision are four interrelated components: student outcomes, instructional climate, philosophy of instruction, and governance and leadership model. Culture is defined as the habits, routines, and behaviors (conscious and unconscious) that reveal the beliefs, norms, and values that build up over time within a school. Within this definition are four subcategories: interpersonal culture, or the philosophy and level of collegiality among members of the school community; organizational culture, or the philosophy and level of internal support for practices and programs; teaching culture, or the philosophy and level of belief in student achievement; and external culture, or the philosophy and level of external support for practices and programs. The art of the principal lies in her ability to orchestrate each element in the environment into a unified culture of shared expectations and accountability. To better understand my vision of leadership, it is necessary to define each component and demonstrate how each is integrated into the overarching school culture.

Student outcomes. The cornerstone of any educational vision is student outcomes. Viewed holistically, students need to develop the academic, social, and personal levels of competence that will prepare them to be productive members of society and contributors to the workforce. All children have the potential to reach high standards of personal competence. My vision is to create a culture that supports all students in realizing their potential by creating an instructional program that supports high academic achievement and that encourages the development of self-discipline, positive self-image, strong personal values, and unilateral respect for all school community members.

Academically, students would develop literacy skills in written and spoken English and apply these skills to the mastery of content area material. This is critical in light of the implementation of the performance standards and the new promotional policy. They would have access to technology and develop the skills necessary to locate, utilize, and evaluate electronic information. Students would have extensive exposure to the arts, so as to develop an appreciation for the richness and diversity of cultures. Learning would be interactive, with ample opportunities for students to experience "real world" applications of knowledge, so as to see the connections between content area materials and between the classroom and life.

Concurrently, students would develop social consciousness and civic responsibility. They would have opportunities to participate in school and community-based service projects whose focus is the development of student awareness of social and political issues, and the relevance of these issues to their lives, the lives of their families, and the life of their community. Ideally, these opportunities would be intergenerational and multicultural, so as to engage students in meaningful and sustained relationships with adults and younger children from all cultural and economic groups, as well as with their peers. In this way, students would be able to develop sensitivity to the needs of others, recognize their similarities, appreciate their differences, and thereby develop a sense of mutual respect. Integral to these service projects should be connections to their classroom content-area learning so as to reinforce the connections between school and life.

Academic and service learning outcomes are intrinsically connected to the developmental outcomes for students. These are crucial for all students, but particularly for adolescents who are grappling with issues of identity and self-worth. Integrated into student outcomes for academic and social learning would be outcomes for personal development and growth. Students should have multiple opportunities to develop self-awareness, self-competence, and self-esteem. Educational experiences would be varied and allow for individual differences, learning styles, and rates of development. Opportunities for student self-expression would abound within the context of social and personal accountability. Character education would be a key component of the educational program and support the development of students who strive to achieve their personal best.

Instructional climate. The realization of student outcomes is inextricably tied to the instructional climate. My vision is of the school as safe harbor or sanctuary in which students, staff, and parents feel safe and nurtured, and in which there is an atmosphere of personal responsibility and mutual respect. The culture of the school would support collaboration, foster reflection, and celebrate accomplishment. Multiple opportunities for celebration of individual and schoolwide success in all areas of achievement would be developed. Student work would be prominently displayed throughout the building, and efforts to acknowledge each student's strengths would be encouraged. Classrooms would be print- and material-rich, and students would have daily access to technology. A code of appropriate behavior would be developed, agreed on, and modeled by all. Consequences for inappropriate behavior would be clear and consistently enforced by all members of the school community.

The school climate would also support professional development that is an outgrowth of self-assessment and reflection and that supports collaboration and collegiality. All staff have the capacity for professional growth. My vision is to create a culture that supports teachers in fulfilling this capacity by providing new teacher training, leadership opportunities, meaningful staff development, and experience in innovative educational practices and strategies. Opportunities for staff to develop and refine their instruction would be organic, teacher directed, and sustained throughout the year. Flexible programming would provide time for teachers to participate in weekly study groups to examine student work and teacher practice in the context of the standards. Each study group would follow specific protocols and be facilitated by a peer coach,

Teachers would participate in weekly peer observations, and classrooms would serve as demonstration sites for specific organizational and instructional practices. Structured opportunities for daily interaction among staff around instructional issues, and ongoing reflection among colleagues about student work and outcomes, would replace one-day trainings and workshops. Ample professional resources would be housed in the professional library so as to support all aspects of the professional development program.

Time and funding for teachers to participate in professional conferences would be provided, with the expectation that they would turnkey this training. In this way, a cadre of in-house specialists would be developed to build school-wide capacity and foster the development of a community of learners.

Parents would also have ample opportunities to develop the capacity to be partners in their children's education. All parents have the responsibility to be active members in their children's educational experience. My vision is to create a culture that supports parents in exercising this responsibility by fostering a dynamic school/family partnership whose focus is active parental involvement in the educational decision-making process and shared, constructive evaluation of learning policies. A parent center with extensive resources in multiple languages would be established. Parent workshops on a wide spectrum of topics, ranging from parenting skills, to literacy strategies, to leadership teams, would be offered throughout the day, as well as in the evening and on weekends to encourage participation. Translators would be provided to facilitate interaction. Parents would be encouraged to participate in the daily activities of the school, to serve on committees and leadership teams, to become volunteers and tutors, and to participate, with teachers and administrators, in study groups around student work. They would be viewed as full and equal partners in the educational process and in the daily life of the school.

Instructional program. The instructional climate is the framework that supports the instructional program. Students would have a variety of learning experiences within and outside of the classroom that focus on the development of the habits of mind of the life-long learner. The schedule would be divided into instructional blocks that are interdisciplinary in focus and that are taught by a team of teachers. These teachers would be a combination of generalists and specialists, and they would develop curriculum that explores the connection between content areas and between the classroom and the world. This curriculum would reflect multiple instructional strategies, so as to accommodate diverse student learning needs and styles. Students would be grouped heterogeneously, and teachers would follow their classes from grade to grade to support instructional and interpersonal continuity. Curriculum would include authentic, project-based learning, and opportunities for community mentorships. Class groupings and scheduling would be flexible, so as to allow for reconfiguration of students and blocks of time as needed. Each student would have an adult adviser and a minimum of 20 minutes of advisory per day.

Opportunities for enrichment, intervention, and extracurricular activities would be offered before and after the school day. Parents and members of the community would be encouraged to offer courses during the extended day, as well as to serve as tutors and mentors. The assessment model would incorporate a spectrum of tools so as to support a holistic approach to evaluation. Foremost among these tools would be student portfolios and student exhibitions. Rubrics for assessing student growth toward the standard, and the tools to assess this growth, would be developed by students and their teachers with the input of the school community. Every aspect of the instructional program would focus on the diverse needs of the students; on their academic, social, and personal growth; and on high standards for student achievement. The school community would be committed to maintaining the same high level of expectations for all students, while acknowledging the individual differences among students in meeting the standards, and to encouraging and nurturing student enthusiasm for learning.

Governance and leadership. Essential to the realization of my educational vision is a model of governance and leadership that supports collaboration and a sense of personal accountability to a set of guiding principles, and that includes and encourages multiple perspectives. In this model, the principal would be responsible for providing the time and the structure for students, staff, parents, and other school community members to openly participate in some aspect of the governance process. This would require identifying specific issues and constituencies and creating multiple governance forums, as well as ensuring that all stakeholders are involved at some point, as appropriate. This includes not only teachers, parents, and students but also custodial and cafeteria staff, health providers, and members of community-based organizations. The principal would also create an environment that fosters open dialogue among the various stakeholders and that provides training in the new paradigm of the shared decision-making process. In this environment, the goals of the school would be developed collaboratively with student achievement as the focus, and the progress toward the goals would be assessed through a process of ongoing reflection. The specific structure of the assessment component would be developed by the school community and would incorporate multiple assessment models, both formal and informal. Responsibility for student achievement would be shared by all stakeholders, and finger-pointing and blaming would be replaced by an atmosphere of collegiality and collaboration in which each member of the school community would take responsibility for the successes and the failures.

As the leader in this school culture, I would model the values, beliefs, and behavior I sought to engender. My leadership style would be proactive, flexible, and reflective. I would be genuine in my commitment to a collaborative approach to leadership and sustain a constant focus on the fundamental belief that student achievement must drive all aspects of the educational process. I would maintain an open door policy, seeking input from members of the school community and participating in the reflective process. I would actively work to secure the resources needed to support the instructional process and to develop and sustain a supportive and open relationship with the district and the community. I would lead by example and demonstrate those qualities of integrity, focus, and mutual respect that are fundamental to my vision of a school community. I would share in both the joys of our successes and in the struggles of our setbacks. I would be coach, facilitator, and exemplar, sustaining the vision and holding the guiding principles continually in the forefront of all our endeavors.

NOTES

1. Although the special supervisor as a specific title disappeared, a host of other supervisors later emerged, such as supervisors of curriculum, instruction, and reading, among others.

2. For a more in-depth historical analysis, see Glanz (1998).

3. This section is informed by the work of Reitzug (1997).

4. Favorite surveys that we use include the Myers-Briggs Type Indicator (Myers & McCaulley, 1985), the Personal Values Questionnaire and Managerial Style Questionnaire from McBer and Company (1994), the Let Me Learn Learning Combination Inventory Professional Form (Johnson & Dainton, 1996), Assessing Your Natural Leadership Qualities (Glanz, 2002), and the Natural Life Energy Survey (Null, 1996). We also encourage our students to read *The Reflective Supervisor* by Calabrese and Zepeda (1997).

5. For a more in-depth discussion of descriptive feedback, see Osterman and Kottkamp (1993), pp. 91–95.

6. This exercise has been adapted from Osterman and Kottkamp (1993), p. 96. See pp. 96–99 for a more detailed discussion of the process.

7. Special thanks to Bruce Barnett of the University of Northern Colorado for sharing this format.

8. Special thanks to Aimee Horowitz (Sample 1) and Fran Macko (Sample 3) for giving us permission to share their vision statements. The second one is anonymous.

2

Three Interpersonal Approaches to Supervision

*A barrier to communication is something that keeps meanings from meeting.
. . . Because so much of our education misleads people into thinking that
communication is easier than it is, they become discouraged and give up
when they run into difficulty. Because they do not understand the nature
of the problem, they do not know what to do. The wonder is not that communicating is as difficult as it is, but that it occurs as much as it does.*

Howe, 1963, pp. 23–24

In the previous chapter you became acquainted with the historical framework of supervision and began to examine your present personal beliefs
within the current context of supervision. This chapter explores and develops
the interpersonal skills that we believe are a prerequisite to all effective supervisory practice. After a brief introduction to the philosophical principles underlying the supervisory beliefs and methods presented in this book, we briefly
discuss the various communication techniques that are essential for all effective
interpersonal relationships: listening, nonverbal clues, and reflecting, clarifying statements. We then offer exercises that hone these techniques. A description of the three interpersonal approaches that we believe are most effective in
working with teachers follows. Before practicing each of the three interpersonal
approaches in a group, we introduce a reflective practice model and provide
guidelines for reflective practice that are used throughout this book to build and
reinforce skills. This chapter concludes with two exercises that permit you to
begin to internalize these approaches prior to implementing them on site.

HOW WE LEARN

People learn best through active involvement and through thinking about and becoming articulate about what they have learned. Processes, practices, and policies built on this view of learning are at the heart of a more expanded view of teacher development that encourages teachers to involve themselves as learners—in much the same way as they wish their students would.

Lieberman, 1995, p. 592

How many lectures have we all sat through during which the speaker expounded at great length about the importance of student-centered learning in the classroom? How many workshops have we attended where the presenter talked on and on about student-centered practices? A district superintendent recently hired one of us to facilitate a teacher-centered retreat, which he began with a 2-hour speech. Ann Lieberman (1995) pointed out that "What everyone appears to want for students—a wide array of learning opportunities that engage students in experiencing, creating, and solving real problems, using their own experiences, and working with others—is for some reason denied to teachers when they are learners." The main goal of this book is to "walk the talk": to enable students of supervision not only to learn teacher-centered supervisory methods but also to have the opportunity to practice the skills and experience the perspectives as they are exposed to them.

The approaches to providing feedback outlined in this chapter and the methods presented for becoming proficient in their use are based on constructivist principles. In the Preface to *In Search of Understanding the Case for Constructivist Classrooms,* Catherine Twomey Fosnot (1993) draws on a synthesis of work in cognitive psychology, philosophy, and anthropology to define constructivism as a theory not about teaching, but about knowledge and learning. Knowledge is defined as temporary, developmental, socially and culturally mediated, and nonobjective. Learning is "a self-regulated process of resolving inner cognitive conflicts that often become apparent through concrete experience, collaborative discourse, and reflection" (Fosnot, 1993, p. 2). In other words, meaningful knowledge and learning are centered around the learner and are best constructed through collaboration and reflection around personal experience.

This belief has ramifications for the two principal focuses of this chapter: interpersonal approaches for providing feedback and the use of reflective practice in working with teachers and in learning supervisory skills. With respect to working with teachers, no matter what the developmental level of the staff member or the interpersonal orientation of the supervisor, the person receiving feedback should be involved in generating ideas and solutions for the situation under discussion. With regard to learning how to provide feedback, it is only through practicing the skills and reflecting on their development that students of supervision will internalize and personalize what they have learned.

LISTENING, REFLECTING, AND CLARIFYING TECHNIQUES

Before we begin learning and practicing the three different approaches to providing feedback, it is important to incorporate skills that promote communication as well as to become aware of those that create barriers. Table 2.1 provides three types of skills that foster bridging the interpersonal gap. Each category can be integrated into any of the feedback approaches. In each approach, we want to encourage the teacher to provide as complete a picture of his or her perspective as possible. The listening techniques and the nonverbal clues are key means to promote open responses. The reflecting and clarifying techniques also are crucial to all the approaches because they facilitate avoiding or clearing up potential misunderstandings and miscommunications. They provide verbal techniques for separating the supervisor's understandings and perceptions from the teacher's without accusing or putting the other person on the defensive. To remind you of appropriate responses, we recommend that you use the crib sheets that summarize the key techniques and steps for practice and actual implementation. Detachable cards for these techniques are provided on a perforated page at the back of the book.

Table 2.1   Communication Techniques

Listening	Nonverbal Clues	Reflecting and Clarifying
"Uh-huh"	Affirmative nods and smiles	"You're angry because . . ."
"OK"		
"I'm following you"	Open body language, e.g., arms open	"You feel . . . because . . ."
"For instance"	Appropriate distance from speaker-not too close or too far	"You seem quite upset."
"And?"		"So, you would like . . ."
"Mmm"		
"I understand"	Eye contact	"I understand that you see the problem as . . ."
"This is great information for me"	Nondistracting environment	"I'm not sure, but I think you mean . . ."
"Really?"	Face speaker and leanforward	
"Then?"		"I think you're saying . . ."
"So?"	Barrier-free space, e.g., desk not used as blocker	
"Tell me more"		
"Go on"		
"I see"		
"Right"		

Table 2.2 contains a summary of common communication spoilers and high-risk responses culled from the interpersonal skills literature. We refer to them as "high-risk" responses because their impact is frequently negative, and as a general rule, they should be avoided. Nonetheless, a few of them can be effective in special circumstances.[1]

The communication techniques and barriers to avoid are critical components of feedback. Effective and appropriate responses are difficult to develop because the barriers to communication are engrained in our language and habits. For these reasons, it is important to practice the communication techniques in class and in your professional and personal lives as much as possible before proceeding to the feedback approaches. As the communication techniques begin to be a part of your repertoire, they will enhance the feedback approaches. The following exercises are an introduction to the type of reflective practice role-plays that you will find throughout the book.

Table 2.2   Barriers to Communication

Barrier Type	Examples
1. Judging • Criticizing • Name calling and labeling • Diagnosing—analyzing motives instead of listening • Praising evaluatively	1. Judging • "You are lazy; your lesson plan is poor." • "You are inexperienced, an intellectual" • "You're taking out your anger on her" • "I know what you need" • "You're terrific!"
2. Solutions • Ordering • Threatening • Moralizing or preaching • Inappropriate questioning or prying • Advising • Lecturing	2. Solutions • "You must . . ." "You have to . . ." "You will . . ." • "If you don't . . ." "You had better or else" • "It is your duty/responsibility; you should" • "Why?" "What?" "How?" "When?" • "What I would do is . . ." "It would be best for you" • "Here is why you are wrong . . ." "Do you realize . . ."
3. Avoiding the other's concerns • Diverting • Reassuring • Withdrawing • Sarcasm	3. Avoiding the other's concerns • "Speaking of . . ." "Apropos . . ." "You know what happened to . . ." • "It's not so bad . . ." "You're lucky . . ." "You'll feel better" • "I'm very busy. . ." "I can't talk right now . . ." "I'll get back to you . . ." • "I really feel sorry for you"

REFLECTIVE PRACTICE

Class Practice

Everyone in the class should find a partner and face that person. Each student will take a turn listening and responding to his or her partner. The goal is to use the communication techniques to foster an effective interchange and to avoid falling into any of the barrier traps. Keep Tables 2.1 and 2.2 handy to facilitate the learning process.

Step 1. Each partner should take a minute to think of a current personal or professional dilemma.

Step 2. Partner No. 1 will recount his or her dilemma.

Step 3. Partner No. 2 will show interest in the speaker's situation by using the listening and nonverbal techniques and avoiding the barriers (Tables 2.1 and 2.2).

Step 4. Partner No. 2 will choose reflecting and clarifying techniques to verify what he or she heard and show understanding of the feelings expressed.

Step 5. Partner No. 1 will give feedback on how well partner No. 2 used the techniques.

Change partners and repeat the cycle. Each cycle should take no more than 5 minutes.

Site Practice

During the next week, target someone who is going to share an experience, problem, or dilemma with you. It can be a spouse, a child, a colleague, or a student. Have your cards with Tables 2.1 and 2.2 on hand, and practice your listening and communication techniques. When the interchange is completed, reflect on what worked well and what areas need improvement. Jot down notes so that you can share your reflections on the experience with your colleagues, first on e-mail, a discussion board, or in a chat room and then in class. You may feel a little uncomfortable at first using these techniques. Remember that because the listeners are involved in their virtually uninterrupted sharing, they won't be aware of your novice status as active listeners.

APPROACHES TO PROVIDING FEEDBACK[2]

With communication techniques now in hand, we can introduce and discuss approaches that are fundamental to providing effective feedback. Some textbooks suggest that individual behavior can be divided into four major groups that require four styles of responses (Glickman, Gordon, & Ross-Gordon, 2004). For example, in his developmental model, Glickman recommends four approaches to working with individuals:

1. Directive control

2. Directive informational

3. Collaborative

4. Self-directed

These approaches range from almost total supervisor control to primarily teacher control. The approach the supervisor chooses is supposed to match the specific teacher's level of development. In reality, many of us tend to favor one approach in our interactions with others. In the directive control approach, the supervisor makes the decision and tells the individual or group how to proceed. The supervisor who uses the directive informational approach frames the choices for the group or individual and then asks for input. In the collaborative approach, the supervisor and the individual or group share information and possible solutions as equals to arrive at a mutual plan. In the fourth approach, the supervisor facilitates the individual or group in developing a self-plan or in making its own decision, Glickman et al. (2004), for example, believe that the teacher's level of development, expertise, and commitment and the nature of the situation determine the choice of approach. We agree that "different folks need different strokes" and that varying school circumstances call for a range of approaches; however, we believe that meaningful learning is dependent on the learner's involvement in constructing that knowledge and so there is no need for the directive control approach. Many supervisors over the years have used this approach, many continue to follow it, and you may favor it yourself. Nonetheless, we think that the collaborative and nondirective models are the most effective, with the occasional application of a modified directive informational approach.

Elena's Dilemma

To illustrate the use of the three approaches, we will present three variations of the same dilemma and offer suggestions on how the different models could be applied to the scenarios (see Table 2.3 for a summary and comparison of the three approaches).

Elena Santiago was appointed principal of New Hope Middle School in September. New Hope Middle School is a large urban school that has a reputation for lax discipline and an unruly atmosphere. In Elena's previous position as an assistant principal, also in a difficult environment, she had gained the confidence of the staff through her high expectations, blended with excellent interpersonal skills and a collaborative manner. The school district's awareness of her effectiveness led to her appointment as principal of New Hope Middle School. In her first weeks at the school, she has been working closely with the school-based planning team to make decisions that will affect the school climate positively.

Passing in the hallways between classes has been a major focus. She has noticed that some teachers are not following the school-based planning team's decision that all teachers should stand at the classroom doors between periods. Elena has decided to discuss the issue with three teachers she has repeatedly observed at their desks during passing times.

Scenario I

Elena approaches Martha before school one morning. Martha also joined the New Hope faculty in September. New Hope is her first teaching job, and despite a solid academic background and an assigned mentor, she seems somewhat overwhelmed.

Elena: Good morning Martha. I've noticed that you haven't been making it to your door between classes recently. Tell me what's been happening.

Martha: I know. I get so bogged down toward the end of class. I can't seem to make it through what I've planned for the class; students come up to talk to me at the end of the period and I'm left with assignments I've either not collected or new homework sheets that I haven't had time to distribute. So, everyone is gathered around me at the end of class, and my next class appears before I get out from behind my desk.

Elena: I remember those days. It took me quite a while until I figured out a system that worked for me. What I did first was to post a sign-up sheet for students to talk to me outside of class so that they didn't bombard me at the end of every period. That way they knew I was accessible but didn't keep me pinned to the front of the classroom. Then I created a system for collecting homework and distributing assignments. I set up individual files, and I made sure I stopped active work 5 minutes early to allow the class to hand in their homework and pick up new assignments. During those few minutes, I was able to pull myself together and take care of an occasional individual emergency. Could any of these ideas work for you?

Martha: I like the idea of having students sign up to talk to me. There's always a group anyway that comes to see me after school. A sign-up sheet might help organize the afterschool chaos, too. I also have to pay attention to ending the lesson before the bell rings so that I can take care of business and get to the door. Maybe I could set a timer that would ring 5 minutes before the end of the period. I have so many students that I don't think I could set up a filing system.

Elena: Do you have any ideas for a system that might work for you?

Martha: What if I appointed two monitors each month in every class to collect homework and distribute assignments at the end of each period?

Elena: That sounds like a good idea. Let's go over your plan. First, you will post a sign-up sheet for students to talk to you instead of coming up to you at the end of the period. Second, you'll set a timer so that you end 5 minutes before the passing bell to allow time for homework distribution and collection. Finally, you will appoint two monitors in each class to take care of the homework so that you can prepare to be at the door during passing. How does that sound to you? Do you want to restate the plan to make sure we're on the same page?

Martha: Sure. I'm going to get a timer so I can end class 5 minutes early to take care of homework. I'm going to appoint monitors to collect homework and distribute new assignments, and I'm going to post a sign-up list so that the students don't detain me at the end of the class. Finally, I'll be at my door at passing time!

Elena: Terrific! How about setting up a time for us to meet and see how this system works for you? I can meet with you at the same time next week so we can catch any glitches that may have surfaced.

Martha: OK. I'll see you after I finish standing at the door at the end of my class!

REFLECTION

How does Elena approach Martha? How does she foster Elena's "buy-in" of her suggestions? What does she do to ensure that the suggestions don't just remain suggestions?

I. The Directive Informational Approach

KEY STEPS—DIRECTIVE INFORMATIONAL APPROACH

1. *Identify the problem or goal and solicit clarifying information.*
2. *Offer solutions. Ask for the teacher's input into the alternatives offered and request additional ideas.*
3. *Summarize chosen alternatives, ask for confirmation, and request that the teacher restate final choices.*
4. *Set a follow-up plan and meeting.*

This approach is used primarily for new teachers or those who are experiencing difficulties that they don't have the knowledge, expertise, or confidence to resolve on their own or collaboratively. These teachers are seeking or need direction and guidance from a supervisor who can provide expert information and experienced guidance. Nonetheless, the supervisor wants the teacher to seek solutions and generate ideas so as to feel at least some ownership of the final choices. Therefore, the supervisor is the initiator of suggestions and alternatives, which the teacher can then revise and refine and to which he or she can add ideas.

1. *Identify the problem or goal and solicit clarifying information.*
    Avoid small talk and focus immediately on the problem or goal in question. Ask the teacher for clarification of the situation so that you are both sure that you are addressing the same problem or goal.

2. *Offer solutions. Ask for the teacher's input into the alternatives offered and request additional ideas.*
    Even though the new teacher might feel overwhelmed, the supervisor's ideas will probably stimulate his or her thinking. Offering input and requesting additional ideas will give the teacher a feeling of ownership and allow him or her to begin constructing a personal perspective. Separating the alternatives from the request for additional ideas allows the teacher to think through the suggestions and then come up with modifications or new possibilities.

3. *Summarize chosen alternatives, ask for confirmation, and request that the teacher restate final choices.*
    Verification that both supervisor and teacher have the same understanding of the final choices is crucial. Two people can easily interpret the same words differently or hear different words. Therefore, if each party repeats his or her understanding, any misunderstandings or differences in perceptions can be cleared before action is taken.

4. *Set a follow-up plan and meeting.*
    A concrete plan (written is preferable) and a scheduled meeting are the only ways that two very busy professionals can be sure of the follow-through that is crucial to the success of any plan.

Scenario II

Ann has been teaching at New Hope for 10 years. Her reputation is that of a cooperative, collaborative, and effective teacher. Elena is therefore surprised to notice that Ann cannot be found consistently at her door between classes. Elena decides to stop by during Ann's free period to find out what's preventing her from carrying out the collective mandate.

Elena: Hi, Ann. I've been checking to see how the staff's decision to post themselves at their doors between periods is working. I noticed that you don't always make it to your door. Anything in particular going on that's keeping you from your post?

Ann: I'm happy you stopped by. I guess two things have been occurring, one of which I can resolve immediately. I'm embarrassed to say it, but sometimes I just get involved with students at the end of class, and since I'm not used to being posted at the door every period, I forget. I do think it's important, so your reminder is really helpful. I'll have to leave a note on my desk to remind myself. The second reason for my negligence is that I've been having difficulty with a couple of students in two classes. They have been causing disruptions that are keeping me from letting the classes out on time.

Elena: So what you're saying is that the combination of your involvement with the students and the newness of the hall monitoring plan have led you to forget to post yourself at the door some of the time. The most important reason seems to be a few discipline problems that are preoccupying you. Is this accurate?

Ann: Sounds right to me.

Elena: Well, I'm happy you already have an idea to resolve the first problem so easily. Tell me more about the disruptive students. Maybe we can figure out something together.

Ann: It's two special needs students in two of my math classes. I haven't discussed the problem with the rest of the team because the students aren't in anyone else's classes. The decision was made to include them in the general ed math classes at their elementary school, and they are having a great deal of difficulty adjusting.

Elena: Have you talked about their behavior with their special ed teachers?

Ann: I know I should, but communication between the special ed and regular teachers hasn't been what it should be. So much of this inclusion is so recent that we just haven't had time to develop proper communication channels. We've had so many initiatives this fall that I can barely keep up with what I have to do.

Elena: I hear what you're saying. However, if two of your classes are being affected by this problem, we have to address it. Do you have any ideas?

Ann: I hate to suggest it, but I can think of one possibility. The school-based planning team might organize a subcommittee of representatives from regular and special ed to figure out what kind of communication we need and how to set it up. In the meantime, I've got to figure out how to handle the short-term dilemma.

Elena: The subcommittee is an excellent idea. I'll bring it up at the next school-based planning meeting. I hope you'll be willing to serve on the committee. In the meantime, I can arrange to free up the special ed teachers and you to meet together to discuss these particular students. Would you mind if I sat in on the meeting to get a clearer picture of what's involved in the realities of inclusion?

Ann: I'd prefer meeting with them on my own the first time. One of the special ed teachers is new and might feel intimidated if you're there. I'd like to get as much honest information as possible.

Elena: I guess it's OK as long as you provide me with written or verbal feedback following the meeting. So, let's see what we've agreed on. First, you'll remember to get to the door on a regular basis. I'll free you and the special ed teachers so that you can talk about the students with special needs. You'll provide me with feedback on that meeting. I'll request to set up a generalized and special ed committee at the next school-based planning meeting and you will serve on it. How does this plan sound to you?

Ann: I'm glad to meet with the special ed teachers and report back to you afterward. I'm not so sure about the committee. I feel like I'm already on overload and am afraid of making another commitment. I wouldn't mind attending one meeting to provide my perspective, but I'm not ready to offer to become a charter member of the committee. Let's hold on that one. In the meantime, I'll already begin trying to get to that door between classes more often.

Elena: Can we look at some times for you to meet with the special ed teachers and to give me feedback on that meeting before I leave?

Ann: Sure. I can stop at your office after school to schedule my meeting with the special ed teachers for sometime next week, and we can meet at this same time the following week, if it's OK with you.

REFLECTION

How does Elena make sure she understands what Ann explains? Does Elena approach Ann differently than Martha? If so, how? How do Ann and Elena deal with their differences?

II. The Collaborative Approach

KEY STEPS—COLLABORATIVE APPROACH

1. *Identify the problem from the teacher's perspective, soliciting as much clarifying information as possible.*
2. *Reflect back what you've heard for accuracy.*
3. *Begin collaborative brainstorming, asking the teacher for his or her ideas first.*
4. *Problem-solve through a sharing and discussion of options.*
5. *Agree on a plan and follow-up meeting.*

In the collaborative approach, the goal is to resolve a problem or reach a goal through shared decision making. The supervisor encourages the teacher to develop his or her ideas first to allow maximum ownership. Nonetheless, the brainstorming and problem solving are shared, and disagreement is encouraged, with assurances that a mutual solution will be reached. The conference always ends with a restatement of agreed-upon plans and setting of a follow-up meeting. Unresolved issues can be included in the planning process and revisited at the follow-up session.

1. *Identify the problem from the teacher's perspective, soliciting as much clarifying information as possible.*

   With the exception of some new teachers and those with problematic practices, the supervisor wants the teacher to initiate the discussion from his or her perspective. The more information provided, the clearer the situation for both parties. Therefore, a more complete description can be drawn out with prompts, that is, eye contact and encouraging open-body language and nonverbal cues, paraphrasing, probing questions, and phrases such as "Tell me more; Uh-huh; I see; I understand."

2. *Reflect back what you've heard for accuracy.*

   It is crucial that you verify that you've heard accurately the content and perspective of the teacher. A summary of what you understood, with the teacher's verification of what you heard, can avoid many misunderstandings and problems down the road. You may feel like you sound silly repeating; rest assured that the teacher is hanging on your every word to be sure that you heard and understood.

3. *Begin collaborative brainstorming, asking the teacher for his or her ideas first.*

   If the supervisor proposes options first, the teacher might not try and develop his or her own ideas and might just follow what the supervisor suggests. Because the teacher is the one most familiar with the situation, it is important to allow him or her to build on that knowledge or to decide to construct a different or new resolution.

4. *Problem solve through a sharing and discussion of options.*

   One of the greatest challenges to a supervisor in a collaborative approach is to encourage disagreement convincingly. Few teachers are accustomed to administrators fostering challenges and encouraging risk taking. Asking for the teacher's suggestions is a first step. Promoting an open dialogue about the options is the second step.

5. *Agree on a plan and follow-up meeting.*

   In the complex lives of teachers and administrators, a written plan on agreed-upon solutions and those yet to be resolved will save a lot of time in the long run. What often seems time consuming can be cost-effective in the final analysis. Taking the time to write out a plan and set up the next appointment are the essential concluding steps.

Scenario III

Will has been teaching for many years. He has his routines down to a science. He teaches in a traditional manner, peppering his well-organized lectures with amusing anecdotes. Although he doesn't provide active resistance to the recently created school-based planning team, he doesn't pay much attention to what comes down from it. As the new kid on the block, Elena wants to solicit cooperation from this veteran teacher without him feeling imposed upon. For this reason, she chooses the self-directed approach to try and encourage him to cooperate with the planning team decision.

Elena: How's it going so far, Will?

Will: It's always fine behind my closed door. It's what goes on outside of my room that leaves something to be desired.

Elena: So, you feel that your classroom is under control, but other parts of the school aren't. Do you want to explain that a little further for me?

Will: Well, I'm sure you know by now. All these new teachers and the problems we have had over the past few years are spilling over into my classroom. They dash to get to my class on time, but the chaotic situation outside of my classroom means it takes longer for them to get settled, and I barely get through my daily plans.

Elena: I think I know what you mean. That's what I wanted to ask you about. Did you see the school-based planning team decision to ask all teachers to be posted at their doors at passing time? The team thought that the whole climate would improve if passing time were orderly. What do you think?

Will: I don't read most of that stuff, but I do try and get to my door when I finish my lesson on time. From the way it looks and sounds, a lot of teachers must be missing in action! (laughs)

Elena: (joking tone) Well, I was looking to your expertise to come up with suggestions to make the new system work.

Will: How about putting a teacher in control on each floor to make sure all the teachers are out there between periods?

Elena: That's a good idea. My only worry is that no one will want to take the job, and there may be some resentment of the teachers who do. What do you think?

Will: You're right. I certainly wouldn't want the job and would resent a first-year teacher telling me what to do. What if it were done on a rotating basis? A different teacher could be in charge every month.

Elena: That's a terrific solution. Would you mind if I brought it to the school-based planning committee this week?

Will: Not at all. Just don't put my name to it. I don't want them coming around asking me to get involved! In the meantime, I'll watch this floor unofficially.

Elena: I'd really appreciate it. To sum up our conversation, I'll bring up your suggestion for peer monitoring of teachers between classes at the next school-based planning meeting; in the interim, you'll unofficially monitor your floor. Can I check back with you in a week and see how you think the hall situation is progressing?

Will: Sure. Same time, same place is fine with me.

REFLECTION

Why doesn't Elena start out mentioning to Will that he hasn't stood at his door consistently? What does Elena do to avoid negativity? What specific words and phrases does she use to encourage Will's participation?

III. The Self-Directed Approach

KEY STEPS—SELF-DIRECTED APPROACH

1. *Listen carefully to the teacher's initial statement.*
2. *Reflect back your understanding of the problem.*
3. *Constantly clarify and reflect until the real problem is identified.*
4. *Have the teacher problem-solve and explore the consequences of various actions.*
5. *The teacher commits to a decision and firms up a plan.*
6. *The supervisor restates the teacher's plan and sets a follow-up meeting.*

The goal of the self-directed approach is to enable the teacher to reflect on the problem, draw conclusions, and construct his or her own alternatives. The supervisor serves more as a coach who does not express his or her point of view or ideas unless the teacher specifically requests them. The supervisor functions as the facilitator of the teacher's development of his or her own ideas. The outcome should always be the teacher's autonomous decision. This approach is appropriate for a very knowledgeable and often experienced teacher. It also can be successful in providing a sense of ownership when the teacher is the primary person responsible for carrying out a decision or when the decision or problem at hand has limited ramifications. A less experienced, but creative, promising teacher can also benefit from the guided ownership that this approach affords.

1. *Listen carefully to the teacher's initial statement.*
   As in the collaborative approach, the starting point is the teacher's perspective of the situation. The techniques and prompts are the same as in the collaborative approach: eye contact, body language, paraphrasing, verbal cues, and probing questions.

2. *Reflect back your understanding of the problem.*
   Again, as in the collaborative approach, verification that you have clearly and accurately understood the teacher's perspective is essential. Reflecting back what has been heard begins to accomplish this task. In addition, paraphrasing can clarify any uncertainty the supervisor may have about what has been expressed and can even allow the teacher to distance himself or herself from what was said and reflect on it from the outside.

3. *Constantly clarify and reflect until the real problem is identified.*
   The crucial prerequisite to solving a problem is to conceptualize accurately what the problem is. Solutions often are hidden in the identification of the problem, thereby limiting the range of resolutions. Thus, the real need must be ascertained. For example, your husband says he's taking the car, and you have a meeting. Your need is not necessarily to take the car but to find a way to get to the meeting. The facilitator's role is to use the reflecting/prompting/questioning process judiciously to permit the teacher to arrive at a crystallization of the need.

4. *Have the teacher problem solve and explore the consequences of various actions.*
   Once the need has been identified, simply ask the teacher to think of possible alternatives. Assist the teacher in walking through the steps, process, and consequences of each action. Ask questions such as "What would happen if . . .?" or "How would you . . .?" Then ask the teacher to explore the advantages and disadvantages of the alternatives. At this point, the teacher may be ready to respond to concluding questions, that is, "Which do you think will work best? Why? In what ways would it be better?"

5. *The teacher commits to a decision and firms up a plan.*
   Once the teacher makes a choice, you can request a plan and encourage a walk-through of the next steps. "What, who, when, how, where" may be part of the plan, or the provision of simple planning forms that the teacher can complete.

6. *The supervisor restates the teacher's plan and sets a follow-up meeting.*
   It is important for the supervisor to restate the teacher's plan before ending the meeting. This verification will avoid future misunderstandings. In addition, even though the teacher owns the plan, the scheduling of a follow-up meeting to see how it's working should always conclude the session.

Table 2.3 includes a summary of each of the three interpersonal approaches to supervision.

Table 2.3   Approach Comparison

Direct Informational	*Collaborative*	*Self-Directed*
1. Supervisor identifies problem, then solicits clarifying information	1. Supervisor seeks to identify problem from teacher's perspective	1. Supervisor asks teacher to identify problem
2. Supervisor offers solutions and then requests input	2. Collaborative brainstorming for solutions	2. Clarification and reflection until teacher identifies problem
3. Supervisor summarizes and then asks for confirmation	3. Problem-solve through sharing and discussion	3. Teacher problem-solves and explores consequences
4. Teacher restates final choices	4. Joint agreement on plan	4. Teacher commits to decision

GUIDELINES FOR REFLECTIVE PRACTICE

We believe that learning is most effective when the learner is actively involved in the learning process, when it takes place as a collaborative activity (Bridges, 1992), and when reflection is the means of observing, analyzing, considering, and reconceptualizing the experience. As we mentioned in Chapter 1, the process used in reflective practice can guide our development of new skills and change ingrained behaviors that may be inconsistent with internalization of the new skills. We first look at the stages of reflective practice and then discuss how they guide our development of supervisory skills.

Reflective practice is based primarily on two learning theories:

- Experiential learning theory, popularly associated with Dewey and Piaget, maintains that learning is most effective and likely to lead to behavior change when it begins with experience, especially problematic experience (Osterman & Kottkamp, 2004).
- The situated cognition perspective that Bridges (1992) popularized in problem-based learning argues that learning is most effective when the learner is actively involved in the learning process, when it takes place as a collaborative rather than an isolated activity and in a context relevant to the learner. This dialectic and cyclical process consists of four stages: experience, observation and reflection, abstract reconceptualization, and experimentation (Kolb, 1984).

In reflective practice, the first stage is to identify a problematic situation; the second is to reflect on the problem or experience—preferably in a collaborative, cooperative environment; the third is to consider alternate ways of thinking and acting; and the fourth is to test the reconceptualized behavior and assumptions. The cycle can begin again with the new concrete experience (see Figure 2.1).

Reflective practice serves two principal purposes in this book:

1. Every idea, tool, and technique to foster internalization of the new learning is accompanied by directions for reflective practice in the course classroom and on site.

2. We hope to instill the ongoing experience of reflecting individually and collaboratively on developing skills as a habit that you carry with you in your personal and professional lives and that you model as an educational leader.

Before you try out your new skills in a classroom or with another teacher, it is important that you have the opportunity to experience and reflect on them in a safe environment. We have developed a method for you to role-play all the interpersonal skills in this book. This method also can serve as a model for experiencing and reflecting on any communication skills or problematic situations you might want to rehearse. The only tools you need are two people who interact and a reflector with a watch or timer. We recommend that you use the "Fishbowl" method outlined in Resource B to model each role play. This method involves student volunteers who model each approach before the whole class attempts each role play. View the accompanying videotape that models the role plays before practicing.

Figure 2.1 Experiential learning cycle.

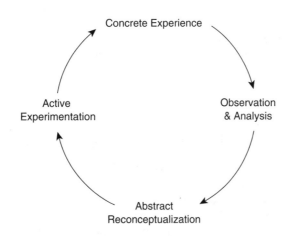

For the purposes of developing supervisory skills, the model presented is limited to the roles of a supervisor and a teacher. We first outline the roles and responsibilities in the process (see Table 2.4) and then provide specific feedback guidelines for the reflector (see Table 2.5).

Table 2.4 Reflective Practice Process—Three Steps, Three Responsibilities

Steps	Supervisor (Person Practicing)	Teacher	Reflector
1. Setting the scene (5 min.)	• Describes situation • Describes other person and possible reactions • Reviews steps on card and mentally rehearses	• Listens Carefully • Asks clarifying questions • Mentally rehearses responses	• Starts monitoring time • Takes notes on key points • Reviews steps on card
2. Practice (10 min.)	• Practices each step	• Responds based on the description of the other person	• Observes practice • Takes notes • Keeps practice on track • Monitors time
3. Feedback and Reflections (10 min.)	• Provides personal reflections first • Follows reflection guidelines	• Expresses personal feedback and reflections second • Follows reflection guidelines	• Facilitates reflections and feedback • Provides personal feedback and reflections last • Gives notes to person practicing

Table 2.5   Reflector's Feedback Guidelines

1. Ask the supervisor:
    *   What went well in each of the steps?
    *   What needs improvement?
    *   What would you do differently next time?

2. Ask the teacher:
    *   What do you feel the supervisor did effectively?
    *   What areas do you feel need improvement?
    *   What suggestions do you have for future interactions?

3. Reflector's feedback and conclusion of process:
    *   Offer your reflections on what went well
    *   Provide your suggestions or alternatives
    *   Ask the supervisor for questions or comments
    *   Give your written reflections to supervisor

Note: To promote self-reflection, make sure that the reflector asks the person role-playing the supervisor for input first. Also, separate carefully the response to "What needs improvement?" from suggestions. The problematic areas need to be thought out before solutions are addressed.

REFLECTIVE PRACTICE

Class Practice

During the next three weeks, each of you is going to create three scenarios. If possible, model the scenarios on existing challenges or dilemmas currently occurring in your school or in real-life situations with which you are familiar.

*   The first scenario involves a supervisor and either a new teacher or a teacher in difficulty for whom the directive informational approach is appropriate.
*   The second scenario takes place between you and a colleague who is an experienced and/or effective teacher with whom you feel comfortable using the collaborative approach.
*   The third scenario involves an interaction with a teacher who is so knowledgeable that he or she just needs prompting to come up with solutions or when you feel it would be beneficial for the teacher to solve the problem on his or her own.

Each week, you should practice a different approach in the course. Observe the appropriate role play on the videotape. Then, three volunteers will model the approach in front of the class before breaking into groups of three. Videotaping at least the three volunteers is recommended. It is very useful for other groups to volunteer to be videotaped so they can observe themselves on tape in the privacy of their homes. All students will have the opportunity to role-play the observer for each approach.

Site Practice

Each week, after you have practiced an approach, try it out by solving a site-based challenge. Where feasible, look for classroom-based problems as the basis of communication. Keep your cards available so that you can refer to them when the occasion arises. Be certain to reflect on how the interchange worked. What went well? What could be improved? What would you do differently next time? Take notes to facilitate class discussion of your experiences.

SUMMARY

In this chapter, we began to lay the groundwork for developing the interpersonal skills that are a prerequisite for all effective supervisory practice. Case studies introduced the three interpersonal approaches for providing feedback: the directive informational approach, the collaborative approach, and the self-directed approach. Before actually learning and practicing these approaches, the listening skills integral to the three approaches were outlined: phrases that show attentive listening, nonverbal cues, and reflecting and clarifying techniques. Class- and site-based exercises for practicing the listening and feedback approaches were accompanied by the introduction of the reflective practice process and guidelines that will be used throughout the book. With these skills and techniques under our belts, we can now tackle the observational tools and techniques for observing classroom teaching and learning that will be presented in Chapter 3.

NOTES

1. *People Skills* by Robert Bolton (1979) is an excellent source of many communication skills.

2. The approaches in this section are adapted from Glickman et al. (2004).

3

Observation Tools and Techniques

You can observe a lot by watching.

Yogi Berra

Teaching is a challenging art and science. Complicating matters are the incredibly fast-paced interactions between teachers and students as well as between students and students. Given the complex nature of classroom life (Jackson, 1990), tools for systematically recording classroom interactions are especially useful to assist teachers in understanding classroom behavior more fully and becoming aware of it (Good & Brophy, 2002). The use of observation instruments, however, has been criticized because of its presumed directive, behaviorist, and positivist orientation (e.g., Eisner, 1994). We heartily agree that use of observation instruments is problematic when directly connected to evaluation. We believe that "life in classrooms" is context bound, situationally determined, and complex. The supervisor is not and should not be the overseer or prescriber but rather the guide, facilitator, or collaborator. Relying on enhanced communication and shared understandings, the supervisor can effectively use observation instruments to encourage interpersonal and collegial relationships.

A major assumption of this chapter is that judicious use of reliable and easy-to-use observation techniques can increase a teacher's awareness of classroom behavior. Moreover, we would be negligent if we didn't include observation instrumentation in a volume devoted to instructional improvement. Through the use of these observation tools and techniques, supervisors and others involved with the supervision process will work more ably with teachers to improve instruction and, hence, promote student achievement.

Another major assumption in this chapter is that instructional improvement is best encouraged through instructional dialogue. Supervision, as a reflective process, is essentially concerned with enhancing teacher thought and commitment to improving instruction. Through the use of observation instruments, supervisors or those concerned with supervision are able to promote such improvement.

Many books or parts of books are devoted to describing various observation instruments, strategies, and techniques (e.g., Acheson & Gall, 1997; Boehm & Weinberg, 1997; Borich, 2002; Pajak, 2000; Willerman et al., 1991). From our experience, we have found that some of these systems are difficult to implement. We have selected for this chapter only those observation tools and techniques that we have personally experienced as easy to implement and effective toward promoting that all-important instructional conversation between supervisors and teachers.[1]

MICROLAB

Describe different kinds of observation techniques or strategies you have personally experienced. Which seemed most effective? Which seemed least effective? What are the primary benefits of the use of observation instruments?

This chapter begins with a transcript of an actual sixth-grade lesson that will be referred to throughout the chapter. Quantitative and qualitative observation instruments highlight the remainder of the chapter. Each instrument is discussed in detail, and examples are provided for implementation. Reflective practice activities will enhance your skill development.

We should note again that many observation instruments are not discussed in this chapter. The reader interested in an overview of other systems should consult Pajak (2000). We have discussed only tools and techniques we have found personally useful. Other tools may, in fact, have equal utility. We also encourage you to develop new tools or adapt the ones we have included to meet your specific needs.

SUPERVISION SCENARIO

Mario Tommasi has just completed his advanced certificate program at a local college and received his state certification as a school administrator and supervisor. A teacher for 10 years, Mario applies to a nearby township for a vice principalship. The board is impressed with his extensive teaching experience and letters of recommendation, as well as his keen insight into instructional improvement. Mario is hired.

The school to which he is assigned is William Heard Kilpatrick Middle School, which has a population of 1,200 pupils in Grades 6 through 8. The school is located in an urban section of the Northeast, and the ethnic makeup of the student body is 45% African American, 40% Hispanic American, 10% Asian American, and 5% others. Mario discovers that teacher morale is quite low, in large measure due to the autocratic practices of the former vice principal, who used strict traditional methods of teacher evaluation and frequently observed teachers without notice. The former supervisor would write lengthy, albeit well-written reports criticizing the teachers' methods and urging them to comply with his recommendations.

Mario is sympathetic toward their resentment of the supervisory practices they have experienced. Initially, he decides to establish rapport with his teachers. Once trust is established, he believes that instructional matters will follow naturally.

Six months pass, and Mario feels proud of the rapport and mutual respect he has developed with his teachers. Teachers, too, are happy that the former vice principal is gone, and they consider Mario to be congenial, articulate, and trustworthy. At a recent sixth-grade conference, Mario presented an overview of his supervisory approach: "Student achievement can be enhanced only when we, as colleagues, discuss matters of instruction in an open, forthright manner." Mario continued,

> The first step toward instructional improvement is for us to describe what is happening in the classroom when we teach. I'd like to present several observation tools and techniques that can help us begin to dialogue about instruction in a nonjudgmental, cooperative way. I'd like to introduce some of these tools to you and then conduct a demonstration lesson in which you will have the opportunity to observe me. You can use any of these techniques you want.

Teachers enthusiastically listened to Mario, and several teachers welcomed him into their classrooms.

REFLECTION

What do you think Mario did within the first six months to demonstrate his "congeniality and trustworthiness"? Consider the ways in which he built trust and confidence in teachers during the sixth-grade conference. What would have been your reaction to Mario's approach to supervision?

Over the course of the next year and a half, Mario made great progress in demonstrating that supervision is less about highlighting teacher deficiencies and more about collegial discussion of instructional matters. The principal and associate superintendent both remarked that a "culture of improvement" was clearly evident in the sixth grade. Teacher morale was high, pupil behavior was markedly improved, and test scores were on the rise.

Not all teachers, however, partook of Mario's "quiet revolution" at Kilpatrick Middle School. Clara Weingarten, a tenured social studies teacher with more than 28 years of classroom experience, was conspicuously absent during Mario's many staff development sessions and instructional workshops. At a recent afterschool faculty conference, however, she lamented the change in the student body, claiming that "these kids today aren't the same as before. They're rowdy, lazy, and disrespectful of authority."

Clara, realizing Mario's growing popularity and effectiveness, finally confided to him that she was at her wits' end. "Can you help?" she asked Mario in a genuine manner. Mario and Clara met several times during her prep periods to discuss not only instructional strategies but the changing student population and demographics of the community. Their informal chats continued over the next several weeks. Discussions included many different topics, such as observation techniques and teaching strategies. They shared their experiences and expertise. Fully cognizant of the fact that Clara had 18 more years of teaching experience than he, Mario nevertheless suggested one day that Clara tape-record a lesson on her own. Never having done so, she could then listen to the tape recording, and if she felt she would like "another ear," she was free to call on him. Call on Mario she did. After listening to the tape, Mario felt it wise to transcribe the tape before he met with Clara.

The transcription follows (visual descriptions were added to enhance readability):

Class: Sixth grade; 16 girls and 16 boys; reading scores are on grade level

Teacher: Clara Weingarten, tenured with 28 years of experience

Description of room: Movable desks are arranged in concentric arcs for this lesson. Student work is exhibited around the room with headings for each topic. A daily plan is outlined on the right panel of the chalkboard. A map of the world is hanging from the center of the wall above the chalkboard.

Curriculum area: Social studies. Topic: The United Nations; lesson in current events given on December 10, 2000

Mrs. Weingarten: What famous place in New York City is having its 55th birthday this year?

Ronald: (volunteering) The United Nations.

Mrs. Weingarten: What do you think we should discuss about the United Nations in class today?

Juanita: (volunteering) Where it's located?

Warren: (calling out) What it's supposed to do?

Mrs. Weingarten: Class, what is it supposed to do?

(At this point she writes on the board: "Can the United Nations prevent war?")

Huan:	(volunteering) I visited the U.N. with my class when I was in the fourth grade in the school that I came from.
Mrs. Weingarten:	What did you see there?
Huan:	It was a tall, flat building with a lot of windows. There was a smaller, round building, too.
Kevin:	I saw the Assembly on television when the President spoke to them on the 55th birthday of the U.N. It was on a news program.
Mrs. Weingarten:	Good. But let's get back to the question I wrote on the board at the beginning of the lesson.

(She asks the class to read the question aloud, which they do.)

Jessie:	(raising his hand) When countries want to go to war, they talk about it in the Assembly. I guess then they vote on what to do about it in the Security Council.
Natasha:	(raising her hand) But when Russia and the United States talk to each other about keeping the peace, they don't speak to each other at the United Nations. Like at Geneva. I saw that on television, too!
Mrs. Weingarten:	That's an excellent observation, Natasha. Class, what's the answer we could give for Natasha's question? (No one responds.) Because problems can be settled in many ways, including the United Nations. (pause) So what do we do about the United Nations? Do you think it can really prevent World War III?
Susan:	(volunteering) Yes, when it gets countries who want to go to war to stop.
Mrs. Weingarten:	That's right, when it gets countries that want to go to war to stop.
George:	(raising his hand) So how come Israel was at war with the Arabs? And what about Bosnia and other places?
Mrs. Weingarten:	Yes, but it's still not World War III. (pointing to the question on the chalkboard) Let's see whether we can answer this question today. How can we go about doing this?
Warren:	(volunteering) Well, we've had World War I and World War II, but so far we haven't had World War III.
Mrs. Weingarten:	Very good. World War I happened between 1914 and 1918, and World War II took place between 1939 and 1945. How do you know that World War II ended in

1945? We have all been given a clue to this question at the beginning of this lesson today. (Teacher looks around the room, waits a short while, with no response forthcoming) Because it was 55 years ago. Don't you remember what we talked about at the beginning of the lesson? (raising her voice) What did we talk about? Let's try to summarize what we have spoken about up to now.

Kevin: (volunteering) The United Nations is 55 years old this year.

Mrs. Weingarten: Rochelle, can you tell us what that means?

Rochelle: I don't know.

Mrs. Weingarten: It means that the United Nations got started at the end of World War II to make sure that World War III would never happen.

Tim: (raising his hand) How can they do that?

Mrs. Weingarten: They have two sections—the Security Council and the General Assembly. Their job is to try to make sure that we don't have World War III. (She then writes Security Council and General Assembly on the board.) Does anyone know how many members there are in the Security Council?

Tatiana: (volunteering) Russia and the United States, because they are the two biggest nations and they are the ones that could start World War III by attacking each other. I heard someone say that on television.

Mrs. Weingarten: No, there are 15 members in the Security Council, and 5 of them are there permanently, forever. The other 10 get elected by the General Assembly from time to time. The General Assembly has all the members, 159, each one of them having one vote. (pause) Class, class, which one—the General Assembly or the Security Council—votes on preventing war? Paul, we haven't heard from you yet.

Paul: I guess it's the General Assembly, because all the members are in it.

Mrs. Weingarten: No, it's the Security Council, because 5 of the 15 members are the great nations: the United States, Russia, China, England, and France. (She writes these countries' names on the board under the title "Permanent Members of the United Nations.") If one of these five says, "No," the

United States can't take action against a nation which is making trouble. That is called the veto power. (pause)

Here is an assignment to be done at home. I want you to look through newspapers and magazines and clip pictures and articles about the United Nations. You have one week to do this, and next Monday, when we have our next weekly current events lesson, we'll go over your clippings. You see, there is much more to learn about what the United Nations has done for the world. There are many other things it gets into besides trying to keep the peace. (pause)

Now, let's sum up what we learned today.

Vivian: That the United Nations could stop World War III before it begins.

Mrs. Weingarten: Thank you. Good. Now, let's turn to the homework which was assigned to you last night. Take out your textbooks, as well as your homework.

MICROLAB

What would have been the former vice principal's reaction (not Mario) to Clara's lesson? Based on our discussion in the previous chapter, what interpersonal approach would work best with Clara? How do you think Mario would react to this lesson? What concrete steps would he take to engage this teacher in instructional dialogue for improvement?

Analysis

Based on our view of supervision, we maintain that Mario is not likely to make subjective judgments about Clara's style of teaching. She has been reluctant to engage in instructional improvement discussions but now, for the first time, has requested some assistance. Mario sees this as an invaluable opportunity to encourage this teacher to become more reflective about her teaching practice. His goal is to encourage Clara to focus more on her lesson aim, questioning techniques, or motivational strategies rather than attributing student lack of motivation and achievement to demographic changes in the community.

The next step Mario takes is to help Clara become aware of how her behavior and teaching style contribute to her classroom effectiveness. Mario realizes that this experienced teacher will view any feedback he might offer with suspicion and, possibly, resentment.

REFLECTION

How would you recommend that Mario approach Clara? Would you use audiotapes? Why or why not? What other ways could the tapes be used?

Seeing a film or listening to an audiotape of oneself teaching is certainly an eye-opening experience. If you haven't had the opportunity to do so recently, we suggest you do.

Site Practice

Tape-record or videotape your next lesson and listen to or watch the tape at home. What's your reaction? After you get over the initial shock, listen to or watch the tape the following week. Imagine that this lesson was not your own. What aspects of the lesson were effective and which areas need improvement? What strategies would you employ to enable this teacher help herself or himself? Record your reflections and share them in small groups in class. Please note that after you read the later chapters in this book, you'll have a better idea of how to analyze your lesson. Still, this activity is useful at this point.

Watching a videotape or listening to an audiotape of your lesson, however, may not be very productive. Interactions in the lesson occur too quickly and are too complex for you or anyone else to pick up teaching subtleties such as effective use of wait time, number of higher-level questions asked, or distribution of questions to all ethnic groups in the class. We believe that videotapes and audiotapes are useful to enhance instructional improvement only if specific teaching behaviors can be highlighted, analyzed, and discussed.

Being familiar with the use of various observation tools and techniques, Mario encourages Clara to choose an observation tool to increase her awareness of what is occurring in her classroom. The ultimate goal is for Clara to be able to monitor herself.

Before Clara is able to become self-monitoring, she will have to learn how to collect data, know what behaviors to look for, and have a conceptual framework to guide her analysis. The remainder of this chapter is devoted to introducing observation instruments that Mario could use with Clara, or with any teacher for that matter. Each observation tool is presented, applied to Clara's lesson, if applicable, and practiced through the use of reflective activities and practice sessions.

TEN GUIDELINES OF OBSERVATION

Before we introduce and explicate each tool, several guiding principles about observation should be kept in mind:

1. Effective supervision is about engaging teachers in reflective thinking and discussion based on insightful and useful observation, not on evaluation.

2. Supervision, relying on the use of observation instruments to provide teachers with information about their classrooms, is likely to enhance teacher thought and commitment to instructional improvement.

3. Observation is a two-step process: first, to describe what has occurred, and then to interpret what it means.

4. Too often, we jump into what has been termed the *interpretation trap.* We jump to conclusions about a particular behavior before describing that behavior. When we interpret first, not only do we lose description of that event but also we create communication difficulties that might result in teacher resistance.

5. The precise observation tool or technique should be chosen collaboratively between teacher and supervisor. However, in most cases, the teacher ultimately should determine the instrument to be used.

6. Observing a classroom is not necessarily an objective process. Personal bias should be acknowledged and discussed. Although two or more individuals may agree on what has occurred (during the description stage), they might interpret its meaning differently. Personal experience, beliefs, and prejudices can lead to misinterpretations. Awareness of the possibility of personal bias is the first step toward interpreting classroom behavior effectively and as objectively as possible.

7. Observing takes skill and practice. Quite often, we interpret as we observe. If these tools of observation are to be effective, then you must practice separating interpretation from description. This chapter provides such practice.

8. Be aware of the limitations of observation. No observer can see or notice all interactions. Attempts to do so lead only to frustration and confusion. Start observations in a limited setting with a small group and observe one specific behavior, such as the quality of teacher questions.

9. Disclosure is an essential element for successful observation. Prior to entering the classroom, the observer should discuss arrangements with the teacher, for example, where to sit in the room, how to introduce the observer to students, and so on.

10. Don't draw conclusions based on one observation, Teachers have "bad" days and lessons sometimes don't work. Students, too, may have "bad" days. Multiple observations with different focuses are necessary.

REFLECTION

How might your biases affect how you interpret what you see, for example, in Clara's classroom? Discuss your answers with a colleague.

TWENTY-SIX TOOLS AND TECHNIQUES FOR OBSERVATION

As we mentioned earlier, many excellent observation systems exist. Our intention is not to review all the systems for observation; rather, we introduce those tools for observation that we personally have used and think can be incorporated easily into almost any classroom situation. The teachers in our classes constantly adapt the tools provided and create new ones, often during the planning conference in collaboration with the teachers they are observing for the course.

Two major categories of observation tools exist: quantitative and qualitative. *Quantitative* approaches reveal the *number* and the ratios of teacher-student behaviors; *qualitative* approaches reveal the *nature* of the observed behaviors. In other words, one category of tools reduces data into fixed or pre-established groups, and the other category describes a situation so that common themes may emerge.

Figure 3.1   Do You See a Musician or a Girl's Face?

Both approaches are valid. Each provides a different and unique lens to view a situation or a classroom. Look at Figure 3.1. What do you see? . . . Ah, so there may be more to "see" and "understand" from a different perspective! Well, that's what each approach offers—just a different, not better, perspective from which to view a classroom.

We have added a third set of tools and techniques to meet the needs of a standards-based environment and other recent educational initiatives. They are a mixture of quantitative and quantitative tools and techniques, including a sample of a quantitative and qualitative tools for the same focus.

Table 3.1 provides an outline of the tools and techniques we discuss next.

Table 3.1   Summary of Observation Tools

Quantitative Approaches

I. Categorical frequency tools
   A. Teacher verbal behaviors (Technique 1)
   B. Teacher questions (Technique 2)
   C. Student on-task and off-task behaviors (Technique 3)

II. Performance indicator tools
   A. Gardner's multiple intelligences (Technique 4)
   B. Hunter's steps in lesson planning (Technique 5)
   C. Johnson & Johnson's cooperative learning criteria (Technique 6)

III. Visual diagramming tools
   A. Diagram of verbal interactions (Technique 7)
   B. Diagram of teacher space utilization (Technique 8)

IV. Tailored tools
   A. Feedback (Technique 9)
   B. Teacher-pupil interaction (Technique 10)

Qualitative Approaches

I. Detached open-ended narrative tool (Technique 11)

II. Participant open-ended observation (Technique 12)

III. Child-centered learning observation (Technique 13)

IV. Nonverbal Techniques (Technique 14)

Tools for a Standards-Based Environment

I. Diversity instruments
   A. Indicators of culturally diverse learners (Technique 15)
   B. Strategies for diverse learners—quantitative (Technique 16)
   C. Strategies for diverse learners—qualitative (Technique 17)
   D. Team teaching in the inclusion (or general) classroom
      (Technique 18)
   E. Accommodations and modifications for English language learners
      (Technique 19)

II. Balanced literacy and standards-based tools
   A. Guided reading—quantitative (Technique 20)
   B. Guided reading—qualitative (Technique 21)
   C. Read aloud/story time (Technique 22)
   D. NCTM content standard 3 (Technique 23)
   E. NCTM process standards 6–10 (Technique 24)

III. Accountable Talk
   A. Teacher Behaviors Keyed to Accountable Talk (Technique 25)
   B. Student Behaviors Keyed to Accountable Talk (Technique 26)

QUANTITATIVE OBSERVATION TOOLS[2]

I. Categorical Frequency Tools

A *categorical frequency tool* is a form that defines certain events or behaviors that can be checked off at frequency intervals and counted.

A. Teacher Verbal Behaviors (Technique 1)

Materials. A watch with a second hand; a Teacher Verbal Behaviors chart (see Table 3.2).

Explanation. Supervisor and teacher collaboratively develop a list of no more than seven teacher behaviors that will be checked off as they occur at frequency intervals of, for example, 1 minute. In Table 3.2, seven teacher behaviors have been agreed upon: information giving, questioning, teacher answering own questions, praising, direction giving, correcting, and reprimanding, You'll notice that during the first minute the teacher gave information, questioned, answered, and reprimanded. Note that the frequency of each behavior is not recorded, merely the fact that the teacher behavior occurred within the time frame.

Site Practice

Find a colleague who will allow you to observe his or her class for 15 minutes. Using the Teacher Verbal Behaviors chart, keep a record of all teacher behaviors observed (use the reproducible version of Table 3.2 in Resource D). Share information with your colleague. What was his or her reaction? How did you find the experience of actually using this technique?

B. Teacher Questions (Technique 2)

Materials. A watch; a Teacher Questions chart (Table 3.3)
Special Prerequisite Knowledge. Familiarity with Bloom's taxonomy
Explanation. Supervisor and teacher collaboratively decide to focus only on the number and quality of questions posed during a specified time period. In the case presented in Table 3.3, both teacher and supervisor agree that Bloom's taxonomy will be used as the principal guide. Six of Bloom's levels are listed: knowledge, comprehension, application, analysis, synthesis, and evaluation. A tally is kept for each instance in which a question is posed. The observer listens to the question and decides into which of Bloom's categories the tally mark should be made. If your knowledge of Bloom's taxonomy is rusty, several Internet sites can refresh your and the teacher's memory. Bring to the observation a copy of the categories, their definitions, and sample questions. At the completion of the observation, totals are computed and percentages are calculated, as noted in Table 3.3. Note that the frequency of each type of question is recorded, but the question itself is not. In addition, many teachers and observers want to observe if there is a progression in the level of questioning during the time period. If the teacher prefers a running record of each question posed and/or a record of the progression in the level of questioning, a tape recorder could be used.

Table 3.2   Teacher Verbal Behaviors

Time began:

	Information Giving	Questioning	Teacher Answering	Praising	Direction Giving	Correcting	Reprimanding
1	X	X	X			X	
2	X	X			X		
3		X			X		X
4	X			X	X		X
5	X				X		
6		X				X	
7	X						
8	X	X			X		
9							X
10	X						
11	X				X	X	
12							X
13							X
14	X						
15	X		X				
16	X				X		

Time ended:

Class:

Date:

Source: C. D. Glickman, S. P Gordon, and J. Ross-Gordon, *SuperVision and Instructional Leadership: A Developmental Approach* (6th ed.). Copyright © 2004 by Allyn & Bacon. Reprinted/adapted by permission.

Postnote: Note that the observer and teacher may collaboratively decide on any kind of teacher verbal behavior, not just the ones listed in Table 3.2. Also, some teachers and observers like to note student questions to ascertain teacher/student interaction. Some observers prefer checking the total number of behaviors over a

Site Practice

Activity 1. Find a colleague who will allow you to observe him or her for 15 minutes. Using the Teacher Questions chart, keep a record of all teacher questions observed based on Bloom's levels (use the reproducible version of Table 3.3 in Resource D). Share information with your colleague. What was her or his reaction? How did you find the experience of actually using this technique?

Activity 2. Refer back to the lesson transcript at the beginning of this chapter. Using the Teacher Questions chart, record the LEVEL of Clara's questions. Discuss

Table 3.3   Teacher Questions

Time began:

Question Category	Tally 5 min.	Tally 10 min.	Tally 15 min.	Total	Percent	Comments
Evaluation		✓	✓	2	.07	
Synthesis				0	0	Where could you have developed synthesis questions?
Analysis	✓✓			2	.07	Discuss placement of analysis questions.
Application			✓		.04	Discuss possible application questions.
Comprehension	✓✓✓	✓✓✓	✓	8	30	How could some of these become application questions?
Knowledge	✓✓✓✓✓✓	✓✓✓✓	✓✓✓✓	14	52	How could these be made higher level questions?

Questions asked:

Time ended:

Class:

Date :

Source: C. D. Glickman, S. P. Gordon, and J. Ross-Gordon, *SuperVision and Instructional Leadership: A Developmental Approach* (6th ed.), Copyright © 2004 by Allyn & Bacon. Reprinted/adapted by permission.

your findings with a colleague. Did your recordings match your colleague's observations?

Postnote. Note that this type of category frequency tool doesn't necessarily have to deal with teacher questions. Any behavior that can be tallied may be observed using this format. Can you think of another example of a teacher behavior that can be tallied using this format?

C. Student On-Task and Off-Task Behaviors (Technique 3)

Materials. A watch with a second hand; a Student On-Task and Off-Task Behavior chart (Table 3.4)

Special Prerequisite Skills. Although using Technique 2 is relatively easy without much practice, we suggest that you practice identifying student on-task and off-task behaviors (Technique 3) prior to actually using the technique in a classroom with a class. Practice is needed because the key used is somewhat complicated. We suggest you memorize and practice using the key prior to any real observation.

Explanation. Supervisor and teacher collaboratively decide to focus on student on-task and off-task behaviors. A list of student names is made as noted in Table 3.4. The students' names are listed according to their seat order beginning from the front row or table and going down each row or table. The observer should be situated to the side of the front of the room. Because the observer will be seen readily by the students, we suggest that the observer come into the class a couple of times prior to the observation to sit up front and make believe that he or she is taking notes to acquaint students with the observer's presence.

Observations are made in 5-minute intervals (depending on the number of students observed). In our case, 15 students are being observed. Thus, each student will be watched for 20 seconds (5 minutes = 300 seconds divided by the number of total students being observed (15) = 20 seconds per student). In a large class, the novice observer may need to reduce the number of behaviors observed. The observer records what he or she sees using the key at the bottom of the chart. Again, familiarity with student on-task and off-task behaviors is essential for this technique to work properly. By the way, the precise on- and off-task behaviors also should be collaboratively developed between observer and teacher.

Site Practice

Activity 1. Find a colleague who will allow you to observe him or her for 15 minutes. Using the Student On-Task and Off-Task Behaviors chart (Table 3.4), keep a record of all on- and off-task student behaviors observed (use the reproducible version of Table 3.4 in Resource D). Share information with your colleague. What was her or his reaction? How did you find the experience of actually using this technique?

Table 3.4   Student On-Task and Off-Task Behavior

Time When Sweep Began

Student	9:00	9:05	9:10	9:15	9:20	9:25	9:30	9:35
Tania	A	A	A	A	A	A	O	A
Manuel	A	A	A	A	A	O	A	A
Vivian	A	TK	TK	A	A	TK	A	TK
Nurit	0	0	P	P	OT	0	0	OT
Joseph	OT	OT	A	P	A	A	P	P
Michael	OT	OT	A	P	0	A	A	TK
Loi	A	P	P	A	P	P	P	OT
Helen	A	A	A	A	A	A	A	A
Mari-Celi	A	A	A	A	O	A	A	A
Wayne	P	P	A	A	P	P	O	O
Virginia	P	A	A	A	P	A	A	A
Colleen	O	A	A	A	TK	0	A	A
Hajime	OT	OT	OT	OT	OT	OT	OT	OT
Kahlid	TK	A	A	TK	TK	TK	A	A
Maria	O	A	A	A	TK	A	A	A

Key: *Total:*

A   = at task
TK = talking (social conversation)
P   = playing
O   = out of seat
OT = off task

Source: C. D. Glickman, S. P. Gordon, and J. Ross-Gordon, *SuperVision and Instructional Leadership: A Developmental Approach* (6th ed.). Copyright © 2004 by Allyn & Bacon. Reprinted/adapted by permission.

Activity 2. The Association for Supervision and Curriculum Development (1990) video, *Another Set of Eyes,* has a number of classroom scenes that you can use to practice this technique. You might also ask a colleague to videotape your own class. Practice and report your ability and comfort in using this technique.

Postnote. Note that this type of category frequency tool refers to student behavior, whereas the previous two formats referred only to teacher behavior. Can you think of another example of student behaviors for which this technique can be used?

II. Performance Indicator Tools

A *performance indicator tool* allows the observer to record whether or not an action or activity listed on the observation instrument has been observed. Many types of performance indicators are possible. In other words, this tool can be applied to any action or activity that can be observed and recorded. We will provide three examples in which a performance indicator tool may be applied.

A. Gardner's Multiple Intelligences (Technique 4)

Materials. A performance indicator chart keyed to Gardner's eight intelligences (see Table 3.5)

Table 3.5   Gardner's Model for Performance Indicators

Elements	Response	Observations
Logical/mathematical	Yes ☑ No ☐ N/A ☐	Mathematical equation examples on board
Bodily/kinesthetic	Yes ☐ No ☑ N/A ☐	No references made
Visual	Yes ☑ No ☐ N/A ☐	Overhead transparencies used
Musical	Yes ☐ No ☑ N/A ☐	No references made
Interpersonal	Yes ☐ No ☑ N/A ☐	No references made
Intrapersonal	Yes ☐ No ☑ N/A ☐	No references made
Linguistic	Yes ☑ No ☐ N/A ☐	Problem-solving examples
Naturalistic	Yes ☐ No ☑ N/A ☐	No references made

Date: 6-28-04

Class: 3-310

Time: 1:15 p.m.

Source: C. D. Glickman, S. P. Gordon, and J. Ross-Gordon, *SuperVision and Instructional Leadership: A Developmental Approach* (6th ed.), Copyright © 2004 by Allyn & Bacon. Reprinted/adapted by permission.

Site Practice

Explanation. Well-versed in Gardner's intelligences theory, both observer and observee have collaboratively decided to record the extent to which Gardner's intelligences are incorporated in a fifth-grade science lesson. A specified period of time to observe the lesson is agreed upon. The observer merely checks off whether or not the teacher addressed in any way each of Gardner's intelligences. The observer may comment on the nature or extent to which each intelligence was introduced and applied. Naturalistic and emotional intelligences are sometimes added to the list of multiple intelligences.

Find a colleague who will allow you to observe their teaching for an appropriate length of time. Using Gardner's multiple intelligences, keep a record of the extent to which Gardner's multiple intelligences are applied in the lesson (use the reproducible version of Table 3.5 in Resource D). Share information with your colleague. What was her or his reaction? How did you find the experience of actually using this technique?

Postnote. Howard Gardner's theory is only one example for which a performance indicator tool may be applied. Can you think of another example for which this tool may be applicable?

B. Hunter's Steps in Lesson Planning (Technique 5)

Materials. A performance indicator chart keyed to Hunter's lesson plan steps (see Table 3.6)

Explanation. Well-versed in Hunter's lesson plan model, both observer and observee have decided collaboratively to record the extent to which Hunter's steps are incorporated into a 12th-grade foreign language lesson. A specified period of time to observe the lesson is agreed upon. The observer merely checks off whether or not the teacher in any way addressed each of Hunter's steps. The observer may comment on the nature or extent to which each of Hunter's steps were introduced and applied.

Table 3.6   Hunter's Steps in Lesson Planning

Elements	Response	Comments
Anticipatory set	Yes ☐ No ☑ N/A ☐	No references made
Objective and purpose	Yes ☐ No ☑ N/A ☐	Unstated-unclear
Input	Yes ☑ No ☐ N/A ☐	Group discussion employed
Modeling	Yes ☐ No ☑ N/A ☐	No references made
Checking for understanding	Yes ☐ No ☑ N/A ☐	Teacher asked "Do you understand?," but did not check
Guided practice	Yes ☑ No ☐ N/A ☐	Teacher circulates
Independent practice	Yes ☑ No ☐ N/A ☐	Sample sheets distributed

Date: 5-18-04

Class: 10-406

Time: 11:15 a.m.

Source: C. D. Glickman, S. P. Gordon, and J. Ross-Gordon, *SuperVision and Instructional Leadership: A Developmental Approach* (6th ed.). Copyright © 2004 by Allyn & Bacon. Reprinted/adapted by permission.

Site Practice

Find a colleague who will allow you to observe him or her for an appropriate length of time. Using Hunter's model, keep a record of the extent to which Hunter's lesson plan steps are applied in the lesson (use the reproducible version of Table 3.6 in Resource D). Share information with your colleague. What was her or his reaction? How did you find the experience of actually using this technique?

Postnote. Again, we are providing only some examples for which a performance indicator tool may be applied. Can you think of another example for which this tool may be applicable?

C. Johnson and Johnson's
Cooperative Learning Criteria (Technique 6)

Materials. A performance indicator chart keyed to the criteria applied to cooperative learning (see Table 3.7)

Table 3.7   Johnson and Johnson's Cooperative Learning

Elements	Response	Comments
Explanation of academic and social objectives	Yes ☐ No ☑ N/A ☐	No explanation of either occurred— just went into lesson
Teaching of social skills	Yes ☐ No ☑ N/A ☐	Teacher merely said, "Cooperate"— no instruction
Face-to-face interaction	Yes ☑ No ☐ N/A ☐	Students sitting quietly facing each other
Position interdependence	Yes ☑ No ☐ N/A ☐	One set of responses required from each group
Individual accountability	Yes ☐ No ☑ N/A ☐	None evident—teacher walked around classroom minimally
Group processing	Yes ☑ No ☐ N/A ☐	Students rated their performance

Date: 3/15/04

Class: 4-417

Time: 9:15 a.m.

Source: C. D. Glickman, S. P. Gordon, and J. Ross-Gordon, *SuperVision and Instructional Leadership: A Developmental Approach* (6th ed.). Copyright © 2004 by Allyn & Bacon. Reprinted/adapted by permission.

Explanation. Well-versed in Johnson and Johnson's cooperative learning format, both observer and observee have decided collaboratively to record the extent to which the criteria of cooperative learning are incorporated in a 12th-grade foreign language lesson. A specified period of time to observe the lesson is agreed upon. The observer merely checks off whether or not the teacher in any way addressed each of the cooperative learning criteria. The observer may comment on the nature or extent to which each cooperative learning criterion was introduced and applied.

Site Practice

Find a colleague who will allow you to observe him or her for an appropriate length of time. Using Johnson and Johnson's cooperative learning, keep a record of the extent to which the cooperative learning criteria are applied in the lesson (use the reproducible version of Table 3.7 in Resource D). Share information with your colleague. What was her or his reaction? How did you find the experience of actually using this technique?

Postnote. We are providing only some examples for which a performance indicator tool may be applied. Can you think of another example for which this tool may be applicable?

III. Visual Diagramming Tools

A visual *diagramming tool* portrays what happens visually in the classroom. Although we present just two examples, please note that several types of visual diagramming tools are possible. Also, the use of videotaping and audiorecording, although easily applied to almost any tool, are particularly useful here to provide visual and/or auditory evidence.

A. Diagram of Verbal Interactions (Technique 7)

Materials. A verbal interaction chart outlining the seating arrangement of the particular class being observed (see, for example, Figure 3.2).

Explanation. A specified period of time to observe the lesson is agreed upon. For purposes of analysis in this case, both supervisor and teacher have agreed on a 30-minute observation period. Six copies of Figure 3.2 in Resource D should be made for the observer to record verbal interactions in 5-minute increments; that is, one chart for *each* 5-minute period. Cross-hatching facilitates the recording of multiple interactions. One of our students effectively used multiple transparencies of the seating chart as overlays for each 5-minute interval. The clear plastic sheets can be superimposed later. She also used different colors of ink to represent each observation interval.

Each arrow indicates a complete statement directed to another individual, and the arrows are numbered in sequence. The observer should have extensive experience applying this technique so that recording can proceed smoothly and accurately. Figure 3.2 is provided as a training tool to interpret the verbal interaction provided.

Site Practice

Find a colleague who will allow you to observe him or her for an appropriate length of time. Using the Diagram of Verbal Interactions, keep a record of the verbal interactions in the lesson (use the reproducible version of Figure 3.2 in Resource D). Share information with your colleague. What was her or his reaction? How did you find the experience of actually using this technique?

Postnote. How might the use of audiorecording assist or hinder interpretation of the nature of verbal interactions in a lesson?

B. Diagram of Teacher Space Utilization (Technique 8)

Materials. A teacher space utilization chart outlining the room arrangement of the particular class being observed (see, for example, Figure 3.3)

Explanation. A specified period of time to observe the lesson is agreed upon. The observer charts teacher movement around the room and, at the same time, records the times.

Figure 3.2   Diagram of Verbal Interaction

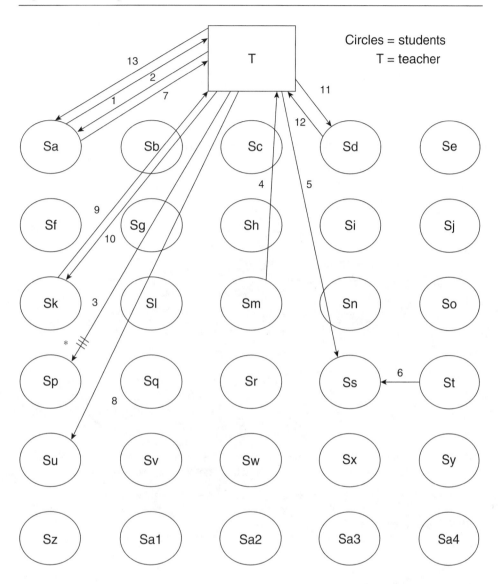

Circles = students
T = teacher

* Example of cross-hatching
Class: 10-517
Date: 11-15-03
TIme: 10:15 a.m.

Site Practice

Find a colleague who will allow you to observe him or her for an appropriate length of time. Using the Diagram of Space Utilization, keep a record of the teacher's movements during the lesson (use the tear-out version of Figure 3.3 in Resource D). Share information with your colleague. What was her or his reaction? How did you find the experience of actually using this technique?

Figure 3.3   Program of Space Utilization

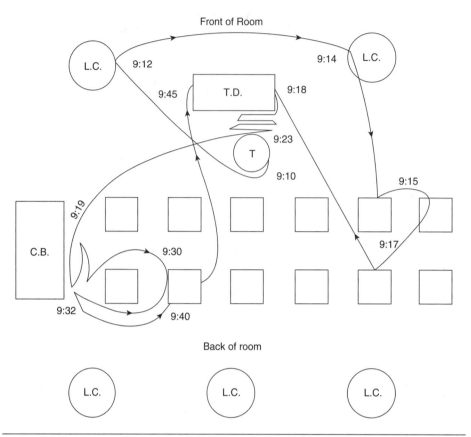

Key: T.D. = teacher's desk; L.C. = learning center; C.B. = chalkboard. Note that, of course, the diagram should be drawn for the room in which the observation takes place.

Source: C. D. Glickman, S. P. Gordon, and J. Ross-Gordon, *SuperVision and Instructional Leadership: A Developmental Approach* (6th ed.). Copyright © 2004 by Allyn & Bacon. Reprinted/adapted by permission.

Postnote. How might the use of videotaping assist or hinder interpretation of the nature of teacher space utilization?

IV Tailored Tools

The term *tailored tools* refer to tools especially developed or created based on a teacher's unique concerns. The teacher, in other words, wants the observer to focus on a specific area or areas. Tailored tools fall into the quantitative approach because numerical data are collected.

Many types of tailored tools are possible. As the name implies, these techniques are tailored to the needs and interests of teachers. Although we present just two examples, please note that others are possible.

A. Feedback (Technique 9)

Materials. A feedback chart outlining the seating arrangement of the particular class being observed (see, for example, Figure 3.4)

Figure 3.4   Feedback

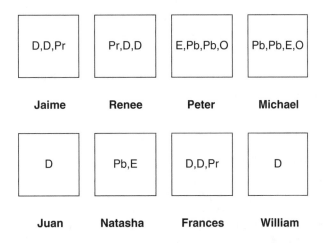

Key: Pr = prompted; Pb = probed; E = encouraged; O = positively reinforced; D = discouraged pupil.

Explanation. A specified period of time to observe the lesson is agreed upon. At a planning conference, the teacher informs you that he or she is interested in whether or not he or she prompts, probes, and encourages student responses. He or she is also interested in how often positive reinforcement is used and how often pupils' responses are discouraged. A key then is developed collaboratively by the observer and the observee during the preconference. Once categories and the key are approved, the observation may be scheduled.

A tear-out version of Figure 3.4 is provided in Resource D as a training tool for interpreting the recorded feedback.

Site Practice

Activity 1. Find a colleague who will allow you to observe him or her for an appropriate length of time. Using the reproducible version of Figure 3.4 in Resource D, keep a record of the feedback the teacher provides in this lesson. Share information with your colleague. What was her or his reaction? How did you find the experience of actually using this technique?

Activity 2. Refer back to the lesson transcript at the beginning of this chapter. Create a tailormade technique to ascertain some aspect of the quality of Clara's teaching style. Discuss your findings with a colleague. Did your recordings match your colleague's observations?

Postnote. Can you develop another chart that might be keyed to another concern a teacher might have?

B. Teacher-Pupil Interaction (Technique 10)

Materials. A Teacher-Pupil Interaction chart (see, for example, Table 3.8)

Explanation. In this case, the teacher wants the observer to focus on an individual student. The teacher informs you that he or she is having difficulty with Steve. The teacher complains that Steve's behavior gets progressively worse during a lesson and that the teacher is at his (or her) wits' end. A specified period of time to observe the lesson is agreed upon. The observer observes and records the student's behavior as well as noting the teacher's reaction.

A reproducible version of Table 3.8 is provided in Resource D as a training tool for interpreting the teacher-student interaction during this particular lesson.

Table 3.8   Teacher-Pupil Interaction

Time	*Student: Steve*	*Teacher: Clara Weingarten*
9:05	Disturbing another students Ceases misbehavior	Moves toward Steve
9:13	Leaves desk; begins wandering around room Returns to seat	Establishes eye contact with Steve
9:18	Playing with friend Throws ruler	Criticizes Steve Tells Steve to see her after class
9:30	Off-task / passive Back on task	Approaches Steve, touches him on the shoulder, quietly asks him to go back to his seat

Class: 2-517

Date: 1-6-04

Time: 9:00 a.m.

Source: C. D. Glickman, S. P. Gordon, and J. Ross-Gordon, *Supervision of Instruction: A Developmental Approach.* Copyright © 1998 by Allyn & Bacon. Reprinted/adapted by permission.

Site Practice

Find a colleague who will allow you to observe him or her for an appropriate length of time. Using the reproducible version of Table 3.8 in Resource D, keep a record of a teacher–pupil interaction during the lesson. Share information with your colleague. What was her or his reaction? How did you find the experience of actually using this technique?

Postnote. What other kinds of tailormade tools can you create?

QUALITATIVE OBSERVATION TOOLS

I. Detached Open-Ended Narrative Tool (Technique 11)

Also known as selective verbatim (Acheson & Gall, 1997) or script taping (Hunter, 1983), the observer records every person, event, or thing that attracts her or his attention. Whatever the observer considers significant is recorded. The observer simply records exactly what is said during the lesson; hence, a verbatim transcript is taken. Not all verbal communications are recorded but only those that the observer feels are significant or those communications agreed upon by both supervisor and teacher beforehand. Hence, only selected portions are recorded. Of course, no prearranged categories or questions are developed.

Selective Verbatim

Materials. A notepad or laptop to record observations

Explanation. Supervisor and teacher collaboratively agree that anecdotal evidence will be collected during a specified period of time. The goal is to <u>describe,</u> as objectively as possible, the key events and actions that occur. It will be impossible to record everything. The observer must try to choose what he or she believes is indicative of the teaching and learning observed.

Open-Ended Narrative

Fifth-grade class; 13 boys and 12 girls; self-contained classroom; Amy Clayman, teacher; 9:45 a.m. I enter as Ms. Clayman tells class to take out their math books. As Ms. Clayman gives instructions for the math assignment, four students (two male and two female) are out of their seats, hanging their clothing in the rear classroom closet. The girl is talking. Ms. Clayman tells her to be quiet and sit down. Teacher takes attendance by reading class roster, name by name. After about 3 minutes, a monitor enters classroom, and teacher is recording daily attendance; noise level in class rises. Monitor leaves room. Teacher walks back and forth as students get quiet. At 9:53 a.m., Ms. Clayman asks a girl to tell the class what the answer to the first math problem is. Student responds; class attentive. Ms. Clayman asks a boy, "Can you answer question No. 2?" Student responds. Teacher calls on a boy who also responds, with a different answer. Ms. Clayman probes and asks boy to explain. Ms. Clayman asks another student to answer the question. Girl responds. Teacher asks another question to a boy and probes. Teacher proceeds this way for the next 15 minutes. Ms. Clayman then asks the class, "How may we figure out how much carpet to buy if the room is 10 feet by 15 feet?" No one raises a hand to answer. Ms. Clayman repeats the question. Still, no response. Teacher draws a diagram on the board and then James calls out, "Oh, I know." Students giggle. Ms. Clayman tells class, "Now, stop that. Pay attention. Go ahead James, tell us." James mumbles something. Ms. Clayman requests that he speak more clearly. James is silent. Teacher then explains to the class how to compute the area of a rectangle. She writes several examples on the board and then calls several students to answer them.

Site Practice

Activity 1. Obtain a videotape of a lesson and practice taking selected verbatim information. After recording is completed, share notes with a colleague.

Then view the video again, taking note of inaccuracies and missed information. Keep practicing until you're satisfied that you've recorded all that you wanted to.

Activity 2. Find a colleague who will allow you to observe him or her for 15 minutes. After completing an open-ended narrative, share information with your colleague. What was her or his reaction? How did you find the experience of actually using this technique?

Postnote. The ability of the observer to accurately and quickly record information is essential. Recording such information may appear simple, but much practice is required. Be certain to practice Activity 1.

II. Participant Open-Ended Observation (Technique 12)

Participant open-ended observation refers to a situation in which the observer partakes in the classroom activities. The observer may assist in the instruction by working with a group or helping individual students.

The observer may take notes or just jot down some ideas for later recall. The advantage of having the observer participate in the class is that many insights may be culled from direct participation that might otherwise be missed from detached observations.

The types of observation possible are similar to detached open-ended narratives. Using this procedure, the observer either makes notes during the activities or simply summarizes events after the observation period. The essential element here is that the observer is in a unique position to better understand classroom interactions because he or she actively is involved.

Observers should feel free to vary their approaches (detached or participant), depending on a given situation. Sometimes, for example, a teacher may feel uncomfortable having the supervisor participate, explaining that it may be distracting. We highly suggest arranging the format of observation with the teacher in advance.

Practice participant open-ended observation as you did previously with the detached open-ended narrative.

III. Child-Centered Learning Observation (Technique 13)

Based on constructivist learning theory, *child-centered learning observation* focuses primarily on the learner, the student, rather than on the instructor. By incorporating a qualitative approach (detached or participatory), the observer may record observations in response to these and other learner-centered questions:

- Were the children learning/thinking?
- What kinds of questions were being asked (e.g., open)?
- How were children treated?
- What opportunities were provided for children to learn in different ways?
- Who is the source of knowledge?

- Were children talking to children?
- Were children designing their own learning?
- Who assesses learning?
- What did we learn about the children?

Child-centered learning observations provide invaluable insights into student learning that would otherwise be overlooked by focusing only on the teacher. They also allow the teacher to reflect on the causes of the student's behavior or response, which may have originated in the teacher's interaction with the student. We suggest you practice this technique as you did the others.

IV. Nonverbal Techniques (Technique 14)

Materials. Nonverbal observation chart (see, for example, Table 3.9)

Proxemics is the teacher's use of perception and space. The closer a teacher is to a student, the less likely the student is to behave inappropriately. For example, the teacher may stand near or move toward a potentially disruptive student as a behavior control strategy. This technique works best with teachers who customarily stand and move about. Another use of proxemics is to arrange classroom furniture in such a way as to convey warmth and closeness.

Kinesics is the teacher's use of facial and body cues, such as smiling, frowning, staring, pointing, or hands on hips. These cues communicate strong messages, work well from a distance, and help signal individuals and groups when they are disrupting others. Kinesic cues should be considered as an aid to conventional classroom management methods. The best way to learn these cues is to practice them with others and in front of a mirror.

Prosody is concerned with tone, pitch, and rhythm of the teacher's voice, and communicates the importance of what is being said. Teachers who use this tool know that yelling and high-pitched voices tend to excite rather than calm students. Effective use of prosody can convey caring, empathy, and warmth as well as a love of teaching and students.

Immediacy is the degree of perceived or psychological closeness between people. Teachers who use this technique are physically close to students, use socially appropriate touching, exhibit warmth, and use open body postures while communicating. For example, lightly touching a student's shoulder or upper arm while explaining an assignment tells that student the teacher cares and wants him or her to be successful.

Explanation. Observations are collaboratively arranged and made in a series of short visits at various times during one day or over several days. Although a checklist can be used noting each time the teacher uses a particular nonverbal technique, we prefer the observer to keep a running record of the types of nonverbal interactions used, along with annotations describing the nature and impact of those interventions.

Table 3.9 in Resource D is provided as a training tool to interpret the teacher-student interaction during this particular lesson.

Table 3.9   An Observation Chart

Nonverbal Technique	Frequency	Anecdotal Observations / Student Responses

Proxemics
  Standing near
   student(s)
  Moving toward
   student(s)
  Touching student(s)
  Moving about room		

Kinesics
a. Affirmation
  Eye contact
  Touching
  Smiling
  Nodding
  Open arm
   movements
b. Disapproval
  Frowning
  Stern look
  Finger to lips
  Pointing
  Arms crossed
  Hands on hips		

Prosody
  Varies voice tone
  Varies pitch
  Varies rhythm		

Immediacy
  Responds with
   warmth		

Class:

Date:

Time:

Source: C. D. Glickman, S. P. Gordon, and J. Ross-Gordon, *Supervision of Instruction: A Developmental Approach*. Copyright © 1998 by Allyn & Bacon. Reprinted/adapted by permission.

REFLECTIVE CLINICAL SUPERVISION IN A STANDARDS-BASED ENVIRONMENT

In the new edition of his book on different approaches to clinical supervision, Ed Pajak (2000) asks "whether clinical supervision is compatible with the principles of systemic reform and exactly how clinical supervision is being implemented in standards-based contexts" (p. 295). In our own work in the field and through feedback teachers and administrators have given us, our impressions are that the revised observation forms that districts often require are variations on the same old theme. Instead of an arbitrary list or categories of behaviors to be observed, the "new" standards-based formats address a range of standards. The supervisor fills out either a checkoff list or short narratives or a combination of both. The result for the teacher is the same: He or she scans the list in relief and files it, or reacts in disbelief to the areas requiring attention. The postobservation conference may provide valuable feedback, but the form itself is of limited value. Too many areas are observed simultaneously. The teacher becomes frustrated because he or she cannot focus on multiple areas effectively at the same time.

We propose that supervisors and coaches use the principles of the reflective clinical supervision cycle in a standards-based environment. Rather than create checkoff lists to verify if learning outcomes are being met, we suggest that each observation focus on one learning outcome, standard, or teaching skill.

In this section, we provide some sample tools that are already in use or that we have created to meet some of the current learning outcomes and standards. The overarching standard, currently expressed as "leave no child behind," is the underlying theme of most of these tools. We have found that performance-indicator instruments, categorical frequency instruments, and focused questionnaires can be easily adapted to meet most outcomes and standards. The samples that we provide are based on these three types of instruments, so that you can see the facility with which you and the teacher can discuss a focus, choose and adapt these tools, or create your own. We address diversity of backgrounds, learning styles, math standards, balanced literacy, and other strategies to enable all children to reach their potential. Since most of these tools are variations of performance-indicator instruments, categorical frequency instruments, and focused questionnaire tools, we have not included site activities or postnotes for these tools.

Another practice in the standards-based environment that we will address is the "walk-through," traditionally termed the informal observation. The walk-through, which was developed as a means to improve instruction through teacher collaboration, will be presented in Chapter 5 as an alternative to traditional supervision. We believe that supervisors often use the walk-through or informal "pop-in" primarily as a monitoring method. In the best-case scenario, the supervisor has met with the teacher at the beginning of the year to talk about goals. Subsequently, the supervisor makes brief visits to a set of classes at regular intervals to ascertain if the agreed-upon goals are being implemented. More often, supervisors pop into classrooms unannounced and follow up the visit with a commendation or recommendation. We believe these informal or formal short visits are evaluation or monitoring practices that do not promote teacher-centered improvement of instruction. Supervisors should be present daily in classrooms and even take on teaching assignments. The goal, however, should be to get to know the children and how they are learning and to build a community of learners.

I. Diversity Instruments

A. Indicators of Culturally Diverse Learners (Technique 15)

As much of the predominantly English-speaking world becomes culturally and linguistically diverse, supervisors need to attend to teachers' awareness of this diversity and their efforts to address it in the classroom. The performance indicator instrument shown in Table 3.10 can form the basis for that discussion and even lead to appropriate professional development.

Table 3.10   Cultural Diversity

Teacher Indicator	Response Yes	No	N/A	Comments
Displays understanding of diverse cultures	☐	☐	☐	
Displays personal regard for students of diverse cultures	☐	☐	☐	
Uses instructional materials free of cultural bias	☐	☐	☐	
Uses examples and materials that represent different cultures	☐	☐	☐	
Promotes examination of concepts and issues from different cultural perspectives	☐	☐	☐	
Intervenes to address acts of student intolerance	☐	☐	☐	
Uses "teachable moments" to address cultural issues	☐	☐	☐	
Reinforces student acts of respect for diverse cultures	☐	☐	☐	

Class:

Date:

Time:

Source: C. D. Glickman, S. P. Gordon, and J. Ross-Gordon, SuperVision and Instructional Leadership: A Developmental Approach (6th ed.). Copyright © 2004 by Allyn & Bacon. Reprinted/adapted by permission.

B. Strategies for Diverse Learners—Quantitative (Technique 16)

This tool has as a focus the teacher's strategies to reach all children in the classroom. It is applicable to all classrooms because diverse learners exist in any environment where people come together. Nonetheless, it is particularly pertinent to teachers who have students with disabilities integrated into the general population.

Table 3.11   Strategies for Diverse Learners

Teacher Indicator	Response			Examples
	Yes	No	N/A	
Proximity to students	☐	☐	☐	
Different ways of encouraging students	☐	☐	☐	
Positive reinforcement techniques	☐	☐	☐	
Modifications for individual children or types of learners	☐	☐	☐	
Use of children's strengths	☐	☐	☐	
Multiple ways in which lesson is unfolding	☐	☐	☐	
Integration of grouping according to needs and skills	☐	☐	☐	
Scaffolding of instruction	☐	☐	☐	

Class:

Date:

Time:

C. Strategies for Diverse Learners—Qualitative (Technique 17)

Those who prefer a qualitative tool can use a focused questionnaire as a basis for ascertaining how the teacher is meeting the needs of all the children. The following brief questionnaire is an adaptation of the performance indicator chart.

1. How does the teacher encourage students?

2. What positive reinforcement techniques does he or she use?

3. What kinds of modifications for individual children or types of learners are evident?

4. How does the teacher use the children's strengths?

5. Where are the students situated in the room and why?

6. What are the opportunities for small-group work?

7. How does the teacher address grouping according to needs and skills?

8. What evidence is there of scaffolding of instruction?

9. How does the teacher adapt materials and instruction to different student learning styles?

10. What is the teacher's proximity to the students?

11. How are the children interacting?

12. What else is special about the treatment of the children?

We hope that these examples of two tools for the same focus will facilitate your ability to create your own tools.

D. Team Teaching in the Inclusion (or General) Classroom–Qualitative (Technique 18)

The integrated or inclusion classroom usually includes a general and a special education teacher. In addition, team teaching has increased with the expansion of the integrated curriculum and longer and flexible time periods. Effective use of two teachers in one classroom is difficult to achieve. The following questionnaire can support collaborative team teaching. You can also create a performance indicator instrument to describe the teachers' roles.

1. Describe the involvement of the general education teacher and the special education teacher with the whole class, with small groups, and with individual children.

2. What is the role of each teacher in the classroom? How is instruction organized between the two teachers?

3. Who guides the curriculum?

4. What is the curricular role of each teacher?

5. Who attends to the individual needs of the children?

6. How are the accommodations for children with special needs handled?

7. How is responsibility for children with special needs divided between the teachers?

Note: Thanks to Claire Wurtzel, Director of Professional Development for the New York City Schools Attuned Initiative, for her suggestions for the inclusion tools.

15

E. Accommodations and Modifications for English Language Learners—Quantitative (Technique 19)

Table 3.12   English Language Learners

Accommodation Modification	Was this element present?			What is the evidence?
	Yes	No	N/A	
Teacher talk is modified: slower speech, careful choice of words, idioms, expressions	☐	☐	☐	
Teacher allows wait time and monitors teacher input vs. student output	☐	☐	☐	
Definitions and language are embedded in content/context	☐	☐	☐	
Real-world artifacts present that support comprehension	☐	☐	☐	
Elicits and draws on students' backgrounds to build prior knowledge	☐	☐	☐	
Teacher uses nonverbal cues to support comprehension	☐	☐	☐	

Class:

Date:

Time:

II. Balanced Literacy and Standards-Based Math Tools

Standards and outcomes for math and literacy can also be observed with performance-indicator instruments and focused questionnaires. We provide a sampling of instruments that our students and colleagues have developed. These tools can serve as a guide for other standards- and outcome-based instruments a faculty can create.

Literacy tools

Universal literacy is the primary focus in all schools. The ability of all teachers in all grades to teach literacy is a nationwide goal. Balanced literacy is one of the major approaches to teaching literacy.

A. Guided Reading—Quantitative (Technique 20)

Table 3.13　Guided Reading—Quantitative

Guided Reading Teacher Indicator	*Yes/No/NA*	*Comments/Examples*
MANAGEMENT		
Was the transition from the mini-lesson to group work implemented in an orderly fashion?	☑ ☐ ☐	• Children for guided reading were told in advance that they would meet • Independent work and book exchange were addressed before splitting up into groups
Were the other children on task while the teacher was in small group instruction?	☑ ☐ ☐	• Teacher did not have to interrupt group to attend to other students until the very end ofsession, after about a 45-minute period • Teacher left guided reading group while they were reading independently to walk around and monitor/ conference withothers
Was the time allotted for the guided reading group appropriate?	☐ ☑ ☐	• Guided reading session lasted for 47 minutes • Recommended time is 15-20 minutes
INSTRUCTION		A. Article for instruction: "Beverly Cleary"
Was the text for guided reading introduced in a manner that provided needed support so that students could read independently and successfully?	☑ ☐ ☐	• Genre—a biographical article, columns, and how to read them • Activated prior—Have you read Beverly Cleary books? • Nontext information—pictures, captions, lists
Were the children interested in and did they grasp the concepts being taught?	☑ ☑ ☐	• Girls seemed more interested than boys • 3 out of 4 students were able to touch on the main idea
Was the text appropriate for the group with respect to the level, content, and interest?	☐ ☑ ☐	• Level seemed too difficult • Interest—boys were not as interested as girls

Guided Reading Teacher Indicator	Yes/No/NA	Comments/Examples
Were support, challenges, and opportunities for problem solving provided	☑ ☐ ☐	• Support—text was introduced with a variety of strategies, main idea was finalized as a group, teacher led students through each paragraph to find details
	☐ ☑ ☐	• Challenge—didn't seem appropriate. The text was challenging in itself as well as the activity
Did the students read independently?	☑ ☐ ☐	
Did assessment take place? What types?	☑ ☐ ☐	• Students wrote main idea in sentence form independently • Students highlighted details and were asked to justify their selections
Did the teacher allow students to be responsible for what they already know?	☑ ☐ ☐	
Did questions include the full range of Bloom's taxonomy?	☐ ☑ ☐	• Knowledge • Comprehension • Evaluation—students had to support and justify answers
Did the teacher help students strengthen their strategies?	☑ ☐ ☐	• Students were asked to justify which details supported main idea. This developed the process behind the strategy • Students were directed through each paragraph to break material into manageable chunks. This modeled how to approach the text • Teacher told students how they can transfer what they did to other reading and writing

Class: 2-3

Date: 5-5-04

Time: Literacy Block

Source: This instrument was adapted from one that Suzanne Dimitri, a Brooklyn, N.Y., literacy coach, created. It is used with her permission.

B. Guided Reading—Qualitative (Technique 21)

A Staten Island staff developer, Maria Casales, created a series of balanced-literacy tools for her work with teachers.

Table 3.14   Teacher Tasks in Guided Reading—Qualitative

Selects appropriate text for small group instruction Teacher uses book, *The Birthday Cake,* written by Joy Cowley. Six students, 4 boys, 2 girls, receive a copy of the same book. They look at the cover of the book with curiosity and await teacher direction.	*Helps children to think, talk, and question through the story* The teacher encourages her students to take a "picture walk" through the story. As they preview the text, Amanda questions an illustration, and Mark questions some of the words in print. Teacher briefly discusses their concerns.
Introduces story to the group as well as vocabulary concepts and text features The teacher brings the students' attention to new vocabulary words and to the ending punctuation. Children give the teacher sentences using the new vocabulary words. Teacher reviews telling sentences and question sentences.	*Allows small groups to read independently with minimum teacher support* The teacher allows the group to read the book independently. She lends support rarely and her students read the whole book (12 pages).
Provides or reinforces reading strategies and provides students with the opportunity to use the strategy Upon completion of reading the story, the teacher asks the students, "How many of you noticed the end of some sentences? Why are some sentences telling sentences and others question sentences?" Children are able to respond to teacher posed questions. The teacher encourages the children to reread the story, focusing on ending punctuation and pauses.	
Records reflections on the students' reading behaviors during and after reading The teacher logs their reading behaviors as they relate to the skill and fluency. After they read, she adds some quick notes.	*Engages students in a brief discussion after reading the story.* The teacher asks the students if they enjoyed reading the book. The students reply "yes." She then asks what they enjoyed the most and why.

Class: 1-2

Date: 6-1-04

Time: Literacy Block

 ### C. Read Aloud/Story Time—Quantitative (Technique 22)

The following balanced literacy Read Aloud tool is adapted from a tool that Lorraine Call, a pre-school teacher on Staten Island created. With slight adaptations, it can be used for any read-aloud lesson.

Table 3.15   Read Aloud/Story Time

Teacher Behaviors	Yes No N/A	Comments/Examples
Introduces book by showing cover and reading title. Encourages students to share thoughts about book based on these features.	☑ ☐ ☐	Teacher showed cover, asked who remembers what book is about. Encourages with "What else?"
Reads name(s) of author and illustrator. Asks students to point to title, author, illustrator, and encourages discussion about these features.	☑ ☐ ☐	Teacher asks, "Who can tell me what the author does? What the illustrator does?
Introduces at least three words that will be in story by showing cards with words and pictures representing them.	☑ ☐ ☐	Teacher covers picture part of word cards and asks who remembers the word. Then shows picture.
Attempts to capture/maintain students' interest. Uses facial expression and changes in tone, pitch, and so on to represent different characters and emphasize words or facts.	☑ ☐ ☐	Teacher uses loud and soft voice throughout. Hesitates when vocabulary word appears, allowing children to fill in word
Involves children throughout the story by encouraging comments and questions.	☑ ☐ ☐	Asks other children if they know response to classmate's question "What's the squirrel doing?"
Asks open-ended questions, such as What if? What would you do if?, and so on, and provides wait time. When voluntary responses are limited, initiates discussion of facts, plot and/or characters.	☑ ☐ ☐	Teacher asks, "What would you do if you were a squirrel?" "What do you think it feels like to roll around in those leaves?"
Involves children in extension activities by creating charts or other visuals, for example, T charts, story maps, word/character webs.	☑ ☐ ☐	Evidence of extension: leaf rubbings, fall collages, KWL chart about fall
Invites children to retell story in their own words (through pretending to read the book to the class, using puppets, etc.)	☑ ☐ ☐	Teacher asks, "Can you tell me something that happens in the fall?" "What's it like outside?"

Class: Title of book:

Date: Author:

Time: Type of book:

                                                  New words:

Other comments:

Mathematics Tools

The mathematics tools included here are based on National Council of Teachers of Mathematics (NCTM) standards for school mathematics.

The NCTM Standards for School Mathematics are divided into two types. Standards 1 through 5 are known as content standards. These standards describe student outcomes along content lines (i.e., number and operations, algebra, geometry, measurement, and date analysis and probability). Since different content standards are emphasized in particular lessons and at certain grade levels, we provide an example of the application of outcomes for one content area: geometry. The supervisor and teachers can create similar performance indicator tools for each area.

D. NCTM Content Standard 3—Quantitative (Technique 23)

Table 3.16   Geometry

Students Can	Response	Observations
Analyze characteristics and properties of two-and three-dimensional geometric shapes and develop mathematical arguments about geometrical relationships	Yes ☐ No ☐ N/A ☐	
Specify locations and describe spatial relationships using coordinate geometry and other representational systems	Yes ☐ No ☐ N/A ☐	
Apply transformations and use symmetry to analyze mathematical situations	Yes ☐ No ☐ N/A ☐	
Use visualization, spatial reasoning, and geometric modeling to solve problems	Yes ☐ No ☐ N/A ☐	

Class:

Date:

Time:

Standards 6 through 10 are known as process standards. These standards describe student outcomes along process lines (i.e., problem solving, reasoning and proof, communication, connections, and representation.) The categorical frequency tool can be used to record evidence of activities in the mathematics classroom that require students to engage in the process named. Each distinct activity should be counted only once in any given standard. However, an activity may meet several of the standards at the same time. For example, students working in cooperative groups may be meeting the problem solving and communication standard.

E. NCTM Process Standards (Standards 6–10)—Quantitative (Technique 24)

20

Table 3.17   NCTM Process Standards 6–10

Activity Category	Tally	Total	Percentage
Problem solving			
Reasoning and proof			
Communication			
Connections			
Representation			

Class:

Date:

Time:

Note: We thank Judy Walsh, an instructor of math methods at the College of Staten Island, CUNY, and a former supervisor and teacher of mathematics, for her lead role in developing the math tools.

III. Accountable Talk   21

A learning concept that has recently emerged from the accountability movement and cooperative learning is accountable talk. It is based on the principle that classroom talk that is accountable to the learning community and to the academic disciplines is essential to learning. The following observation tools are based on the four ways that student talk should be accountable: accountability to the community (polite listeners), accountable to knowledge (use evidence), accountable to standards of reasoning, and accountable to standards of reasoning appropriate to a subject area. For further information on accountable talk, contact the Institute for Learning at the Learning Research and Development Center at the University of Pittsburgh.

A. Teacher Behaviors Keyed to Accountable Talk—Quantitative (Technique 25)

Table 3.18   Teacher Indicators of Accountable Talk—Quantitative

Teacher Indicators	Response	Observations
Engages students in talk by: • Providing opportunities for students to speak about content knowledge, concepts, and issues. • Using wait time/allowing silence to occur • Listening carefully • Providing opportunities for reflection on classroom talk	Yes ☑ No ☐ N/A ☐ Yes ☑ No ☐ N/A ☐ Yes ☑ No ☐ N/A ☐ Yes ☑ No ☐ N/A ☐	Teacher consistently waited for students to answer. You could see her thinking about the response. At the end of the class, group reflectors reported on the process in their groups.
Assists students to listen carefully to each other by: • Creating seating arrangements that promote discussion • Providing clear expectations for how talk should occur • Requiring courtesy and respect • Reviewing major ideas and understandings from talk	Yes ☑ No ☐ N/A ☐ Yes ☑ No ☐ N/A ☐ Yes ☑ No ☐ N/A ☐ Yes ☐ No ☑ N/A ☐	The class reviewed the guidelines for discussion before going into circles of small groups where a reflector and facilitator were chosen. No time remained at the end of class to review group work.
Assists students to elaborate and build on others' ideas by: • Modeling reading processes of predicting, looking for key words, engaging prior knowledge, and so on. • Facilitating rather than dominating the talk • Listening carefully • Asking questions about discussion ideas and issues	Yes ☑ No ☐ N/A ☐ Yes ☑ No ☐ N/A ☐ Yes ☑ No ☐ N/A ☐ Yes ☐ No ☑ N/A ☐	The introductory whole-class discussion of the topic allowed the teacher to model the skills the students needed in their small-group discussions. She asked the class what reading process she had just used at least three times. No time to debrief about the discussions at the end of class.
Assists in clarifying or expanding a proposition by: • Modeling methods of restating arguments and ideas and asking if they are expressed correctly • Modeling and providing practice at responding appropriately to criticism • Modeling expressing own puzzlement or confusion	Yes ☑ No ☐ N/A ☐ Yes ☑ No ☐ N/A ☐ Yes ☑ No ☐ N/A ☐	The teacher modeled all these methods in the introductory discussion and encouraged them as she walked from group to group.

Class: 9.2

Date: 4-17-04

Time: Humanities Block

B. Student Behaviors Keyed to Accountable Talk—Quantitative (Technique 26)

Table 3.19   Student Indicators of Accountable Talk

Student Indicators	Response	Observations
Students are engaged in talk when they: • Speak appropriately in a variety of classroom situations • Allow others to speak without interruption • Speak directly to other students	Yes ☑ No ☑ N/A ☐ Yes ☐ No ☑ N/A ☐ Yes ☑ No ☐ N/A ☐	The whole and small-group class discussions were very lively. Many students spoke, primarily to each other. Sometimes they interrupted each other.
Students are listening attentively to one another when they: • Make eye contact with speaker • Refer to a previous speaker • Connect comments to previous ideas	Yes ☐ No ☐ N/A ☑ Yes ☑ No ☐ N/A ☐ Yes ☑ No ☐ N/A ☐	It was often difficult to determine if eye contact was being made. Students usually referred to the person whose ideas they were addressing
Students elaborate & build on others' ideas when they: • Make comments related to the focus of the discussion • Introduce new, related issues • Listening carefully • Talk about issues rather than participants	Yes ☑ No ☐ N/A ☐ Yes ☐ No ☑ N/A ☐ Yes ☑ No ☐ N/A ☐ Yes ☐ No ☑ N/A ☐	Students stayed on topic, listened to each other. They were so engrossed in the issue that they did not bring up any related or new issue. One or two students referred to each other.
Assists in clarifying or expanding a proposition by: • Modeling methods of restating arguments and ideas and asking if they are expressed correctly • Modeling and providing practice at responding appropriately to criticism • Modeling expressing own puzzlement or confusion	Yes ☑ No ☐ N/A ☐ Yes ☑ No ☐ N/A ☐ Yes ☑ No ☐ N/A ☐	The teacher modeled all these methods in the introductory discussion and encouraged them as she walked from group to group.

Class: Social Studies

Date: 2/2/04

Time: 2:15

SUMMARY

We have described two approaches to observation: quantitative and qualitative. We have also included a section on how these approaches can be applied to standards-based observation tools. A total of 26 techniques were reviewed and practiced. We have not included videotaping and audio-recording as separate tools; rather, they are valuable instruments that can be used with any of the tools and techniques described in this chapter. According to Acheson and Gall (1997),

> Video and audio recordings are among the most objective observation techniques. . . . They allow teachers to see themselves as students see them. . . . [T]hey can pick up a great deal of what teachers and students are doing and saying. A good recording captures the "feel" of classroom interaction. (p. 111)

Videos and audios, according to Acheson and Gall (1997), are examples of "wide lenses" that are particularly useful "in supervising teachers who are defensive or who are not yet ready to select particular teaching behaviors for improvement" (p. 107). Acheson and Gall conclude, "After reviewing wide-lens data, these teachers may be more ready to reflect on their teaching, identify specific teaching behaviors for focused observations, and set self-improvement goals" (pp. 107-108). We agree.

CONCLUSION

Research demonstrates that teachers are likely to change their instructional behaviors on their own after their classroom has been described to them by an observer. Observation is a mirror and thus a stimulus for change. Effective supervision is about engaging teachers in reflective thinking and discussion based on insightful and useful observation tools and techniques. In the next chapter, we place these observation tools within the context of a clinical supervision program.

NOTES

1. We would like to acknowledge Glickman et al. (2004) for their excellent discussion of observation instruments. Our framework is drawn, in large measure, from their work. Their division of instruments into quantitative and qualitative approaches makes the most sense.

2. These categories were developed by Glickman et al. (2004).

4

An Introduction to Clinical Supervision

The way in which supervisors try to bring about change largely determines how teachers respond to the challenge. Supervisors can mandate change externally; or they can, together with teachers, build collaborative cultures that encourage the seeds of change to take root and grow.

Grimmet, Rostad, & Ford, 1992, p. 185

The first chapter traced the emergence of clinical supervision in the 1960s. In this chapter, we first present and explain our definition of clinical supervision and then offer an adaptation of clinical supervision we call *reflective clinical supervision.* An outline of the steps for each part of the cycle (except the actual observation) is accompanied by brief case studies. Opportunities to practice each phase are included. Finally, we detail how the whole process can be simulated in the course before trying it out on site. By the end of this chapter, you will be prepared to complete the final assignment of conducting a whole cycle in your schools.

A DEFINITION OF CLINICAL SUPERVISION

Although the sequence of a preconference, classroom observation, and postconference already existed in the 1920s, during the era of democratic supervision, Morris Cogan is credited with developing the elaborated concept and techniques of the clinical supervision cycle, which has emerged as a major force in educational supervision since the 1960s.

Edward Pajak (2000) said that Cogan "viewed clinical supervision as a vehicle for developing professional responsible teachers who were capable of analyzing their own performance, who were open to change and assistance from others, and who were above all, self-directing" (p. 76). This definition encompasses some of the assumptions that we believe underlie effective supervision: It does not explicitly restrict supervision to the supervisor, opening up the possibility that change and assistance can come from many sources; and it emphasizes self-analysis and self-direction, important components of reflective practice. We expand the definition to include classroom teaching and learning as the focuses of improvement and collaborative as well as individual analysis and reflection.

Before we define supervision, and learn and practice an adaptation of the clinical supervision cycle, it is important to understand that clinical supervision is not only a structure but a concept, and as such, it contains a series of assumptions. Goldhammer, Anderson, and Krajewski (1993) outlined nine major characteristics of clinical supervision that we believe are consistent with any of the approaches and structures in this book:

1. It is a technology for improving instruction.

2. It is a deliberate intervention into the instructional process.

3. It is goal oriented, combining the school's needs with the personal growth needs of those who work within the school.

4. It assumes a professional working relationship between teacher(s) and supervisor(s).

5. It requires a high degree of mutual trust, as reflected in understanding, support, and commitment to growth.

6. It is systematic, although it requires a flexible and continuously changing methodology.

7. It creates a productive (i.e., healthy) tension for bridging the gap between the real and the ideal.

8. It assumes that the supervisor knows a great deal about the analysis of instruction and learning and also about productive human interaction.

9. It requires both preservice training (for supervisors), especially in observation techniques, and continuous inservice reflection on effective approaches. (pp. 52–53)

REFLECTION (INDIVIDUAL AND SHARED)

Formulate a definition of clinical supervision based on the preceding ideas and assumptions. Work in class in groups of three to five; share your definitions and come up with joint ones that designated group leaders will report out to the whole class.

THE REFLECTIVE
CLINICAL SUPERVISION CYCLE

Richard Weller's (1971) formal definition of clinical supervision provides a basis on which we can develop our cycle of supervision:

> Clinical supervision may be defined as supervision focused upon the improvement of instruction by means of systematic cycles of planning, observation, and intensive intellectual analysis of actual teaching performances in the interest of rational modification. (p. 11)

Weller referred to the three phases of the clinical supervision cycle as represented in Figure 4.1.

Figure 4.1   Three Phases of the Clinical Supervision Cycle

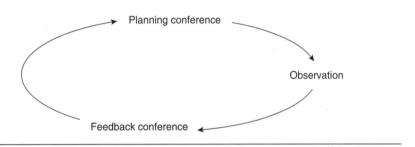

We add a fourth phase to the three activities of planning, observation, and analysis through a feedback conference that includes a collaborative reflection and analysis of the process and its findings. The fourth phase is professional development. If you juxtapose the four steps that we propose with the four steps of the reflective practice cycle (see Figure 4.2), you will observe that they are correlated: The planning phase of the clinical supervision cycle is similar to the concrete experience or problematic or indeterminate situation of reflective practice (the goal is to pinpoint an experience for examination and analysis); we have also included professional development related to the observation focus as a possible part of the planning phase; the observation phase of clinical supervision, which is followed by individual analysis, is analogous to the observation and analysis stage of reflective practice; the feedback conference, which involves the joint analysis of the data and the reconceptualization and planning for the next cycle, is comparable to the abstract reconceptualization stage of reflective practice. The collaborative reflection concludes the third phase. It allows the supervisor and teacher to reflect on how the supervision process and its results worked before proceeding. In the fourth phase of the reflective practice model, the reconceptualized ideas are actually put into action, completing the cycle and simultaneously beginning another (Osterman & Kottkamp, 2004). In our fourth phase, professional development, the reconceptualized ideas are developed further. Thus, in the next cycle, the combination of the discussion of the observation and the further development through professional development prepare the teacher for a new planning cycle. If the observation did not result in a need for change in the practice, professional development can focus on a new instructional strategy.

Figure 4.2   Comparison of Reflective Clinical Supervision With Reflective Practice

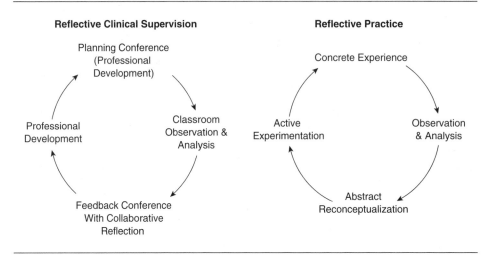

It is apparent that in our model, the reflective process takes center stage in the clinical supervision cycle. The planning conference is the first step in the process and is crucial in determining the tone, content, and approach to the cycle.

The Planning Conference

Elena Santiago, the newly appointed principal of New Hope Middle School, whom we met in Chapter 2, began her first set of classroom observations as early as possible in the fall. She hoped to develop trusting relationships that would permit her and the teachers to focus on the improvement of teaching and learning, and not on the bureaucratic process of evaluation. Because her assistant principal could only accomplish some of the required observations and Elena wanted to be actively involved with what was going on in the classroom, she decided to meet with and observe the newest teachers herself first.

We have found that the change process often begins during the planning conference. Therefore, we believe that two types of planning conferences can be effective. In the simpler form (see Scenario A), the teacher and supervisor identify the focus, choose an appropriate tool, and set the date and time of the observation and postconference. The supervisor can choose either the directive informational, collaborative, or self-directed approach to determine focus and tool. In the second type of planning conference (see Scenario B), the change process actually begins in the initial conversation. The discussion and choice of focus frequently lead to a decision to try new strategies. The teacher can practice the innovations(s) before the actual observation or implement them for the first time during the observation. Again, the supervisor chooses one of the three interpersonal approaches to determine focus and tool. In either case, some kind of professional development may also take place before the actual observation. That professional development could be as simple as a conversation and an intervisitation with a teacher expert in the chosen focus area.

Elena set up a planning conference with a brand-new language arts teacher. She had heard that Sylvia, a recent graduate of a high-quality master's program, was having difficulty implementing her student-centered practices. Some of the students had not been exposed to cooperative learning groups before, and rumor had it that some of her classes were out of control. Nonetheless, Elena decided to query Sylvia about what she felt her concerns were. To make Sylvia comfortable, Elena set up a meeting in Sylvia's classroom, not in the principal's office.

Scenario A

Elena: Hi, Sylvia. How's it going?

Sylvia: OK, I guess.

Elena: Since I will be beginning nontenured teacher observations, I thought we could discuss a particular area, interest, or concern that could be the focus of the observation.

Sylvia: Gosh, I wouldn't know where to start. You pick it.

Elena: I know that you use a lot of exciting innovative teaching methods. Is there any one in particular that you'd like some feedback on?

Sylvia: Mmm. . . I've been trying to have the students work in cooperative groups to discuss their writing, and it doesn't seem to be working in some classes. I have a rambunctious seventh-grade class that doesn't work well in groups at all, and I can't seem to get control of the process. Could you sit in on that class?

Elena: Sure. Let me show you a couple of tools I could use to observe the groups and see which one you think might pinpoint your concerns.

They decide to use the cooperative learning performance indicator instrument created by Johnson and Johnson (1989).

Elena: What is a convenient time for me to visit when you will be using cooperative groups with the seventh graders?

Sylvia: How about third period next Tuesday? They're usually awake by then but not yet completely out of control.

Elena: Fine. Next Tuesday, October 1, third period. While we're at it, could we set a time to meet after the observation? How about during your professional period the following day?

Sylvia: Sounds OK to me.

Elena: Agreed. Third period on Tuesday and second period on Wednesday. By the way, if you have any other input that would be helpful before I visit, don't hesitate to stop in and share it with me. I'm looking forward to seeing students using this wonderful method.

REFLECTION

What does Elena do to make Sylvia feel relaxed and at the same time focus on instruction? How does she get Sylvia to reflect on her own perceptions of her needs?

Scenario B

Sylvia: I'm at my wit's end.

Elena: How long have you been doing cooperative groups with the seventh-grade class?

Sylvia: I began last week. I explained the process to them, handed out guidelines, and asked them to study the steps and rules for their homework assignment. We tried groups the next day and they were *so noisy.* I made one more attempt the following day and had to abandon the process midway. It was so frustrating!

Elena: Did you model the process before you divided them in groups?

Sylvia: I thought that the sheets and my explanation would be sufficient. Maybe the change was too abrupt and extreme. Do you think one group could model without my losing control of the rest of the class?

Elena: Have you ever tried the fishbowl technique, where a volunteer group models the process in the middle of the classroom while the others watch and then comment at the end? If all the students keep their instructions in front of them, it will improve the fishbowl process and the ability of the rest of the class to comment.

Sylvia: Your suggestion could really help. It gives me another idea. I could have them make name plates for each role with a summary of the responsibilities on each card so the class would know who had each role in the fishbowl, and the list of steps on the other side would help everyone remember them. The list would also help them give feedback in the fishbowl and later in their small groups.

Elena: Your idea is very creative. Would you like me to visit when you do the fishbowl or when the whole class is in groups?

Sylvia: I think I could do both the fishbowl and cooperative groups in the double period we have the day after tomorrow. If I assign the name plates tomorrow, could you come the following day third and fourth periods?

Elena: I will make sure to be there. I'm very excited to see how it works.

They decide to use Johnson and Johnson's (1989) cooperative learning performance indicator instrument to observe the fishbowl and the subsequent groups. They confirm the time and location and set up a postconference time and place.

REFLECTION

What are the major differences between Scenario A and Scenario B? What would help determine whether to use the approach depicted in Scenario A or B?

KEY STEPS—PLANNING CONFERENCE

1. *Decide the focus of the observation (choose a general approach: directive informational, collaborative, or self-directed).*
2. *Determine the method and form of observation.*
3. *Set the time of the observation and the postconference.*

The goals of the planning conference are

- To identify teacher interests and concerns in an appropriate manner (directive informational, collaborative, or self-directed).
- To clarify that the primary purpose of the observation is to improve teaching and learning.
- To reduce stress and make the teacher feel comfortable about the process.
- To choose an observation tool and schedule the visit and postconference.

The three steps of the planning conference are:

1. *Decide the focus of the observation.*
   Whereas the chief purpose of the observation is to improve instruction, it is essential to have the teacher's perspective on his or her concerns and interests. Even a new teacher can help identify the primary or most urgent concerns. Change occurs most easily if the teacher has a role in providing the focus. The supervisor will use one of the three interpersonal approaches to guide the planning conference. Wherever possible, begin the problem-solving process related to the chosen focus of observation and include professional development.

2. *Determine the method and form of observation.*
   Once the focus is determined, the supervisor can discuss the appropriate tools. The supervisor will decide whether to include the teacher in making the choice of the observation tool. A newer or less secure teacher may have enough to cope with without taking part in that decision.

3. *Set the time of the observation and post conference.*
   It is important, wherever possible, to provide the teacher with the opportunity to choose the day and time. The teacher knows in which class the focus that he or she has chosen can be observed best. Once he or she has had a role in deciding the focus, the choice is simplified. It

becomes a learning experience with less likelihood of the visit being an occasion to put on a show.

Class Practice

During the week, think about two teachers in your school: an experienced, confident teacher and a novice. Imagine a planning conference with each one, and write a short dialogue based on the imaginary planning conference. In class, you will practice at least one of the scenarios in groups of three using the reflective practice guidelines. Keep your key steps cards and practice guidelines handy. Volunteers will model at least one scenario, which CAN be videotaped for their personal use and reflection.

Site Practice

Begin to think about a teacher who would be receptive to participating in a clinical supervision cycle with you. Once you have found a volunteer, you can rehearse the planning conference in class and then actually schedule the site planning conference.

The Observation

KEY STEPS—THE OBSERVATION

1. *Finalize the choice of observation tool.*
2. *Conduct the observation.*
3. *Verify the postconference meeting time, and offer a copy of the observation tool to the teacher wherever appropriate.*
4. *Analyze facts of the observation and begin thinking of interpretations.*
5. *Choose a postconference interpersonal approach from Chapter 2.*

---

1. *Finalize the choice of observation tool.*
   The supervisor finalizes the choice of an observation tool from those described in Chapter 3, preferably after consultation with the teacher during the planning conference.

2. *Conduct the observation.*
   The observation takes place at the agreed-upon time. The teacher should be less anxious about your presence and your writing because he or she has chosen the focus and is familiar with the instrument you are using to document it.

3. *Verify the postconference meeting time, and offer a copy of the observation tool to the teacher wherever appropriate.*
   At the end of the class, the supervisor reminds the teacher of their scheduled postconference. Where appropriate and feasible, the supervisor

supplies the teacher with a copy of the completed observation tool so that they both can examine it individually before the conference.

4. *Analyze facts of the observation and begin thinking of interpretations.*
   It is preferable for the supervisor to analyze and interpret the observation tool as soon as possible after the class, while the observation is fresh in his or her mind. Study and analyze the facts and then begin to think about an interpretation of the findings. Don't jump to conclusions before meeting with the teacher. It is important to get the teacher's perspective before finalizing an interpretation.

5. *Choose a postconference interpersonal approach from Chapter 2.*
   Now that the supervisor has held the planning conference with the teacher and actually observed the teacher in the classroom, the supervisor should be able to determine which interpersonal approach is appropriate for the postconference.

The Postconference

We now provide three scenarios based on the interpersonal approaches presented in Chapter 2. Before briefly reviewing the steps, try to identify which approach the supervisor chose.

Scenario A

In the first scenario, we return to Elena and Sylvia. You will remember that Elena is the recently appointed principal of New Hope Middle School, and Sylvia is a new, young language arts teacher who is trying to implement the cooperative learning methodology she learned in college and who is running into some difficulties. She asked Elena to observe her rambunctious seventh-grade class during a cooperative learning workshop on the writing process. Elena chose Johnson and Johnson's cooperative learning performance indicators as the observation tool (Table 3.7) and shared a copy of the results with Sylvia immediately, so she could review it before the postconference the following day. The scheduled meeting was in Sylvia's classroom during her professional period. This postconference is based on Scenario A of the planning conference.

Elena: Did you get a chance to look at the cooperative learning performance indicators?

Sylvia: I was devastated! Despite your attempts to write positive comments, it looks like I didn't get any of the responses right.

Elena: They seemed to know what they were supposed to be doing because they kept on arguing about how they weren't following the rules! I didn't see them referring to written guidelines or following a clear sequence. How much preparation did they have before they began using the process?

Sylvia: I handed out a sheet one day for them to study at home, and then I had them try it out the next day.

Elena: Maybe it was too much too soon. Don't forget that some of these students haven't had much opportunity to work collaboratively. They are fortunate to have you as a teacher with all your current knowledge! This class in particular may need much more practice and role playing of the different roles before they can run their own groups. Have you ever tried the fishbowl technique, where a volunteer group models the process in the middle of the classroom while the others watch and then comment at the end? They also need to keep their instructions in front of them and make sure that the reflector has time to provide feedback at the end. Perhaps the reflectors can share who performed the roles most effectively in each group before the end of class. What do you think? Do you have any ideas?

Sylvia: I love your ideas, and they made me think of others. I can assign them as homework the job of making 3 × 5 cards for each job. They can then use the cards to direct their group work. And I could get a volunteer to videotape a group so they can see for themselves how they did.

Elena: Effective ideas! Let's review your plans and jot them down on the observation sheets so that we don't forget. First, you'll give them the 3 × 5 card assignment. The next day, a group will model the process using the fishbowl technique. Then you'll ask for a volunteer to videotape a group and ask the reflectors to identify who performed most effectively in each group. We can think of further incentives if these work. Do you want to go over them so we're sure we are on the same wavelength?

Sylvia: Sure. I can't wait to try these ideas. I'll give them the card assignment tomorrow. The next day, we'll do the fishbowl technique. Then I'll ask for videotaping volunteers. The following day, I'll explain the reflector's new role, and we'll try our first practice. How does that sound to you?

Elena: Terrific. How about meeting next week at the same time to touch base on how it's working? If it's going as planned, we can brainstorm some other refinements. Your feedback can help us decide if I need to revisit that class or if we can move on to another area.

REFLECTION

What does Elena do to take some of the heat off of Sylvia? What strategies does she use in giving suggestions? Why do you think Sylvia gets so excited? Which approach did Elena choose and why?

KEY STEPS—DIRECTIVE
INFORMATIONAL APPROACH

1. *Identify the problem or goal and solicit clarifying information.*
2. *Offer solutions. Ask for the teacher's input into the alternatives offered and request additional ideas.*
3. *Summarize chosen alternatives, ask for confirmation, and request that the teacher restate final choices.*
4. *Set a follow-up plan and meeting.*

Scenario B

Judy has been a French and Spanish teacher at New Hope for five years. As part of a state grant, all the foreign language teachers have a bank of computers in their classrooms for the first time. Very little staff development accompanied the grant, so the teachers have been struggling to use the computers effectively. Elena is trying to get some funds to pay the foreign language teachers to work on lessons for the wired foreign-language classroom.

In the meantime, Elena thought she might get the dialogue started by observing one of Judy's classes. At the planning conference, they decided that Elena would use the student on-task, off-task behavior tool (Table 3.4) to determine what is going on in the groups working on projects while Judy is helping the students on the computer. Elena gave a copy of the observation to Judy after class.

Elena: Did the on-task, off-task tool provide any helpful information?

Judy: It was actually pretty depressing. The students were off task much more than I had thought while I was helping at the computers. I guess that I was so immersed that I didn't realize how little work was getting done. On the other hand, when I left the computer group, they really stayed on task. I wonder what that means?

Elena: The students really can get involved in the computer work. It really has a lot of potential for foreign language work. Your guiding them is so important. They are getting off on the right foot. What do you think you can do to get the rest of the class to stay on task while the computer group still needs assistance?

Judy: I guess I'm going to have to develop clear roles and processes for them to work together so I don't have to watch them all the time. I thought that writing and practicing scenes for a play they're going to perform would keep them on task. I have to remember that they're middle school students. Can you think of how I can organize them?

Elena: How about using some simple cooperative learning techniques—in French, of course—to keep the groups focused?

Judy: I guess they do need that structure. One could be the recorder for the scene and another the group leader. Do you think they need a reflector to report on how the group worked?

Elena: Maybe to start off with. Once you see that they are on task most or all of the time, you may or may not choose to do away with the reflector. If this strategy works well, do you think one of the other foreign language teachers could observe it?

Judy: I'd prefer not. I'm not comfortable with either the technology or leaving the groups on their own. And I'm the least experienced of the foreign language teachers.

Elena: OK. We can wait till the funding for your meetings comes through and start from there. So, you'll start training the students in cooperative learning techniques so they can work more effectively while you're working at the computers. Do you need any literature on cooperative learning?

Judy: No thanks, I've got plenty.

Elena: Can we meet again next week at the same time to see how it's going? I'd also like your input on how the observation process worked for you. Would you like me to observe the groups again before we meet?

Judy: Let's meet first and see how it's working. I wouldn't want you to observe until I've gotten some of the kinks out.

REFLECTION

How does Elena respond to Judy's rejection of Elena's request? What do you think is Elena's ultimate goal? How can you tell which approach is being used?

KEY STEPS—COLLABORATIVE APPROACH

1. *Identify the problem from the teacher's perspective, soliciting as much clarifying information as possible.*
2. *Reflect back what you've heard for accuracy.*
3. *Begin collaborative brainstorming, asking the teacher for his or her ideas first.*
4. *Problem-solve through a sharing and discussion of options.*
5. *Agree on a plan and follow-up meeting.*

Scenario C

Several parents have already come in to complain to Elena about John O'Connell's class. A few have been trying to switch their children out of his class. As a result, Elena has decided she'd better see what's going on. It is going to be a difficult task because John has been teaching math at New Hope for more than 25 years, and from all accounts, he is teaching the exact same way he did 25 years ago.

Elena has an idea. At the planning conference, she asks John, as the senior math teacher, to try out some techniques that a math teacher in her previous school found exceedingly successful, especially in preparing students for the new state math test. Depending on how they work for him, they could discuss recommending them to the other math teachers, she says. Elena also offers John the opportunity to visit the math teacher from her previous school so he can see the techniques at work and talk about them with their originator. After much hesitation, John reluctantly takes her up on the suggestion. Elena then asks if she can observe him using the techniques and use the visit as her official observation. When Elena mentions observation tools, John immediately says that he prefers that she use the traditional narrative form. Elena convinces John to allow her to record verbatim as much as she sees, and he agrees that each of them will analyze the verbatim narrative separately.

Elena: Did you get a chance to look at the transcript of my observation?

John: No. I've been too busy. The visit to your old school really set my schedule off.

Elena: Can you take a few minutes now and give me your reactions?

John: (after a few minutes) Having the students work in twos to solve problems and then share their answers and process with the closest set of twos just doesn't work for me. The desks got all messed up, the class was disorderly, and then it took me a long time to get them back to their regular work. It may work for your colleague, but not for me. Look at all the confusion and lost time.

Elena: I hear what you're saying. Besides the noise and confusion, how did the students work together?

John: They had a ball because they could talk away, but I had no way of knowing what was going on.

Elena: Do you have any ideas on how you could get rid of the glitches?

John: Your math teacher friend has the room set up differently, so she doesn't have to deal with students moving all over. I can't have them working at tables all the time. I can't teach that way.

Elena: How could you get around that?

John: Maybe I could have them rearrange the desks on Friday so the custodians could get them back in rows for Monday. But that would mean teaching the whole day with them in groups.

Elena: Could you arrange your schedule to do that?

John: I guess I could do problems on Friday and have them go over their tests for the rest of the period. They always have trouble concentrating on Friday anyway, so I won't have to deal with trying to make them listen all period.

Elena: Good suggestion. What do you think about getting feedback on their problem-solving processes and solutions?

John: I don't know. Your colleague has one student from each group write the solution and explain the process on the board. I'm afraid I'll lose control on a Friday if they're at tables. Maybe I'll have each table be responsible for writing one problem's solution and process on the board, and then ask for other suggestions. I don't know if it'll work. They may not stay as quiet as I like.

Elena: I think it's a terrific start. Let's go over what you're going to do. If it works, maybe some of the new math teachers can sit in on your class to see how it works.

John: I don't think so. They should concentrate on keeping order in their own classrooms. Some of the noise I hear coming out of those rooms. . . . So, I'm going to ask my homeroom to arrange the desks on Friday morning in tables of four. The students will first work in twos solving a problem, then they'll share their process and answer with the other two at the table. Then one person will put one process and solution on the board, and I'll ask for comments. Then they'll go to the next problem. If I've time at the end of the period, they can go over their weekly tests. The custodian will put the desks back in rows for Monday.

Elena: Fine. So Friday will be problem-solving day with the students at tables. If you make this an ongoing schedule, I could ask the custodian to rearrange the desks when he cleans on Thursdays. Can we meet a week from Monday to see how it's going?

John: Let's wait for two weeks. It'll give me a better idea if I want to continue with it. Since I get here early, you could come to my classroom on Monday before school starts.

REFLECTION

What does Elena do to avoid feeding into John's negativism? How is she responding to the parents' complaints? How does she react to his resistance to do certain things? Which approach did Elena choose and why?

KEY STEPS—SELF-DIRECTED APPROACH

1. *Listen carefully to the teacher's initial statement.*
2. *Reflect back your understanding of the problem.*
3. *Constantly clarify and reflect until the real problem is identified.*
4. *Have the teacher problem-solve and explore consequences of various actions.*
5. *The teacher commits to a decision and firms up a plan.*
6. *The supervisor restates the teacher's plan and sets a follow-up meeting.*

Collaborative Reflection

The purpose of the collaborative reflection is to think about the value of the supervision cycle just completed. This discussion can take place toward the end of the postconference, at a scheduled time after the postconference, informally soon after the postconference, or, if schedules are really tight, as written feedback. The questions asked are simple; in fact, they are a variation of the reflector's questions in the reflective practice guidelines presented in Chapter 2—What went well? What needs improvement? What would you do differently?—and are the prototype for most effective feedback processes. Remember that the focus of the collaborative reflection is the process between the supervisor and the teacher, not the teaching that took place in the observation.

COLLABORATIVE REFLECTION

1. *What was valuable in what we have been doing?*
2. *What was of little value?*
3. *What changes would you suggest for the next cycle?*

Class Practice

If you are able to schedule the planning conference or observation with your teacher volunteer before the next class meeting, be prepared to role-play the postconference in class. Decide on an interpersonal approach and create a description of the teacher you met. Using the reflective practice guidelines, groups of three will practice as many of the scenarios as possible.

Site Practice

If the colleague on site with whom you practiced the planning conference is not the participant for the whole clinical supervision cycle, find another teacher who will volunteer to do the complete cycle. Complete the cycle on site and prepare the following written report:

A. Summarize or recount each phase of the cycle: planning conference, observation, postconference, and collaborative reflection. A video- or audiotape can substitute for the written description.

B. Analyze the data from each approach choice you made and then interpret the data.
   1. How much teacher input was there in the planning conference? Would you recommend a change in the approach to this teacher in another planning session? Why?
   2. Did the observation tool reveal the behaviors on which you and your colleague agreed to focus? How or why not? Was the observation tool you chose appropriate and effective? Is it a tool you would use again? Why or why not? What other tool would you suggest?
   3. Which interpersonal approach did you use in the postconference? Why? What was the teacher's response? How well did it work?
   4. What were the teacher's reactions to the process? How effective was the collaborative reflection? What did <u>you</u> learn?

C. Provide a final reflection on the whole process, that is, your personal evaluation of what worked and was of value and what you will think about doing differently in the future.

CONCLUSION

This chapter has permitted us to expand our understanding of clinical supervision and become acquainted with the authors' version of reflective clinical supervision. The cycle presented consists of four stages:

1. The planning conference

2. The observation

3. The postconference

4. The collaborative reflection

Scenarios for some phases based on actual school contexts were presented, and exercises to practice the stages in class and on site were created. Now that you are familiar with and have practiced various interpersonal approaches, tools and techniques of observation, and the clinical supervision cycle, you can begin to think about the different ways improvement of classroom instruction can be configured in a department, grade, team, or school. In Chapter 5, we present some of the significant alternatives and variations on the traditional procedures for improving classroom instruction.

5

Alternative Approaches

Case Studies and Implementation Guidelines

We have laid the foundation for a sound supervision program by discussing interpersonal approaches, reviewing observation instruments, and introducing a framework for a complete cycle of reflective clinical supervision. You also have had the opportunity to practice and reflect on each facet of this supervision program. In this chapter, we provide a unique compendium of alternative approaches to supervision. Each approach is presented through an actual case study[1] that highlights the successful implementation of six alternative approaches to supervision of classroom instruction:

1. Standards-based walk-throughs

2. Mentoring

3. Peer coaching

4. Portfolio assessment

5. Peer assessment

6. Action research

Stages for implementation accompany each approach. In addition, a few of the case studies focus primarily on the organizational processes that the individuals or group instituted to develop their procedures. Thus, these studies illustrate the way that instructional leaders introduce innovative supervisory strategies in the context of unique school settings. We are broadening the picture—until now we have concentrated on the development of supervisory skills and practices; now we are beginning to look at supervision as one facet of instructional leadership.

STANDARDS-BASED WALK-THROUGH

The standards-based walk-through is unique because it does focus on enabling teachers to learn by exploring and relating to what other teachers are doing in their classrooms.

Roberts & Pruitt, 2003, p. 121

Case Study 1[2]

Dr. Christina Russo is an instructional supervisor in the Laurelton School District in El Dorado Hills, California. She's been in that position in her district for the past three years and has a superb reputation as a constructivist educator who relates well to teachers and principals. As an innovative educator, Dr. Russo explored a range of alternatives to supervision and staff development. Having read about Sylvia Roberts' and Eunice Pratt's "walk-through" approach to promote a culture of collaborative inquiry among teachers, Christina volunteered to offer professional development workshops in the district. Mohammad Alauddin, principal of a K–5 elementary school, was particularly interested in nurturing a culture of collaborative instruction for his teachers. As a new principal whose predecessor was the classic administrator-bureaucrat, Mr. Alauddin wanted to implement alternatives to traditional supervision. First, however, he wanted to engage teachers in meaningful staff development. Having worked with Christina in the past, he invited her to conduct a walk-through in his school during a professional development day in November. Mohammad was particularly interested in the standards-based walk-through because principals in the district, as in many other locales, were required to pay close attention to the standards-based curriculum.

During her opening address to the faculty, Dr. Russo explained the walk-through as follows:

> The walk-through is a structured process for opening up classrooms so that you can observe one another and learn from what occurs in other classrooms. How often are we isolated? We rarely have the opportunity to visit other classrooms in order to systematically observe what our colleagues are doing. Each of us can learn from one another. Great ideas are meant to be shared so that all students will learn. The walk-through is a great tool used by teachers for teachers. My role and that of Mr. Alauddin are meant uniquely to facilitate the process. The ultimate form and shape of the walk-through will be up to you.
>
> Several models of the walk-through exist. I'd like to discuss the standards-based model since, as you very well know, our district has

implemented an assessment system for the standards-based curriculum. Please note that after the approach is explained and tried at least once, you as a faculty will have the opportunity on your own to revise or even adopt another walk-through model.

Dr. Russo then explains the connection between the walk-through and standards.

Our model of the walk-through, based wholly on the work of Roberts and Pruitt (2003), is driven by the implementation of the content standards that have been adopted by school districts. This does not preclude a school from using the process to focus on other areas of interest. We initiated the process because building principals, with whom we were working, were struggling to identify ways of getting teachers to become comfortable with and respond to the standards that had been mandated as the focus of instruction in their districts.

We view schools as professional learning communities. Clearly, instructional practice and educational reform efforts have been profoundly influenced by the standards movement. Standards provide teachers with a blueprint for setting goals, planning curriculum, identifying effective instructional strategies, and assessing student performance. Once standards have been set, if teachers are to know what to do with them, they need ongoing direction and adequate support. We view the school walk-through as a strategy that serves this purpose by permitting teachers to observe their colleagues' work in relation to the standards, as they seek ways of improving learning opportunities for their students.

One of the teachers at the staff development introductory meeting interrupts Dr. Russo and asks, "What do we do on the walk?" Dr. Russo explains:

The tour is conducted on a professional development day when the students are not present in the school building. During the walk-through, the team members visit the classrooms to which they have been assigned and record their observations. They review student work for evidence of standards-related activities. They identify instructional activities, teacher-made instructional materials, and learning centers that might have implication for standards-based teaching in their own classrooms. They look for instructional activities that develop students' higher level thinking skills. They make note of the layout of classrooms and content of bulletin boards and other displays in the classroom. If they are available, visitors may also review the teacher's lesson plans to see the scope and sequence used by the teacher for standards-related instructional planning.

As a team of teachers reviews the various artifacts in the classrooms, they share their perceptions with each other. It's important to remember that this process is not meant for evaluation.

Dr. Russo explains what happens after the walk-through:

After the walk-through, the teachers attend grade-level meetings to discuss their observations. Finally, they prepare a brief summary sheet listing (a) the things that they have learned about standards-based teaching and learning as found in their notes and (b) the ideas they would like to replicate in their own classrooms. All summary sheets are then submitted to the principal, and a brief report, indicating what the teachers have learned from the process, is prepared for dissemination to the faculty. This process will also cultivate classroom observation as a facet of your role as teacher leaders and enhance your overall leadership capacity.

The faculty committed to implementing the walk-through that year. The following comments were culled from the assessment Dr. Russo distributed to the participants at the end of the academic year:

- I ended up looking forward to the walk-through. We walked through twice, and most teachers enjoyed the process and learned a lot. It made me feel good about being a teacher.
- Finally, we spent valuable time on a professional development day. The walk-through is fun and a tremendous learning experience.
- The walk-through lets me see the teachers in my school in a different light. I am always surprised at the creative ways I see of teaching to and reinforcing the standards.
- I am motivated to try new things with my class when I see how innovative some of the teachers can be.
- I believe every good teacher is a thief. We all steal good ideas from one another. After the walk-through, I accumulate loads of new ideas.
- After our last walk-through, a teacher from another grade level, whom I don't know too well, asked if she could come to my room to discuss how I used some of the instructional materials that I had made. I think the school walk-through is one of the better ideas that the principal has introduced to our school (Roberts & Pruitt, 2003).

A Definition

The *standards-based walk-through* provides for an organized tour of the building by teams of teachers, who visit their peers' classrooms; observe the classroom environment and learning centers; review student work samples, special projects, and portfolios; and examine other classroom artifacts that the teacher has put on display for the walk-through (Roberts & Pruitt, 2003). Roland Barth (1990), noted educator, has pointed out that "teachers also need to be able to relate their classroom behavior to what other teachers are doing in their classrooms. Teachers *think* they do that. Many do, but many do not do it very systematically or regularly" (p. 49).

The standards-based walk-though is unique precisely because it focuses on enabling you to learn by exploring and relating to what other teachers are doing in their classrooms. Because it is designed and carried out by you, it helps to develop your leadership capacity. Please note that neither students nor supervisors are present during the walk.

The walk-through is a model or approach used to promote a culture of collaborative learning. Used as professional development or supervision, the walk-through engages teachers in meaningful activities to enhance the instructional process. Teaching can be a lonely experience. The walk-through gives colleagues an opportunity to see each other's work, reflect on the instructional process, and to collaborate on developing new and better ways to improve instruction and thus promote student learning (Roberts & Pruitt, 2003).

Stages for Implementation

Various formats of the walk-through are possible. Although the case study above focuses on using the walk-through to enhance professional development during professional development days, other models use it directly as an alternative to traditional observation (evaluation). For instance, a principal can forgo traditional observations of teachers who implement a walk-through, as described below. The walk-through can easily be done during the regular school day (not a professional development day), where a small group of teachers plan on walking through each other's classrooms when class is in session. What makes the walk-through successful is that it is a well-planned and systematic process.

Here are some general steps for implementing a walk-through as an alternative to supervision:

1. Meet with a supervisor and a teacher colleague to discuss using the walk-through as an alternative to traditional supervision.

2. Articulate a specific purpose for the walk-through.

3. Establish and maintain trust.

4. See the walk-through as an opportunity to collaborate in order to grow and learn as a professional.

5. Develop objectives for the walk-through.

6. Develop a form to guide the observation (based on the objectives).

7. Decide when and how the walk-through will take place. Will students be in the room during the walk-through?

8. Prepare your classroom for the visit by showcasing the aspects of the curriculum you want seen. For instance, if you decide that you want to show the science curriculum in action, make sure you put on display lessons and unit plans, student projects, science materials in use, student bulletin boards that focus on science, seating arrangements used, and so on.

9. Plan to meet during a common preparatory session or before or after school to share experiences.

10. Develop a plan of action. If the process is used as an alternative to supervision, the supervisor will likely want to see an action plan that summarizes the walk-through, what each teacher learned through the process, and the steps that will be taken to improve classroom instruction.

Reflective Practice

Activity 1. Groups of two or more research the walk-through. Can you find a school to visit that has implemented the walk-through? If so, interview the participants. What do you think are the advantages and disadvantages of the walk-through? How might you implement a walk-through with a colleague or an entire faculty at a given grade level?

Activity 2. Find a colleague who wants to develop a plan for the walk-through as an alternative to supervision. Assume the supervisor has agreed to the walk-through in concept but wants to see a plan for implementation. Develop concrete objectives and, using the steps listed above in the Stages for Implementation section, establish a specific plan you would present to your supervisor. Be sure to demonstrate what you will do, what you might learn, and how the walk-through will contribute to your professional development and ultimately change teaching to improve student learning.

MENTORING

The mentor-mentee relationship is, indeed, a transformative one that can forever change the course of one's life.

Cienkus, Grant Haworth, & Kavanagh, 1996, p. 2

Case Study 2

Mari Celi Sanchez is an experienced teacher in Northern Valley Regional High School District. After consulting with her assistant principal, James McDonnell, Mari Celi has decided to mentor Eric Jones, a nontenured second-year teacher. Mari Celi is a dedicated teacher who has received two Outstanding Teacher of the Year awards over the course of her 18 years at the high school. As part of the professional development program, she opts for mentorship and receives released time to work with Eric.

Mari Celi meets with Eric to discuss their plans. She explains to Eric that she has no evaluative authority and will keep their conversations confidential. Although Eric will have to undergo at least three formal observations over the course of the semester, Mari Celi will not in any way participate in the evaluation process. "My job," she explains to Eric, "is to work with you as much as you'd like on areas that you feel may need improvement." Eric and Mari Celi develop a close professional relationship over the course of the next several months. He realizes that she in fact does not have any evaluative input, and his confidence in her grows daily. "You know," says Eric, "I feel I can really open up to you. More so than to a supervisor who I know will eventually evaluate me."

Eric's skills have improved dramatically. "You know," explains Mari Celi, "you are really a natural teacher. The kids love you, and your enthusiasm is infectious." Certainly Eric's evaluation reports in the year and a half he has been at the school have been exceptional. Eric attributes much of his success to the "expert and friendly assistance" he has received from Mari Celi.

While working on their second-semester instructional plans, Mari Celi shares some research she recently completed on gender bias in the classroom as part of her doctoral work. "Gender bias is quite common in many classrooms, you know," explains Mari Celi. Eric responds: "Oh, I believe that's overstated. I treat everyone equally in my class." "OK," says Mari Celi. "Let's see. I'll observe you." They discuss plans for an upcoming lesson during which Mari Celi will observe as both as an independent observer and a participant observer using a qualitative research approach (Glanz, 1998). Mari Celi records the following notes during one segment of the lesson:

11th-grade class: 13 boys and 12 girls; self-contained classroom. Eric starts lesson at 9:45 a.m. I enter as Eric tells class to take out their readers. As Eric gives instructions for silent reading, three students (two male and one female) are out of their seats hanging their coats in the rear classroom closet. The girl is talking. Eric tells her to be quiet and sit down. During silent reading, students are reading quietly. After about 3 minutes, a monitor enters classroom and the teacher records the daily attendance. Noise level in class rises. Monitor leaves room. Teacher walks back and forth as students get quiet. At 9:49 a.m., Eric asks a boy to tell the class what the story was about. Student responds. Class attentive. Eric asks a girl, "Why do you think Billy in the story was so upset?" Student responds. Teacher calls on a boy who also responds, albeit differently. Eric probes and asks the boy to explain. Eric asks a girl another thought-provoking question. Girl responds. Teacher asks a boy another question—"Why was Jane so angry with Billy?—and probes. (10 minutes elapse and I note that it appears that Eric calls on boys and girls evenly, but that he consistently probes male responses but rarely probes a female response. Curious, ask Eric about this!) Time elapses. Teacher divides class into study groups; I join one of the groups with two boys and one girl. Teacher circulates. Students answer reading questions and discuss story. I ask them if they liked the story and to explain why or why not. Teacher requests attention from class. Eric continues by asking many thought-provoking questions and follows the same pattern of probing more for boys than for girls. Interestingly, when the boy sitting to my right in the group was asked a question, he was probed, but the girl to my left was not. I could not discern any concern among the students.

After the class, Mari Celi shares her observations with Eric. Eric, not defensive at all, was surprised. "Really? That's interesting. What do you think it means?" he asks. Mari Celi and Eric explore various possibilities in an atmosphere of trust, candor, and mutual respect.

A Definition

Mentoring is a process that facilitates instructional improvement wherein an experienced educator works with a novice or less experienced teacher collaboratively and nonjudgmentally to study and deliberate on ways instruction in the classroom may be improved. Mentors are not judges or critics but facilitators of instructional improvement. Like Northern Valley Regional High School, many schools have developed mentoring programs in which an experienced teacher is assigned or volunteers to work with a novice teacher for the purpose of "providing individualized, ongoing professional support" (Glickman et al., 1998, p. 353). In some parts of the country, such as Toledo, Ohio, mentoring is actually negotiated into the union contract as an alternative supervisory approach. Although some people in the field equate mentoring with supervision (Reiman & Thies-Sprinthall, 1998), we assert that mentoring is an alternative form of supervision.

Stages for Implementation

To implement mentoring effectively, the reader is advised to read *Teachers as Mentors: A Practical Guide* by Field and Field (1994) and to view the videotape that the Association for Supervision and Curriculum Development (1994) has produced on mentoring. We strongly recommend that mentors develop and use the supervisory skills presented in the preceding chapters. The stages for implementation that follow were developed at Northern Valley Regional High School District (1996) and are excerpted from a manual titled *Differentiated Supervision*.

Description: This model can incorporate a variety of possible applications. In all cases, an educator would agree to provide assistance, support, and recommendations to another staff member or staff members. A mentor could work with a nontenured teacher or share expertise in a specific area with other educators. For example, a staff member with specific technical training may share this expertise with others. All interactions and recommendations between the mentor and staff members will be confidential.

Approach: The following guidelines are highly prescriptive, however, mentorship has proven successful as an alternative means of supervision at Northern Valley High School.

1. Any educator may volunteer to be a support mentor. A supervisor or administrator, knowing of a certain staff member's expertise, may request that that individual serve in this capacity. If asked, a staff member must agree, not be directed, to serve.

2. A mentor plan is developed by the educator, approved by the supervisor, and shared with those individuals to be mentored.

3. The mentor implements the plan and reports on the plan activities to the supervisor.

Reflective Practice

A group of three students should develop a mentor plan. Describe the plan. Role-play a mentoring session in which the mentor shares his or her plan. What feedback approach would you use? Use the guidelines for reflective practice to provide feedback to the mentor and mentee,

PEER COACHING

When two teachers observe each other; the one teaching is the "coach" and the one observing is the "coached."

Showers & Joyce, 1996, p. 15

Case Study 3

The International Institute is one of four minischools or institutes that are part of a large New York City middle school. It was previously one of the lowest-performing middle schools in the district. Nancy Brogan, an assertive, go-getter principal was brought in to improve both achievement and image. Open to innovation and aggressive in pursuing funds, she broke up the 1,200-plus students into four theme institutes. The International Institute is composed primarily of Haitian, Russian, Spanish, Chinese, Bengali, and Urdu bilingual students. Because of the bilingual focus, the staff of the institute mirrors the diversity of the student body.

Through one of her outreach efforts, Nancy secured the assistance of one of the authors of this text. My (the author's) initial project was to help organize the governance committee of the institute. This task completed, our conversations veered more toward curriculum and teaching and learning issues. All of the teachers on the steering committee were committed, enthusiastic, effective, and creative teachers, and along with the institute director, Lynne Pagano, were open to anything that would promote student achievement. Because peer coaching was an approved choice in the new union contract's weekly period for professional development for each teacher, we decided to pursue the possibility of using this staff period to develop and implement the skills and practices of peer coaching. A second recently approved union provision included the option of alternative assessment for tenured teachers. The director's reaction was,

> These teachers are the best. They can all use the peer coaching as their
> official observations—even the one who is just shy of tenure. This way
> I can concentrate on the teachers who really need help. By the way,
> would you mind if I sat in on your meetings?

The prospective participants and I then made a site visit to a school that had developed a very sophisticated system of peer assessment. The teachers came back excited and ready to take on the challenge.

Next, we had to decide the focus of the peer coaching. Two of the teachers had been trained during the summer in the new standards required by the city and the state, and one teacher had been involved in developing the Spanish curriculum and city adaptation for the standards. Their enthusiasm about the work they had been doing and the need for implementation triggered conversation about two possible coaching models:

1. Peer observations based on the implementation of the curriculum for the new standards

2. Coaching where teachers would discuss classroom challenges or interests and conduct interclass visitations

Mannor Wong, the English as a Second Language (ESL) teacher, commented, "Since I'm not tenured yet, I'd prefer honing my general instructional techniques. I'd like someone to be able to give me feedback on the strategies I'm working on in the classroom and how the students are responding to them."

Farooqui Nasreen, the Urdu bilingual teacher, had the following conversation with Madeline Castaneda, the Spanish bilingual teacher:

Farooqui: Since you've already developed a curriculum in Spanish for the new standards, could I see how you're going to implement it in the classroom? Then maybe you could observe me as I try to use the adapted curriculum in my Urdu classes.

Madeline: That's a good idea. And the students will feel comfortable with you there because of the multicultural sharing we've been doing.

Lynn Lavner, an English Language Arts teacher with a strong performing arts background began sitting in on our meetings unofficially. Her reactions were somewhat different: "I could use help as I try to develop our Facing History Through the Arts curriculum this spring, but I don't know about observing another teacher's class. I don't think that's for me."

The plan that emerged was for the participants to learn and practice interpersonal, observation, and feedback skills through observations of videotaped classroom instruction and role plays of interpersonal techniques and feedback approaches. They would then be prepared to help each other more effectively and become turnkey trainers for future coaching groups. A date for the first orientation and training meeting was set. In the interim, the volunteer group was to be finalized.

The Best-Laid Plans of Mice and Teachers

We began meeting in the director's office during the teachers' 40-minute lunch hour. There were constant interruptions, time lost getting lunch, and teachers arriving late or not at all. Lynn Lavner hadn't been in on the original planning, which may have been the reason for her initial spotty attendance. Mannor Wong had not been involved in the early meetings either and may have had some initial apprehension. I decided that we needed to go back to the drawing board to look for a longer block of time at a different point in the day. Luckily, this particular group was involved in implementing a grant with some flexible funding. The coordinator of the grant, Elke Savoy (one of the participants), figured out that she could compensate the teachers to come after school for a series of two-hour workshops.

We had one more setback before launching the afterschool workshops. Through her ongoing outreach efforts, Nancy Brogan had procured additional professional development help to increase achievement scores. One strategy included daily brief observations by the directors in all classrooms and completion of checklists for each teacher. All staff were to follow certain procedures that the directors would verify in their visits. I met with the principal and Lynne Pagano to explain that this method was at odds with our peer coaching goals. They agreed that the teachers involved in our project would be exempt from this requirement. In fact, Lynne was relieved because she was "going crazy" trying to keep up with the marathon visiting schedule.

Uninterrupted quality time, snacks, and compensation were a few of the elements that fostered time on task. The following weeks were spent perfecting the participants' interpersonal and feedback skills and using various techniques to observe videos of teachers and students. As the group simulated and role-played the skills in class, they began to practice observing colleagues' classes. Finally, they went through the clinical observation cycle with each other and other volunteers in the International Institute. Discussions and feedback took place at each session to fine-tune the process as we went along. Open communication about reactions to the process was encouraged.

Once the participants were comfortable with their observing and feedback skills, the next step was to set up individual or paired plans for their dialogues around curriculum implementation. The initial plans were set up at the last workshop because it was the last opportunity for quality time. We decided that each teacher or pair of teachers would write an action plan for his or her focus. Brief meetings would take place every two weeks to share experiences, provide feedback on what was and was not working, troubleshoot, and modify plans as needed.

I kept a running record of the process and provided both a qualitative and quantitative evaluation at the end of the semester. The participants were so enthusiastic that it was decided to involve more volunteers the following Fall and share the experience with another institute.

REFLECTION

What are the lessons to be learned from the initial meetings of the coaching group? What are a couple of underlying assumptions that the facilitators of this type of project must maintain for successful implementation?

A Definition

Peer coaching is an umbrella term for the many different configurations of teachers helping teachers that have emerged primarily since the 1980s. Some of the other terms often used interchangeably with peer coaching are peer assistance, collegial coaching, technical coaching, cognitive coaching, challenge coaching, and peer supervision. Most of these models pertain to variations of peer-to-peer assistance of equals and do not involve evaluation. Mentoring programs that consist of master teachers helping less experienced or less well-trained colleagues are not included in our categorization. In this case study, peer coaching is defined as teachers helping teachers reflect on and improve teaching practices or implement particular instructional skills introduced through staff or curriculum development. Joyce and Showers (1980) specified the process as two or more teachers who meet regularly for problem solving using planning, observation, feedback, and creative thinking for the development of a specific skill.

Stages for Implementation

Goals for peer coaching include:

- Refine teaching practices
- Stimulate self-initiating, autonomous teacher thought
- Improve school culture
- Increase collegiality and professional dialogue
- Share in the implementation of new or common instructional skills

Key steps. Teresa Benedetti (1997) outlined a simple set of procedures for teachers to initiate a peer coaching system in their schools. The following procedures are an adaptation of her recommendations:

1. After obtaining permission from the appropriate administrators, suggest that your colleagues choose a peer whom they trust and with whom they feel they will work well.

2. Make sure that everyone is familiar with and able to engage in the cycle of clinical supervision. Ask assistance from supervisors or others familiar with clinical supervision.

3. Peers may have to help each other cover classes while their colleagues observe each other. Interested supervisors also can facilitate freeing up of teachers. If scheduling conflicts occur, videotaping a class can provide the additional experience of viewing the class together. If both teachers teach the same content to similar classes, combining classes and observing each others' application of skills or team teaching can be very effective.

4. Organize weekly or biweekly seminars for peer coaching. The first sessions can be used to learn and review observation and feedback

techniques. The opportunity to share experiences and brainstorm new ideas as well as modify the existing structure is essential.

Through the ongoing discussion of teaching and learning, curriculum development, and implementation, peer coaching can become the heart of professional development.

Reflective Practice

Site Practice

Each student will recruit a colleague who is interested in exploring peer coaching. Brainstorm with the teacher or teachers, if possible, about how peer coaching could be developed at your site. Record your ideas on chart paper and bring the actual sheets to class.

Class Practice

Divide the class into groups. Share the brainstormed ideas. Make a group list of the most promising ideas. The list can be developed by having each participant choose two or three favorites. The final choices will be the strategies that receive the most votes. Each group will report out its results to the whole class. Students will then record their preferred strategies.

PORTFOLIOS FOR DIFFERENTIATED SUPERVISION

Case Study 4[3]

When Carmen Farina became principal of the New York City elementary school PS 6, she faced many challenges, some more familiar to suburban principals than to urban ones. She entered a school long renowned for academic excellence, located in one of the most elegant neighborhoods in the city. The previous principal presided over a building known as the private public school. Many of the parents had the means to send their children to private schools but preferred to send them to PS 6, generously funding the PTA to provide some of the extras wealthy districts and independent schools often provide.

In her previous positions as a building principal and district staff developer, Carmen had transformed her school's language arts/social studies curriculum into an exciting interdisciplinary program called Making Connections and had overseen its implementation in the whole district. Carmen described the challenge at PS 6:

> My dilemma upon assuming the principalship was that the students scored high on the standardized tests while little student-centered learning was going on. Veteran teachers, for the most part, ran traditional classrooms. How could I effect change in an environment where many parents and teachers were content with the status quo?

The approach I took was to begin visiting teachers on a daily basis and engaging them in conversations around their teaching practices. These visits allowed me to assess school strengths and weaknesses. Through constant class visits and discussion of successes and challenges, areas of concern and/or interest began to emerge. By the end of the year, we had been able to designate three priorities around curriculum needs and an area of interest for each teacher.

At that point, Carmen selected 10 teachers to participate in the first-year implementation of Portfolios for Differentiated Supervision. Although it was emphasized that participation was open to all faculty, a total of 16 teachers volunteered and subsequently took part in the process.

Laura Kotch, a staff developer, was key to the successful development and implementation of the model. The following remarks are some of the thoughts she shared in greeting a group of visitors to the school:

Each participating teacher is involved in creating a portfolio, a container for his or her area of inquiry. The decisions about which topics to study came from questions teachers had, their areas of interest, their curiosity, and experimentation with new classroom strategies and techniques. Some questions have lingered over time. A first-grade teacher's investigation originated with her question about practice that wasn't working. Her inquiry led to research on the most effective way to create competent and curious first-grade spellers. Other teachers began their portfolios by taking a risk and experimenting with new ways to integrate curriculum, such as Making Connections, author studies, and math/cooperative learning.

Laura concluded a workshop with these thoughts:

Teachers have been spending time talking together, reading articles and books written by the experts, and reflecting on their beliefs and practices. The task of writing ideas down in a portfolio requires us to clarify thoughts and ideas, refine our language, and find our writer's voice. The process of creating text has been both challenging and exciting. Writing together has allowed us the wonderful opportunity of forming a writing network, relating to each other not only as teachers but as authors as well. It will be worth all the hard work if the portfolio serves as a practical resource, while continuing to change and grow as our learning continues. As a facilitator, adviser, and friend working alongside the dedicated, hard-working and talented professionals of PS 6, I am proud to be part of this exciting and innovative model of staff development.

A Definition

A professional portfolio can serve many different purposes. It can be, as it is at PS 6, a container for a particular area of inquiry. At PS 6, the portfolio not only documents the development of innovative and effective practices, it is a central vehicle for the growth of the teacher through self-reflection, analysis, and sharing with colleagues through discussion and writing. Although each PS 6 portfolio is different, each one includes teacher resources and references, professional articles, and practical suggestions.

Portfolios also can be used to support and enrich mentoring and coaching relationships. Although the portfolio does not replace the classroom observation, it extends and enhances the professional discussion by going beyond what is observed in the classroom on a given day. The advent of the electronic portfolio opens even more opportunities for sharing practices within a school, between schools, and beyond the teacher's district. When a teacher is applying for another position, an annotated collection of materials on a teacher's best classroom practices and work with colleagues supplements and strengthens the interview process (Danielson, 1996). One of us has repeatedly witnessed the influence that a well-crafted portfolio has on hiring committees.

Stages for Implementation (based on the PS 6 process)

Phase 1

   A. Curriculum Prioritizing
      1. Assessment of school strengths and weaknesses and development of a set of prioritized curriculum needs for the building

   B. Portfolios for differentiated supervision
      1. Designation of an area of expertise in each teacher's classroom built through intensive class visitation and conversation around teaching practices
      2. Solicitation of a group of volunteers or selection of staff to reflect on an area of expertise and share and provide materials for the school faculty and visiting colleagues
      3. Criteria for inclusion of participants:
         a. Outstanding expertise in a certain area
         b. A teacher who has not refined or reflected on a special talent
         c. Teachers likely to respond to a collegial environment for self-improvement

      4. Professional development to lay groundwork for the creation of portfolios. Possible outcomes of the workshops:
         a. Reflection on and analysis of the areas of expertise
         b. Decision of some teachers to collaborate on their efforts and create a joint portfolio
         c. Use of a letter format as a means of beginning faculty journals

      5. First drafts of the portfolios are submitted the following fall, and an administrator reviews the drafts and gives oral and written comments and suggestions
      6. When portfolios are completed, the principal writes a "dear author" letter to each participant

Phase II

    A. New portfolio cycle
        1. Additional teachers choose to participate in the process
        2. Specialty faculty, such as ESL teachers, can complete their portfolios by adding to individual portfolios

    B. The reflective teacher
        1. The process now involves semiannual "conversations" with the principal, for a minimum of one uninterrupted hour to discuss portfolios and other areas of interest
        2. Teachers receive a summary of their conversation with the principal

Advantages and limitations of process (according to PS 6).

    A. Advantages
        1. Affords the staff the opportunity to be reflective and analytical
        2. Encourages the teachers to work cooperatively together
        3. Allows the administration to get to know the teachers better and to encourage their growth in many areas
        4. Encourages the staff to read professional journals
        5. Gives a purpose for intervisitations
        6. Fosters professionalism in teachers
        7. Encourages teachers to apply for grants in areas of their expertise
        8. Enhances parents' view of the school
        9. Provides a focus for the two-way conversation with teachers
      10. Gives teachers more input
      11. Produces the "Hawthorne effect" when visitors come to the school
      12. Provides a vehicle for continuous inclusion of strategies (e.g., ESL, multiculturalism)

    B. Challenges
        1. Administration must develop a trusting relationship with the staff.
        2. A lot of time is required.
        3. Principal must be aware of what is going on in the classroom.
        4. Teachers must be accepting of the process.
        5. Inordinate amount of time is required for planning and writing.
        6. Materials must be available.
        7. Change is not immediate—it takes time.

REFLECTION

How does this process differ from peer coaching? What are the similarities?

Reflective Practice

Each student reflects on an area of classroom practice in which he or she has expertise or talent, about which he or she has questions, or with which he or she would like to experiment. Once everyone has come up with an idea, the class divides into small groups. After each person shares his or her area, the other members of the group offer suggestions of resources, professional articles and references, and strategies for creation of the portfolio.

PEER ASSESSMENT: SELECTION, SUPPORT, AND EVALUATION

Shared leadership can foster the professional growth and development of teachers, which in turn leads to the empowerment of students as successful learners.

Personnel Committee, International High School, 1991

Case Study 5

The International High School, located on the basement floor of LaGuardia Community College, was a joint venture of the then-New York City Board of Education and the Board of Higher Education of the City of New York. It is an alternative high school founded in 1985 to serve the needs of students with limited English proficiency. It describes itself as "alternative in its admissions policy, population served, school governance, teaching methodology, setting, and opportunities for both students and staff."

Some of the unique learning experiences for students developed over the last 13 years are

- A focus on content-based English as a Second Language instruction
- Heterogeneous, collaborative groupings
- Career-oriented internships
- Organization of the entire curriculum around thematically based inter-disciplinary cycles
- Team teaching
- Performance-based alternative assessment standards for course work and graduation
- The opportunity to take college courses with matriculated college students for both high school and college credit

The school is open to all students with limited English proficiency who reside in New York City, who have lived in the United States for fewer than 4 years, and who are entering 9th or 10th grade in the next school year. The diversity of languages, dress, and ethnicities that fills the halls dazzles the first-time visitor.

In a conversation, Eric Nadelstern, the founding principal of International High School, retraced the road that the staff traveled to reach their singular level of faculty and student empowerment:

The first years. In reflecting back, it was less about trying to figure out how to structure a school than trying to figure out how kids learn best—and through our discoveries, figuring out what a school would need to look like if it were built around our understanding about how kids learn best and in a way that allowed us to continue that level of inquiry, and then designing the school based on new learnings.

Given that, it's not surprising that the first year we opened, our school looked not too dissimilar from a traditional New York City public high school. We divided all knowledge into the same six arbitrary disciplines everyone else has been confined to for centuries. Periods were exactly 40 minutes long; we had eight of them a day. We made the mistake of thinking that if eight periods were good, nine must be better. So, going into the second year, we shaved five minutes off each instructional period and that gave an additional class.

The staff did meet together for two hours a week. Back then, it was as a paid-per-session afterschool activity. Since it was part and parcel of working here, it wasn't necessarily voluntary, although no one was forced to be here. We shared our insights on this common exploration about learning. And on the basis of those insights, we continued to rethink the way the school needed to be structured.

The first major step in that direction, or at least a milestone in it, was something we referred to as the Student for a Day Project. Everyone on staff was given the opportunity to be relieved of responsibilities, teaching and otherwise, for an entire school day, to spend a day with a kid. The staff member was to travel through the school as that kid did and attempt to see the school from the student's perspective. To avoid stacking the experiment, we selected 40 kids who were not as successful as we would have liked and asked the volunteers to spend the entire day with the student they chose. If that student had lunch during a particular period, they had to go to lunch with that student. If that student had gym, they had to bring their sneakers.

Over a three-month period, everyone on staff volunteered for this exercise. We facilitated the shadowing opportunity by covering their classes. At the end of the experiment, we got together and shared our findings. In discussion, comments surfaced like, "The most interesting thing that happens in this school happens in the hallway in between classes." Or "Thirty-five-minute periods are insane. You can't do anything meaningful in 35 minutes, and to have to shift your focus every half hour is a crazy way of learning something."

So the curriculum committee decided to look at the structure and subsequently built a new one based on the 70-minute periods at LaGuardia Community College. I created a two-hour block on Wednesday afternoon for the staff to meet. On Wednesdays, students can choose to stay at the school if they wish—the computer room is open, athletic and club activities are offered, or they can participate in college activities.

The key is that the staff meet together to identify their successes, failures, and kids' problems. As the staff learns what it isn't doing, the students learn from the staff's experience of trying to meet the kids' needs through inquiry. A principle emerged: Teachers best offer learning experiences for students that they experience first themselves. Therefore, peer assessment for children developed only after the teachers did it themselves.

Peer assessment. The peer assessment itself grew out of a small-school necessity. I realized that because of my small administrative staff, I needed to share responsibility. I was working a 70-hour week, seven days a week. So I started with personnel. I asked teachers if they wanted to participate in hiring. Prior to opening the school, I had interviewed 60 people for seven positions with each interview lasting two hours. In our first year, all seven staff members agreed to join the personnel committee and decided on a chair. They staffed the school for the second year. It did take time for them to become effective. By the end of that first school year, they weren't able to fill all the vacancies.

Having hired most of the staff, they had a vested interest in their hires becoming successful. The underlying assumption is that when staffing is a shared activity, the entire faculty accepts responsibility for orienting and supporting new members. Thus, the third year, the staff initiated peer support during the Wednesday afternoon meetings. Initially, peer support took place on Wednesdays without involving evaluation. Once the faculty became accustomed to providing support, they began visiting each other's classes. As the observations increased, some written feedback began. Trust had to be built, and it took time. Providing written feedback to each other did not become widespread until the fourth year. And it wasn't until the fifth year that the personnel committee wrote and codified the schema for evaluation. Based on research showing that ideas from colleagues carry more weight than traditional evaluation procedures, the committee members concluded that a combination of self-evaluation and peer evaluation would be the most effective means to promote professional growth. By that time, my role was to meet weekly with the chair of the committee. The message to the faculty is that they are autonomous professionals who are trusted. The key to consensus in the school is that it is the faculty that shapes policy.

Ongoing development. Over the last few years, the staff has evolved into instructional teams that have become increasingly autonomous and have taken on more and more responsibilities. They schedule themselves for free periods, and they do their own hiring. These instructional groups have replaced the peer groups. The personnel committee has taken on more of a coordinating function. A coordinating committee oversees governance. I am a member of the coordinating committee and create my own portfolio, which my peer group evaluates.

At the time of the interview, Eric Nadelstern saw his own leadership role as threefold: First, he felt that his job was to model professional development, as in the portfolio that he created for his own assessment; second, he considers that training his staff to be leaders was one of his central roles; and third, a major piece of his responsibility was an external one—to protect and advocate for his school. In that role of advocate and liaison to the outside, he promoted the creation of an in-house, unpublished handbook titled *Personnel Procedures for Peer Selection, Support, and Evaluation* that International High School shares willingly with other professionals. We summarize some of the main assumptions and procedures for International's peer process as well as provide information on how you can request a copy of the complete handbook.[4]

Peer Support Groups

A Definition

The purpose of the peer support group is to provide a place for staff to exchange ideas, learn from each other, and support each other in reaching their professional goals. Groups composed of three to four members from at least two subject areas, one of whom is tenured, and including support staff, meet regularly and rotate every year.

Stages for Implementation

- Goals are established collectively at the beginning of the year.
- Meetings are scheduled to discuss progress and problems and provide timely feedback throughout the year.
- Staff visit each other's classes several times a year and write peer observations that reflect the goals of each staff member.
- Everyone in the group, including nontenured and provisional staff, writes at least one peer observation.
- The group provides support and feedback in the writing of self-evaluations, in the completion of the portfolio, and in the preparation of presentations before the peer evaluation teams.

Self-Evaluation

Self-evaluations can be as varied as the individuals on staff. The only requirements for the self-evaluations are that nontenured teachers must provide at least two every year and that tenured staff submit one at the end of the year. The self-evaluations can range from discussing growth to expressing disappointment, from looking at one course to comparing several, from focusing on content to examining skills. Because the portfolios are in a central location and open to all staff, faculty members can derive benefit from the insights of their colleagues.

Peer Evaluation

A Definition

The idea behind the peer evaluation team is that when a staff member needs feedback from the school at large, the staff member will make a presentation to a larger group of peers who represent the whole school. These presentations, as differentiated from the peer support group, often take place in passing through the gates that lead to tenure; that is, for appointment to a position, at the end of the first two years of teaching in the school, for continuation and completion of probation, and for granting of tenure. Tenured staff present every three years, a process that represents a form of renewable tenure.

Stages for Implementation

- The peer evaluation team is composed of staff members who have been in the school for a full school year, and the members are chosen from the following groups at random: a teacher or guidance counselor from the personnel committee to serve as team leader, a member of the subject area and other staff members, and the candidate's choice from his or her peer support group.
- The candidate prepares a portfolio that contains goals and objectives for the year; self-, peer, and administrative evaluations; two out of three student class evaluations for each semester; any professional work of the candidate's choice; and the annual end-of-term evaluation review.
- In the presentation, the team examines the portfolio materials, discusses the candidate's accomplishments and goals for the future, and makes a recommendation based on the portfolio, feedback from the peer support groups, and the discussion with the candidate.
- The following day, the candidate meets with the principal, the personnel committee chair, and the peer evaluation team leader to discuss the committee's recommendation and to develop a plan to meet the coming year's goals.

REFLECTION

How does the portfolio in this process differ from the portfolio in PS 6? Where does the responsibility lie at the International High School for selection, support, and evaluation? To whom is each staff member accountable?

ACTION RESEARCH

Although action research is not a quick fix for all school problems, it represents a process that. . . can focus the brain-power of the entire instructional staff on maximizing learning.

McLean, 1995, p. 5

Case Study 6

Doris Harrington is a tenured math teacher at Northern Valley Regional High School, a school that comprises 1,100 students. Having taught in the school for 18 years, Doris is excited about the new program that Principal Bert Ammerman spearheaded to enhance professional development and instructional improvement: "I think it's neat that we now have a system in place in which we feel empowered. I mean, having an option, a choice in determining my professional development is certainly new and much appreciated."

Doris selects an action research plan as a part of the supervisory program that teachers, supervisors, and administrators collaboratively developed. "I've read so much about action research," she says, "and am so excited that others now appreciate how important it is to provide time for teachers to reflect about what we do every day in the classroom." Doris's observations confirm the views of many educators, who maintain that encouraging reflective teaching is one of the most important responsibilities of instructional supervisors (Schon, 1988).

Familiarizing herself with the literature on action research (Elliott, 1991; Glanz, 2003; Stringer, 1999), Doris reviews the four basic steps:

1. Selecting a focus for study

2. Collecting data

3. Analyzing and interpreting the data

4. Taking action

She wonders about her classroom. "What has been successful? How do I know these strategies are successful? What needs improvement? What mistakes have I made? In what ways can I improve my instructional program?" In collaborative conversations with her assistant principal, Jim McDonnell, Doris frames her project.

She wonders whether or not the time and energies expended on cooperative learning activities are worth the effort. Although she is familiar with the extensive research on the subject (Johnson & Johnson, 1989), Doris decides to compare her fourth-period math class with her sixth-period class in terms of how cooperative learning strategies affect student achievement and attitudes toward problem-solving in mathematics. She chooses these two classes because they are somewhat equivalent in mathematical problem-solving ability. She selects a nonequivalent control group design commonly associated with ex post facto research because the study involves the use of intact classes (see Glanz, 2003, for an explanation of this research design).

She randomly assigns cooperative learning as the primary instructional strategy to be used with the fourth-period class, whereas the other class will work on mathematical problem solving through the traditional textbook method. After six weeks of implementing this plan, she administers a posttest math exam and discovers, after applying a t-test statistic, that the group exposed to cooperative learning attained significantly higher mathematical problem-solving scores than the group that was taught math traditionally. Doris also keeps an anecdotal record throughout the research project on how students seemed to get along socially in both classes. Independent observers are utilized to ensure more reliable findings. She also administers an attitude questionnaire to ascertain how students felt about learning math using cooperative learning groups as compared to learning math in the more traditional format.

Based on her findings, Doris decides to incorporate cooperative learning procedures into all her classes. She still wonders whether or not, for example, cooperative learning will work for all math topics and whether cooperative learning is uniquely effective for problem-solving activities. In consultation with Jim McDonnell, she develops a plan to continue assessments throughout the year. Jim asks Doris to present her findings at both grade and faculty conferences.

Doris's enthusiasm for action research was emphatic:

> Employing action research engenders greater feelings of competence in solving problems and making instructional decisions. In the past I never really thought about the efficacy of my teaching methods to any great extent. The time spent in this project directly impacts on my classroom practice. I'm much more skeptical of what really works and am certainly more reflective about what I do. Action research should, I believe, be an integral part of any instructional improvement effort. No one has to convince you to change an instructional strategy. Once you gather and analyze your own data, you'll be in a position to make your own judgments about what should or should not be done. Action research empowers teachers!

A Definition

Action research is a type of applied research that has reemerged as a popular way to involve educators in reflective activities about their work. Action research is not a narrow, limited practice but can use a range of methodologies, simple and complex, to better understand one's work and even solve specific problems. Action research, properly used, can have immeasurable benefits such as:

- Creating a systemwide mind-set for school improvement—a professional problem-solving ethos
- Enhancing decision making
- Promoting reflection and self-improvement
- Instilling a commitment to continuous instructional improvement
- Creating a more positive school climate in which teaching and learning are foremost concerns
- Empowering those who participate and promoting professional development

Action research is an ongoing process of reflection that involves four basic cyclical steps:

1. Selecting a focus
   a. Know what you want to investigate
   b. Develop some initial questions
   c. Establish a plan to answer or better understand these questions

2. Collecting data
   a. Primary
      i. Questionnaires
      ii. Observations
      iii. Interviews
      iv. Tests
      v. Focus groups
   b. Secondary
      i. School profile sheets
      ii. Multimedia
      iii. Portfolios
      iv. Records
      v. Others

3. Analyzing and interpreting data

4. Taking action

Stages for Implementation

To effectively implement action research, the reader is advised to read Glanz's (2003) *Action Research: An Educational Leader's Guide to School Improvement* book, view videotapes produced by the Association for Supervision and Curriculum Development (1995) on action research, and even take a course at a local university or attend a workshop. Another resource is Hubbard and Power's (1993) *The Art of Classroom Inquiry: A Handbook for Teacher-Researchers.* The following stages for implementation were developed at Northern Valley Regional High School District (1996) and are paraphrased from a handout titled *Differentiated Supervision.*

Action Research

Description. The model allows the educator the chance to increase his or her scholarly background by encouraging the examination and analysis of pertinent documents. The educator might complete this independent study in one year. To complete the project, the educator will have periods designated for research and development during the year.

Before beginning the Action Research Project, the educator will discuss the project with his or her supervisor. . . . [consultations with supervisor are elaborated.]

At the end of the year, the researcher will submit a report to the supervisor. The report will highlight the project's significance, content, and conclusions, as well as pedagogically sound methods to teach the materials.

If the project's scope warrants an extension, the supervisor can recommend granting an additional academic year to complete the project. This model is applicable to all tenured staff and, in an exceptional case, could apply to an experienced but non-tenured staff member.

Approach

1. Identify the importance of the research and suggest ways the project will enhance students' knowledge or improve services offered by the school district.

2. Identify the specific materials (primary and secondary sources) the educator will research.

3. Develop a schedule.

4. Limit the project's scope. Such delimitation will promote thorough rather than superficial research.

5. Study and analyze all materials for the project.

6. Develop and implement a unit or program based on the project.

The Northern Valley High School District uses a prescribed set of guidelines that have resulted in a number of valuable research projects. In our experiences, without a formal structure to support such efforts, action research projects rarely, if ever, are successful. The implementation of this alternative means of instructional improvement in Northern Valley has furthered the efficacy of action research as an invaluable means to promote professional development. Action research as used at Northern Valley does not necessarily replace other traditional forms of supervision.

Reflective Practice

Groups of three to six students can consult Glanz's (2003) book, *Action Research: An Educational Leader's Guide to School Improvement*, and develop a workable research project whose aim is to improve classroom teaching. Describe the project and be as specific as possible. Incorporate both quantitative and qualitative approaches. Each group will present its project in a fishbowl. Sitting in a circle surrounded by the rest of the class, members of the group will describe different facets of the project. At the end of the presentation, the observers, or outer circle, will provide feedback, ask questions, and offer suggestions.

CONCLUSION

With these six case studies of alternative approaches and the guidelines for creating a supervisory program that encompass alternatives to traditional supervision, you are now ready to consider what your next steps might be to improve the supervision of classroom instruction in your school and district.

NOTES

1. Most of the faculty in the schools involved in the case studies have encouraged us to use their real names.

2. This scenario is based on Sylvia Roberts's model and work with schools.

3. The information for this case study was gathered from materials distributed at workshops held at PS 6 and through conversations with the then-principal, Carmen Farina. Names have not been changed.

4. Copies of the complete set of procedures can be obtained from The Personnel Committee, The International High School, LaGuardia Community College, 31–10 Thomson Avenue, Long Island City, New York.

6

Supervision to Improve Classroom Instruction

Next Steps

Assume that any significant innovation, if it is to result in change, requires individual implementers to work out their own meaning.

Fullan, 1991, p. 105

In the preceding chapters of this book, we have tried to provide you with a foundation of knowledge, theory, and practice to permit you to formulate your own supervisory platform. With this goal in mind, we have provided you with an overview of the history of classroom and instructional supervision, guidance in developing an initial personal educational vision statement, a description of the more recent approaches to supervision that aim to improve classroom instruction, strategies and techniques for developing the skills needed to implement the different models and approaches, and case studies that illustrate how individuals and schools have operationalized these models.

We think that you now have the requisite knowledge, skills, and experience to draft your personal supervisory platform and begin to reach out to others. The goal of this final chapter is to facilitate the development of a personal plan to put improvement of instruction at the center of supervision in your professional environment. In the subsequent sections, we provide a framework for you to develop your personal next steps, a synopsis of an actual case study that elucidates the bottom-up, top-down development of peer supervision in a Vermont school district, and suggestions and guidelines for initiating an alternative supervisory process in your department or your grade, in your school, or

Table 6.1   Supervisory Development Plan: Next Steps in Putting Improvement of Classroom Instruction at the Center of Supervision

For me, personally	
For my inner circle	
For the rest of the school	
For the district in the future	

Source: The late Nancy Mohr, former principal and leadership consultant, gave us permission to adapt her planning sheet.

in your school district. These suggestions are designed to serve as a springboard for your own creativity, not as a recipe to follow.

NEXT STEPS

At this juncture, we encourage you to formulate your own beliefs related to supervision of classroom instruction and integrate them into your initial personal vision statements. Thus, next steps begin with "me," the clarification of your own supervisory beliefs. Once you have worked out your own meanings, you can begin to think about the next steps in your school environment. You can contemplate sharing them with your inner circle at school, be it the teachers on your grade level, in your department, in your cabinet, and so forth. After the inner circle has worked out a joint direction for itself, this small group can think about consequences and ideas for the whole school and eventually for sharing, dissemination, and development in the school district. The planning outline might look like Table 6.1.

GUIDELINES FOR CREATING A SUPERVISORY PLATFORM

Because we have focused primarily on supervision of classroom instruction in this book, we limit our guidelines for the development of a personal supervisory platform to classroom supervision. Although we recognize that it is impossible to isolate supervision of classroom instruction from the other facets of supervision of instruction, such as staff, curriculum, and group development, for the purposes of this book, we have placed supervision of classroom instruction at the center of professional development.

Your supervisory platforms probably will be as varied as your vision statements. We include some questions and sample supervisory platforms to facilitate the process of clarifying your beliefs and ideas. We suggest you use the same process that we outlined for your vision statement in Chapter 1:

- Prepare a first draft.
- Bring three copies to class.
- In groups of three, read each other's platforms one at a time.
- Provide descriptive feedback to the author after reading each platform.
- Revise your platform based on feedback and further reflection.

You can approach the following questions in at least two ways: (a) You can use some or all of your responses to these questions as a basis for your supervisory platform or (b) you can write your platform first and verify that you have included some of the ideas contained in these questions.

1. How do you define supervision of classroom instruction?

2. What should be the ultimate goal of supervision of classroom instruction?

3. What assumptions, values, and beliefs underlie your goals and definition?

4. Who should make the decisions about supervision of classroom instruction for the school?

5. How do you envision the process developing?

6. What would the structure(s) of supervision of classroom instruction look like?

7. Who should be involved in the supervisory process? What should each party's role be? How would the roles differ?

8. What skills are needed for effective supervision?

9. What activities would be included in instructional supervision (e.g., staff development)?

10. How would you address the question of supervision versus evaluation?

11. What are your beliefs with respect to the role of the district in supervision of classroom instruction?

12. How would you assess the implementation of your ideas? What would be the indicators of success?

The following supervisory platform statements represent the thinking of students after one semester of developing their supervisory beliefs and practices. Christine Drucker, a Staten Island, New York, high school teacher at the time, wrote the first platform; Linda Herman, a Brooklyn, New York, early childhood teacher at that juncture, submitted the second one; the third platform was written by Chris Ogno, then a Brooklyn, New York, elementary school teacher.

Supervisory Platform 1 (Christine Drucker)

Educating our children is not the job solely of the teacher. It is a result of a community of people working together to provide students with the skills they need to succeed in the world. This community includes parents, students, teachers, and supervisors.

Supervisors of curriculum and instruction hold a very important job—to ensure that students are receiving the best possible instruction they can from their teachers. Educators often discuss the role of the teacher as a mentor, inspirer, and facilitator for students. A supervisor holds that same role for the teacher—a mentor, inspirer, and a facilitator of learning.

The major role of a supervisor is to enhance the instruction of teachers. In order to perform this task, it is necessary for a supervisor to be a master teacher. This means the supervisor must have a working knowledge of instructional techniques and curriculum. Teachers must have confidence and respect for their supervisor's knowledge in order to rely on that supervisor for assistance and advice. One way to accomplish this is for the supervisor to encourage teachers to visit the supervisor's own classroom. This is not only an opportunity to model teaching techniques, but it demonstrates the supervisor's confidence in teaching methods and classroom management.

Having knowledge of teaching and curriculum is only helpful if a supervisor has the ability to communicate. This is the key to successful supervision. The supervisor must develop relationships with the teachers where the teachers feel comfortable having discussions about their instruction. The relationship between the supervisor and teacher must be one of trust and mutual respect. Furthermore, teachers should be encouraged to communicate with each other. Creating the "open community" can lead to successful working relationships such as mentoring, team teaching, or coaching. It allows both teachers and the supervisor to be avenues of support, encouragement, and learning to their colleagues.

Most discussions between teachers and the supervisor are informal, and a comfort level should be developed between the teacher and supervisor through informal observations. The supervisor's presence should be commonplace—a consistent factor in the classrooms and hallways. This is very important in creating a comfortable atmosphere for the teacher and students during formal and informal observations.

Classroom observations are a key part of effective supervising. For observations to be effective, they must include communication. The communication process for classroom observations has three basic parts: the planning conference, the observation, and the feedback conference. During the planning conference, the supervisor and teacher confer about the purpose of the observation and they decide on a focus for the lesson. It should be the goal of the supervisor that the teacher be comfortable and knowledgeable enough about his or her teaching to decide what the observation should focus on.

It is important that observations be focused. When the supervisor and teacher decide to discuss, observe, and evaluate one piece of a lesson, that one piece can go into more depth. Furthermore, the teacher can feel more at ease when the focus is on a topic or issue that the teacher has selected. The teacher can also feel secure in knowing that there is a valuable purpose to this observation.

In addition to deciding on a focus, the tool used for observation should be decided upon. The supervisor must have knowledge of a variety of observation tools that will assist both parties in focusing the observation and later evaluating it.

In order for the supervisor to be effective during the actual observation of a lesson, objectivity is essential. The tool selected by the teacher and the supervisor should act as a guide in focusing the supervisor and assist in maintaining the supervisor's objectivity. The supervisor's role in this step is to observe the behaviors, techniques, or issues discussed in the planning conference.

The supervisor should attempt to make the teacher as self-directed as possible during the feedback conference. At this point, the teacher, with the guidance of the supervisor, evaluates the lesson using the observation tool. If the teacher needs assistance in evaluating or understanding the observation tool, the supervisor assists while still trying to push the teacher toward independent reflection. This is the key to having successful observations. Once a teacher can look independently at observation tools and reflect on them, that teacher can continue the process without the supervisor, either alone or with a colleague.

The teacher should feel comfortable at feedback conferences and be able to discuss any difficulties he or she may be having. The feelings of trust, support, and respect discussed earlier are imperative if any suggestions the supervisor makes to improve any difficulties are discussed. The focus of the feedback conference should be on the issues or topics that the teacher and supervisor agreed on earlier. This prevents the teacher from feeling overwhelmed and helps maintain the concept that the observation is to improve the instructional process, not pick on things that went wrong.

Part of enhancing the instruction of teachers is professional development. Not only should teachers be encouraged to attend workshops offered by outside organizations and through the school, but also the supervisor must create a variety of professional development activities. As the supervisor's classroom is open for teachers to visit, the teachers should be encouraged to do the same with each other. Teachers need to learn how to work with one another to share ideas, support, and advice. All teachers can learn from each other. Newer teachers can benefit from the seasoned teachers' experience in the classroom, and the seasoned teachers can learn from the new theories and practices that new teachers learned in college. Mentoring and coaching relationships can be created, and teams of teachers can work together on developing and expanding their instruction. Multiple possibilities of professional development should be available to the teachers. It demonstrates an appreciation of the diverse learning and communication styles of teachers—the same understanding of diversity teachers are expected to have of their students.

Communication and community are the key elements of supervising instruction and curriculum. When a supervisor creates the sense of togetherness, the feeling that teachers and the supervisor are colleagues working to meet one mission—the successful education of students—there will be success.

Supervisory Platform 2 (Linda Herman)

I believe that the most important element of supervision is the tone that the supervisor sets in the school. When you walk into the building, you should feel the cooperation, support, care, common short-term goals, common long-term vision, lack of competition, safety, hard work, trust, and high expectations. It is in this kind of atmosphere, I believe, that teachers, supervisors, students, parents, and community leaders can do their best work to educate children.

I believe that supervision of classroom instruction is collaborating with teachers, helping them set their personal goals and classroom goals; helping teachers meet these goals; supporting and guiding teachers to be better teachers; helping teachers to see how their children are learning, and supporting teachers to help their children do even better. I also see supervision of classroom instruction as helping teachers enjoy teaching more, and realizing that they are not in this alone, that teaching is a "we" project. We can do together what we cannot do alone.

The ultimate goal of supervision of classroom instruction is that children learn and grow. We hope to help children not only do well on tests, but become life-long learners who love books and discovery and see learning and school as an exciting adventure.

In order for my supervision to be effective, all or most teachers in the school need to be on board. They also, like myself, will want to improve as teachers and as co-workers. They will want to grow. They will want to see their students improve. They will want to see the parents and community become more a part of children's education. They will view education as a process. Hopefully some will realize that we are on a wonderful path—working with children, helping them learn and grow, and that we are all on this path together.

When I begin supervising in a school, I will make an appointment with each teacher—to get to know them. I will ask them about their ideas for the school. What they think has worked. What they think can work. What hasn't worked. I will ask them how I can help them. I will ask them what their goals for themselves and their students are. I will ask them how I can help them realize their goals. I would set up a schedule with each teacher, where I could be in their classrooms once a week to assist them in their teaching. I feel that supervisors need to know kids and groups. Hopefully, it will begin to open up a dialogue and teachers will really feel comfortable coming to me for help. Teachers can hopefully see that I am really there for them, for I truly am, for if

I really support the teachers, they can really do their jobs, which is my ultimate goal: to help the children.

For supervision of classroom instruction, I will meet with the teachers individually, talk about what they want to achieve, what they want to work on, what they want to know about their teaching. I will give them a copy of the supervision book, so they can decide what tool they want me to use when I observe them. We will set up a time for me to come visit. I will use the tool they have chosen. I will then give the teacher a copy of my observation and make an appointment for discussion. We will meet and discuss what I have observed, how they felt, what they felt they would like to do differently, the same, what worked and what didn't. I will try to keep this experience positive, so that the teacher can feel safe and truly grow. I would tell the teacher that I would like to visit again in a month or so and maybe he or she could try another tool and look at a different area. Hopefully, I would be able to visit each teacher four times a year.

What I would really love to encourage in my school is peer observation, using the different supervision tools. I would like each teacher to have a partner to work with and help each other improve. They could observe each other's class often, learning and growing from each other.

I think that effective supervisors need to be good listeners. They need to be good observers. They need to be experienced teachers. They need to be compassionate. They need to be able to create a positive, open energy in the school. They need to be supportive. They need to be able to see teachers' successes and celebrate them, even the small ones. They need to be able to pat teachers on the back. They need to be able to pick teachers up when they are having a hard time, encourage them to see the light, and move forward. They need to have a lot of energy.

I also think that supervisors also need to really know the curriculum in the school. They need to know what is being taught. They need to think about different ways to teach so that they can be a resource. Supervisors need to be able to go into a class and teach. A supervisor should be able to model lessons. If teachers are going for workshops for a new curriculum, the supervisor should go also. It should be clear that this is a learning community for all.

There should be much professional development to help teachers grow. Teachers should be encouraged to go to workshops at colleges, at the district office. A supervisor can invite a guest speaker in on a topic that the faculty is working on. Teachers in the building can develop their own workshops for each other, teaching what they feel passionate about to their peers. A schoolwide educational journal can be started—maybe twice a year—where teachers can write about their thoughts about teaching, ideas they have tried, or books or articles they have read. There should be a teachers' library where there are curriculum books, professional magazines, and articles. Teachers should be given the time to watch each other teach. Teachers should be encouraged to team teach. Supervisors should model a lesson. Teachers should be given time to visit other teachers in other schools. Teachers can watch an educational movie together and then have a discussion afterward. An instructional supervisor should make sure that there is a space for dialogue, where teachers can share ideas and grow.

Supervision for growth and evaluation should be separate. Supervision for growth should feel safe, so that the teacher can try new ideas and experiment and learn and grow.

I hope that I can work with other principals in the district to brainstorm ideas about how to supervise teachers better, to help children learn better, to include parents in the process. I hope that I can be instrumental in helping schools be less competitive and more cooperative, for we are truly all in this together.

I would feel successful if children liked coming to school. I want children to do well on tests. I want an active PTA where parents are involved in their children's education. I want teachers to feel happy working the best they can, but not stressed; to feel supported, to feel comfortable coming to me, to collaborate, to share ideas. I want a school that is always humming, always excited, always trying something new, alive. I think I would feel that I had really done a good job if my second year, teachers walked in the first day and said how happy they were to be back in school!

Supervisory Platform 3 (Chris Ogno)

There is no more prodigious challenge than that of educating children. The role of the administrator must not be underestimated in this process. Educators are entrusted with the greatest gift the world can offer—the future. For educators are sculptors; they create and mold the minds of the future world. This is an awesome responsibility, especially in a world where drugs, technology, and the degeneration of the nuclear family have forced schools to take on new responsibilities. Teachers, as "the frontline soldiers," need support in undertaking such an enormous task. That support should come in the form of collaboration. The school, at all levels, must work together toward the common goal of educating children. Administrators must guarantee that these lines of communication both exist and stay open.

If the teachers are the "frontline soldiers" in the battle to educate our youth, then classroom instruction must be seen as the true "front line" of education. This is where the action and learning takes place. It is here that the education process comes to its fruition, and it is the place where the administrator needs to be. The administrator can no longer be the field general on the hill (in an office) telling his or her troops what to do. The administrator needs to be in the "trenches" (classrooms) offering support, promoting communication between teachers, and encouraging professional development.

Communication must be the fundamental goal of any good administrator, for without communication no growth can occur. As a leader, he or she must establish an environment that is free of fear and conducive to the sharing of ideas. The administrator's task is to ensure that teachers are afforded the opportunity to share ideas and work cooperatively toward the improvement of classroom instruction. Administrators cannot be critical and look for mistakes, or else they risk irreparable damage to this process by instilling fear and hindering dialogue. A good administrator cannot put him- or herself above the teacher. They must treat teachers with mutual professional respect. The administrator needs to foster an open, trusting relationship with his or her teachers. It is the administrator's function to serve the teacher as a resource in helping to improve instruction. He or she must be available to help and support the teachers of the school.

The administrator must "get dirty" by going into classrooms and working cooperatively with teachers on improving instruction. By being in the classroom, the administrator gets hands-on experience and can better understand the needs of the teacher. The leader can then offer resources that will be effective in helping the teacher improve instruction. This in turn will keep the administrator's fingers on the pulse of the educational process.

Another way that having the administrator in the classroom can improve instruction is through observations. He or she can work collaboratively with teachers and set up observations to improve their teaching techniques. The key point in the observation process is to create an environment where positive feedback is promoted and fear and criticism are eliminated. During this process, administrators need to engage teachers in dialogue about their classroom instruction. It is through this personal reflection, which should be encouraged by the administrators, that teachers can do self-evaluation and real professional growth can occur. Classroom instruction then becomes a learning experience for the student, teacher, and administrator.

Finally, I believe that a good administrator should foster staff development. Teachers should be going into each other's classrooms and observing teaching. Ideas need to be shared and the classrooms are once again the "front line" of the educational process. The administrator should promote intervisitation by teachers for the enhancement of classroom instruction. I believe that by doing this, teachers will begin to see observations as a tool for improvement rather than a terrifying event that degrades and demeans the work that they do. Teachers and administrators can finally unite in a common effort to promote a system that strives to always improve classroom instruction in an effort to guarantee each child the finest possible education.

Peer Assistance at Windham Southeast Supervisory Union[1]

Before suggesting some general guidelines for the development of next steps for your inner circle, school, and district, we provide an example of how peer supervision developed in a Vermont school district. The Windham Southeast Supervisory Union (WSESU) spent several years attempting to improve its supervision and evaluation practices through research and discussion. This climate promoted the creation of two projects, one in the English department of the high school and a second one at the district level.

In June 1986, the Brattleboro Union High School English department staff members decided that evaluation and supervision would be the department's theme for the following school year. The faculty felt that the department head, who was responsible for evaluation, budget, program development, curriculum, and scheduling and who taught two classes, could not provide substantive, clinical supervision for 16 department teachers. One of the teachers suggested that, given the expertise and professionalism of the department members, peer supervision could permit them to help each other with professional issues and provide mutual aid.

After considerable discussion, the English faculty decided that the department head should be an active support in the process without direct involvement. They felt that the inclusion of an evaluator would compromise a purely helpful, growth-oriented process. His help was, however, crucial in procuring the time, money, substitutes, and support services to make the experiment work.

Despite additional apprehension about the actual peer observation process, all members of the English faculty decided to serve at least once as an observer and once as an observee. After the first round, the full department discussed what had transpired and expressed nearly universal enthusiasm for the peer process. The members made two decisions based on their initial experiences:

- They decided to form small groups. Members of a group would have a clearer picture of whom they were working with and could develop commitment and closeness. They could also cover classes for each other more easily.
- They also set up a clear clinical structure that included a preconference and postconference with specific goals.

Other challenges that were eventually resolved were

- The establishment of voluntary participation
- The acquisition of district funds to permit training in observation and conference techniques and to relieve nonprofessional time
- The establishment of confidentiality and documentation for district approval through questionnaires, videotapes, and personal anecdotal records

The following year, a group of administrators, frustrated with the amount of time that evaluation consumes without improving instruction, initiated a district-level committee of volunteer teachers and administrators. The goal of their action plan was to establish a supervisory process for all staff members in the district that would both encourage professional growth and enhance learning. The supervisory process would be nonevaluatory and a separate administrative evaluation would determine job status. A district committee member discussed the pilot project with administrators, teachers, and paraprofessionals at each site and collected the names of volunteer pairs. Training was held at the district office; the number of participants was so large that each site had to provide financial support for the afterschool sessions. At the end of the pilot project, all the volunteers indicated that they wanted to continue their involvement. The district committee decided to design a plan for expansion in the next school year.

The lack of funds to support a district-level peer assistance coordinator was instrumental in the decision to move coordination of the project from the district level to each school and department. Each site's peer assistance leader would participate in a monthly meeting of a district Peer Assistance Steering Committee, which would facilitate communication between schools and departments and keep the process active. All of the district and school administrators made a commitment to finding the time and money for three clinical supervision cycles for each participant and for training of new participants.

Despite setbacks due to unforeseen external circumstances, peer assistance survived and the steering committee introduced a cyclical evaluation model for the next year. Summative evaluation would occur every three years, with the two years between evaluations devoted to no evaluative supervision.

This model developed under the most propitious conditions: the stewardship of two supportive superintendents and the buy-in of the individual school leaders.

"FOR ME, PERSONALLY": MY SUPERVISORY PLATFORM

We believe that the following ideas and suggestions for your inner circle, your school, and/or your district can be implemented in most school districts under many types of leadership and in diverse settings.

For My Inner Circle

Once you have completed your personal supervisory platform, you can reach out to colleagues in many ways. What we consider most important of all is to begin from the bottom up, that is, to find one or more colleagues who are amenable to beginning a conversation about transforming classroom supervision from a required, primarily evaluatory process to one of shared growth in teaching and learning. It is also essential that project participation be voluntary.

The following suggestions are some of the innumerable strategies that can open up the conversation. Some of these ideas are teacher initiated; several can emanate from either teachers or supervisors.

- Share case studies from this book with one or more colleagues and then brainstorm possibilities for your inner circle.

- Invite a colleague to observe a challenge or success in one of your classes and provide you with feedback.
- Discuss with a colleague a curriculum area or approach you would like to try, and plan to team-teach a lesson or observe each other teaching the innovation and give mutual feedback.
- Offer to present an introductory workshop on alternative ways to look at supervision of classroom instruction.
- Discuss the possibility of building a peer coaching component into an annual personal, department, or grade-level goal.
- Look into grant possibilities to support your project.

For My School

Although we advise that you begin the conversation about classroom supervision with a small group, it is sometimes possible to make inroads at the school level as you introduce the idea to your immediate colleagues. Some of the "inner circle" suggestions also are applicable to the school level. Therefore, a few of the following ideas are variations on the inner circle:

- Request that this book and other articles and books about innovative supervisory practices be purchased for your school's professional library.
- Spearhead a voluntary professional reading and sharing group in which alternative supervision is a topic.
- Suggest that innovative classroom supervision be a school goal for the year.
- Ask that a subcommittee on your school's site-based planning team be formed to discuss innovative classroom supervision.
- Offer to develop a series of workshops on observation techniques, feedback approaches, and alternative supervision for a group of volunteer teachers.
- Offer to set up a visit for interested colleagues to schools where successful alternative supervisory practices are being implemented.

For the District in the Future

Michael Fullan (1993) concluded that "effective schools are ones that are plugged into their environments. . . . a systematic, symbiotic relationship is required between schools and local agencies. . . . leadership in successful systems *conceptualizes* the problem as continually negotiating school and district codevelopment" (p. 16). We endorse the idea that for reform to be successful, the district and school must support each other. If alternative supervisory methods are to succeed, the district will need to support them philosophically and financially.

Therefore, even as you begin to explore alternative supervisory methods with your inner group, it is important, wherever possible, to explore connecting with the district office. The district can facilitate the process at the site level from the outset. We recommend that you consider the following suggestions, but *only* after taking into consideration (1) that the individual, inner group, or school committee needs to consult with building supervisors before making contact with district-level employees and (2) that the careful application of problem-solving and decision-making skills is essential to determine if, when, and how to proceed.

- Offer to give an introductory workshop or a series of workshops on innovative supervisory practices.
- Request staff development funds so that teachers can be released for intervisitation or staff development.
- Apply for staff development funds or a grant to facilitate developing a pilot program.
- After completing a pilot program, request permission to ask other district faculty to visit implementation of your project.
- Request permission to offer a presentation to other interested schools.
- Ask to set up a district schedule of intervisitation to other schools and districts involved in innovative supervisory practices.
- Procure funding to attend conferences on innovative practices.
- Apply to be a presenter at a conference as a representative of your school and district.
- Explore the feasibility of setting up a district-based committee on innovative supervisory practices.
- Discuss the possibility of including innovative supervisory practices as a district goal.
- Request district support in apprising you of grant possibilities and in writing proposals.

CONCLUSION—OR JUST A BEGINNING?

A major premise of this volume has been that supervisors can become a potent vehicle for the improvement of classroom instruction. We have attempted to highlight the tools, techniques, and strategies that we think are crucial in promoting instructional excellence. Yet, the challenge remains in your hands. We affirm what Harold Spears (1953) articulated more than a half century ago: "Supervision is and always will be the key to the high instructional standards of America's public schools" (p. 462). To ensure that supervision will continue as such, we have presented our modest proposal for effective supervision. We hope that you use our suggestions as a springboard for the improvement of teaching and learning in your professional environment. Please contact us (Susan Sullivan at Sullivan@mail.csi.cuny.edu or Jeffrey Glanz at jglanz@ wagner.edu) to share your experiences, comments, and suggestions.

NOTE

1. This synopsis is based on a case study in *Supervision in Transition* (James, Heller, & Ellis, 1992).

Resource A

Microlab Guidelines[1]

Microlab is a term for a planned and timed small-group exercise that addresses a specific sequence of questions and promotes active listening skills in the process. Its structure is about equalizing communication and withholding judgment. It affirms people's ideas and helps build community.

Aim

The aim is to help participants learn more about themselves and others and deepen the quality of collegial sharing using a timed small-group exercise.

Setup

All groups should consist of three to five people and be about the same size. It helps if people can pull chairs into a tight private group. The following techniques can be used to divide participants:

- Use cards with numbers on them such as three 1s, 2s, and so on. If the numbers come out uneven, avoid groups of five. Make two groups of four instead.
- Count off by three, four, or five.
- Group by level or category.

Time

It takes 15 to 40 minutes to complete a microlab; less time for groups of three addressing two to three questions; more time for groups of four to five addressing four questions. Allow time for the whole group to debrief at the end.

Directions for Leader

I'll be directing what we're going to be sharing. It's not an open discussion. It's about listening and sharing nonjudgmentally. I will pose one question at a time. Each person gets approximately one minute to answer it in turn. No one else is to talk or ask questions when it's someone else's turn. The goal is active listening. I will use a timer and tell the group when they should be halfway around. I also will tell you when the time is up for that question and what the next question is. If a person gets short-changed on time for some reason, he or she can go first in the next round. It's about being open and honest and also about respecting confidentiality. What someone says in your group is not to be repeated by anybody else. Can you agree to that?

Guidelines

- Speak from your own experience. Say *I* when speaking about yourself.
- Stay on the suggested topic.
- Listen and discover rather than give advice.
- Avoid being judgmental.
- Respect shared confidences.
- It's OK to pass.

Debrief at the End

The whole group should discuss: What do we now know about each other's ideas or experiences? Commonalities? Differences? What was helpful or positive about the process? What was difficult? Is it something to revisit in our work? How could you use the process in your work?

NOTE

1. We thank Emily White of Bank Street College of Education and Linda Lantieri of Educators for Social Responsibility for allowing us to adapt their guidelines.

Resource B

Fishbowl Guidelines

The fishbowl can be used either to discuss ideas generated in small groups in a large-group setting or to provide feedback to a small group that is modeling a role play, simulation, or another group process.

Aims

The aim of the fishbowl as follow-up to small-group discussions is to provide a forum for reporting out, sharing, and discussing the ideas generated in small groups. The fishbowl also allows a new process to be modeled with the goal of the volunteers learning the process, getting feedback, and helping the observers learn from the model's experience.

Setup

Discussion fishbowl. Place one chair per small group in a circle in the middle of the room. Provide an additional chair. Each small group chooses a representative for the circle to report on the group's discussion. The rest of the class observes without participating in the debriefing. If a class observer feels strongly about making a particular point, that person can sit temporarily in the additional chair in the circle to express that point. The observer then returns to his or her seat to free the empty chair.

Model fishbowl. Students volunteer to model a particular role play, simulation, or process. The players and an observer sit in the middle of the room surrounded by the rest of the class. Videotaping of the model is highly recommended. The volunteers model the process following the Guidelines for Reflective Practice. Once the observer in the small group provides feedback, class members can make additional observations. If a number of students want to comment, it is preferable to go around the outside circle in order, allowing the students to pass if they wish.

Time

The discussion fishbowl should be given a precise time limit; 10 or 15 minutes should be sufficient. The model fishbowl also should not take more than 10 or 15 minutes and should be abbreviated when necessary. Additional observations from the outer circle in the model fishbowl exercise should be limited by going in order and allowing only one comment per person.

Resource C

Technology
in the Classroom

*Tips That Span the Traditional
to the Virtual Classroom*

Feedback from instructors who have used the text in virtual or distance education environments confirms that careful planning can result in an almost oxymoronic success story: a hands-on virtual classroom. Lynn Doyle's distance classroom at Old Dominion University provided the impetus for some of these suggestions for the virtual and distance education models. Most of these ideas can be adapted to enrich the traditional college classroom. School and teacher leaders can also use them for training in any of the alternatives to traditional observations. The suggestions are organized according to their versatility in different types of college classrooms or schools.

1. E-mail, discussion boards, chat rooms. The materials in the book and the assignments are an effective source for myriad online activities. Discussion boards and chat rooms are a perfect means for students to obtain rapid assistance and feedback on site assignments. From the first school assignment on listening skills to the final reflective supervision cycle, students can query (through e-mail, discussion boards, and chat rooms) their colleagues and their instructors on how to approach a situation, how to handle the next steps, and how to discuss challenges and successes that took place. Microlabs can be organized online asynchronously or in chat rooms.

2. Videotapes or DVDs and to a lesser extent audiocassettes can substitute for classroom feedback from instructors in the distance or virtual classroom. Viewing of the role plays on the videotape that accompanies the

book can facilitate role playing and the practice of observation tools in the college classroom. Virtual classroom students can purchase the videotape and re-create the role plays with willing colleagues.

3. A highly developed technological environment can allow an actual classroom to be viewed in a *smart* college classroom or streamed online for a virtual course. The joint observation provides a common base for analysis and discussion.

4. If students are required to do paper or electronic portfolios, taping or videotaping site practice conferences and assignments creates ideal portfolio artifacts. The DVD or videotape of the conference can be included in the paper portfolio or viewed live in the electronic portfolio.

5. Online professional development for peer coaching, mentoring, and other alternatives to traditional observations can be organized for a school district at individual school sites to avoid teacher travel during or after school.

Resource D

Observation
Practice Sheets

Table 3.2   Teacher Verbal Behaviors

Time began: 9:15

	Information Giving	Questioning	Teacher Answering Own Question	Praising	Direction Giving	Reprimanding	Correcting
1	X	X		X	X		
2	X	X		X			
3		X		X		X	X
4		X					
5	X	X		X	X	X	
6		X		X	X		
7	X			X	X	X	X
8				X	X		X
9				X			
10						X	
11						X	X
12		X			X	X	
13		X		X	X	X	
14		X		X			
15		X			X		X
16				X	X	X	

Time ended: 9:30

Class: K

Date: 5-15-12

Source: C. D. Glickman, S. P Gordon, and J. Ross-Gordon, *SuperVision and Instructional Leadership: A Developmental Approach* (6th ed.), Copyright © 2004 by Allyn & Bacon. Reprinted/adapted by permission.

Table 3.3   Teacher Questions

Time began:

Question Category	Tally 5 min.	Tally 10 min.	Tally 15 min.	Total	Percent	Comments
Evaluation						
Synthesis						
Analysis						
Application						
Comprehension						
Knowledge						

Total number of questions asked:

Time ended:

Class:

Date:

Source: C. D. Glickman, S. P. Gordon, and J. Ross-Gordon, *SuperVision and Instructional Leadership: A Developmental Approach* (6th ed.), Copyright © 2004 by Allyn & Bacon. Reprinted/adapted by permission.

Table 3.4   Student On-Task and Off-Task Behavior

Class:
Date:
Time when sweep began:

Student	9:00	9:05	9:10	9:15	9:20	9:25	9:30	9:35

Key: Total:
A   =   at task
TK =   talking (social conversation)
P   =   playing
O   =   out of seat
OT =   off task

Source: C. D. Glickman, S. P. Gordon, and J. Ross-Gordon, *SuperVision and Instructional Leadership: A Developmental Approach* (6th ed.), Copyright © 2004 by Allyn & Bacon. Reprinted/adapted by permission.

Table 3.5   Gardner's Model for Performance Indicators

Elements	Response			Observations
	Yes	No	N/A	
Logical/mathematical	☐	☐	☐	
Bodily/kinesthetic	☐	☐	☐	
Visual	☐	☐	☐	
Musical	☐	☐	☐	
Interpersonal	☐	☐	☐	
Intrapersonal	☐	☐	☐	
Linguistic	☐	☐	☐	
Naturalistic	☐	☐	☐	

Class:

Date:

Time:

Source: C. D. Glickman, S. P. Gordon, and J. Ross-Gordon, *SuperVision and Instructional Leadership: A Developmental Approach* (6th ed.), Copyright © 2004 by Allyn & Bacon. Reprinted/adapted by permission.

Table 3.6   Hunter's Steps in Lesson Planning

Elements	Response Yes	No	N/A	Comments
Anticipatory set	☐	☐	☐	
Objective and purpose	☐	☐	☐	
Input	☐	☐	☐	
Modeling	☐	☐	☐	
Checking for understanding	☐	☐	☐	
Guided practice	☐	☐	☐	
Independent practice	☐	☐	☐	

Class:

Date:

Time:

Source: C. D. Glickman, S. P. Gordon, and J. Ross-Gordon, *SuperVision and Instructional Leadership: A Developmental Approach* (6th ed.), Copyright © 2004 by Allyn & Bacon. Reprinted/adapted by permission.

Table 3.7   Johnson and Johnson's Cooperative Learning

Elements	Response Yes	No	N/A	Comments
Explanation of academic and social objectives	☐	☐	☐	
Teaching of social skills	☐	☐	☐	
Face-to-face interaction	☐	☐	☐	
Position interdependence	☐	☐	☐	
Individual accountability	☐	☐	☐	
Group processing	☐	☐	☐	

Class:

Date:

Time:

Source: C. D. Glickman, S. P. Gordon, and J. Ross-Gordon, *SuperVision and Instructional Leadership: A Developmental Approach* (6th ed.), Copyright © 2004 by Allyn & Bacon. Reprinted/adapted by permission.

Table 3.8   Teacher-Pupil Interaction

Time	Student: _____	Teacher: _____

Class:

Date:

Time:

Figure 3.2   Diagram of Verbal Interaction

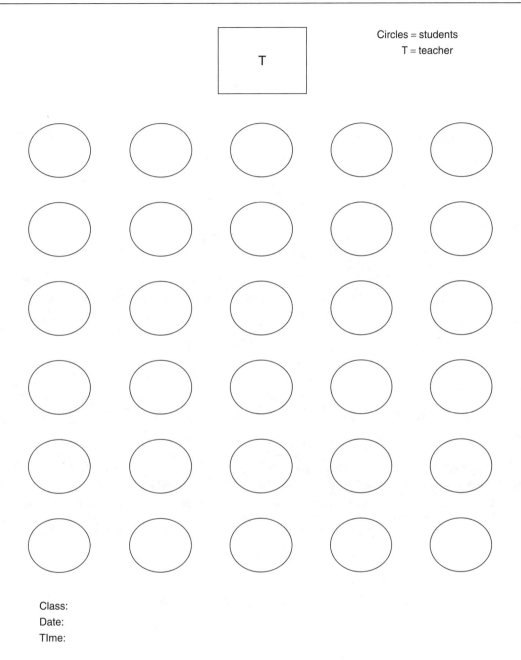

Figure 3.3   Program of Space Utilization

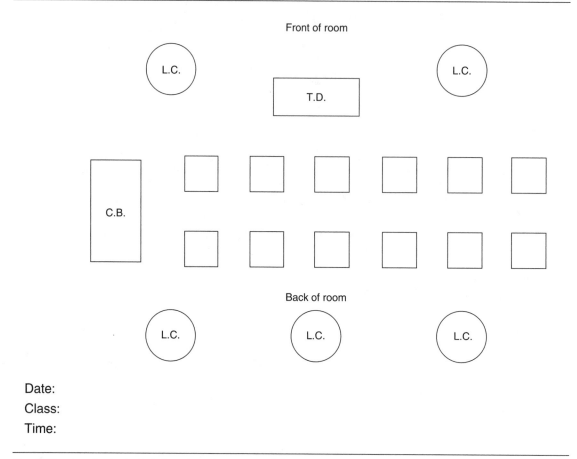

Date:

Class:

Time:

Key: T.D. = teacher's desk; L.C. = learning center; C.B. = chalkboard; W.A. = work area. Note that, of course, the diagram should be drawn for the room in which the observation takes place.

Source: C. D. Glickman, S. P. Gordon, and J. Ross-Gordon, *SuperVision and Instructional Leadership: A Developmental Approach* (6th ed.). Copyright © 2004 by Allyn & Bacon. Reprinted/adapted by permission.

Figure 3.4   Feedback

Key: Pr = prompted; Pb = probed; E = encouraged; O = positively reinforced; D = discouraged pupil.

Table 3.9   An Observation Chart

Nonverbal Technique	Frequency	Anecdotal Observations / Student Responses

Proxemics
  Standing near
  student(s)
  Moving toward
  student(s)
  Touching
  student(s)
  Moving about
  room		

Kinesics
a. Affirmation
  Eye contact
  Touching
  Smiling
  Nodding
  Open arm
  movements
b. Disapproval
  Frowning
  Stern look
  Finger to lips
  Pointing
  Arms crossed
  Hands on hips		

Prosody
  Varies voice tone
  Varies pitch
  Varies rhythm		

Immediacy
  Responds with
  warmth		

Class:

Date:

Time:

Source: C. D. Glickman, S. P. Gordon, and J. Ross-Gordon, *Supervision of Instruction: A Developmental Approach.* Copyright © 1998 by Allyn & Bacon. Reprinted/adapted by permission.

Table 3.10   Cultural Diversity

Teacher Indicator	Response			Comments
	Yes	No	N/A	
Displays understanding of diverse cultures	☐	☐	☐	
Displays personal regard for students of diverse cultures	☐	☐	☐	
Uses instructional materials free of cultural bias	☐	☐	☐	
Uses examples and materials that represent different cultures	☐	☐	☐	
Promotes examination of concepts and issues from different cultural perspectives	☐	☐	☐	
Intervenes to address acts of student intolerance	☐	☐	☐	
Uses "teachable moments" to address cultural issues	☐	☐	☐	
Reinforces student acts of respect for diverse cultures	☐	☐	☐	

Date:

Class:

Time:

Source: C. D. Glickman, S. P. Gordon, and J. Ross-Gordon, *SuperVision and Instructional Leadership: A Developmental Approach* (6th ed.), Copyright © 2004 by Allyn & Bacon. Reprinted/adapted by permission.

Table 3.11   Strategies for Diverse Learners

Teacher Indicator	Response Yes	No	N/A	Examples
Proximity to students	☐	☐	☐	
Different ways of encouraging students	☐	☐	☐	
Positive reinforcement techniques	☐	☐	☐	
Modifications for individual children or types of learners	☐	☐	☐	
Use of children's strengths	☐	☐	☐	
Multiple ways in which lesson is unfolding	☐	☐	☐	
Integration of grouping according to needs and skills	☐	☐	☐	
Scaffolding of instruction	☐	☐	☐	

Class:

Date:

Time:

Table 3.12   English Language Learners

Accommodation Modification	Was this element present?			What is the evidence?
	Yes	No	N/A	
Teacher talk is modified: slower speech, careful choice of words, idioms, expressions	☐	☐	☐	
Teacher allows wait time and monitors teacher input vs. student output	☐	☐	☐	
Definitions and language are embedded in content/context	☐	☐	☐	
Real-world artifacts present that support comprehension	☐	☐	☐	
Elicits and draws on students' backgrounds to build prior knowledge	☐	☐	☐	
Teacher uses nonverbal cues to support comprehension	☐	☐	☐	

Class:

Date:

Time:

Table 3.13   Guided Reading–Quantitative

Guided Reading Teacher Indicator	Yes	No	N/A	Comments/Examples
MANAGEMENT				
Was the transition from the mini-lesson to group work implemented in an orderly fashion?	☐	☐	☐	
Were the other children on task while the teacher was in small-group instruction?	☐	☐	☐	
Was the time allotted for the guided reading group appropriate?	☐	☐	☐	
INSTRUCTION				
Was the text for guided reading introduced in a manner that provided support needed for students to read independenlty and successfully?	☐	☐	☐	
Were the children interested in and did they grasp the concepts being taught?	☐	☐	☐	
Was the text appropriate for the group with respect to the level, content, and interest?	☐	☐	☐	
Were there support, challenges, and opportunities for problem solving from the teacher?	☐	☐	☐	
Did the students read independently?	☐	☐	☐	
Did assessment take place? What types?	☐	☐	☐	
Did the teacher allow students to be responsible for what they already know?	☐	☐	☐	
Did questions include the full range of Bloom's Taxonomy?	☐	☐	☐	
Did the teacher help students strengthen their strategies?	☐	☐	☐	

Class:
Date:
Time:

Source: This instrument was adapted from one that Suzanne Dimitri, a Brooklyn, N.Y., literacy coach, created. It is used with her permission.

Table 3.14   Teacher Tasks in Guided Reading

Selects appropriate text for small group instruction	*Helps children to think, talk, and question through the story*
Introduces story to the group as well as vocabulary concepts and text features	*Allows small groups to read independently with minimum teacher support*
Provides or reinforces reading strategies and provides students with the opportunity to use the strategy	
Records reflections on the students' reading behaviors during and after reading	*Engages students in a brief discussion after reading the story.*

Class:

Date:

Time:

Table 3.15 Read Aloud/Story Time

Teacher Behaviors	Yes	No	N/A	Comments/Examples
Introduces book by showing cover and reading title. Encourages students to share thoughts about book based on these features.	☐	☐	☐	
Reads name(s) of author and illustrator. Asks students to point to title, author, illustrator, and encourages discussion about these features.	☐	☐	☐	
Introduces at least three words that will be in story by showing cards with words and pictures representing them.	☐	☐	☐	
Attempts to capture/maintain students' interest. Uses facial expression and changes in tone, pitch, and so on to represent different characters and emphasize words or facts.	☐	☐	☐	
Involves children throughout the story by encouraging comments and questions.	☐	☐	☐	
Asks open-ended questions, such as What if? What would you do if?, and so on and provides wait time. When voluntary responses are limited, initiates discussion of facts, plot and/or characters.	☐	☐	☐	
Involves children in extension activities by creating charts or other visuals, for example, T charts, story maps, word/character webs.	☐	☐	☐	
Invites children to retell story in their own words (through pretending to read the book to the class, using puppets, etc.)	☐	☐	☐	

Class: Title of book:

Date: Author:

Time: Type of book:

                                  New words:

Other comments:

Table 3.16   Geometry

Students Can	Response			Observations
	Yes	No	N/A	
Analyze characteristics and properties of two-and three-dimensional geometric shapes and develop mathematical arguments about geometrical relationships	☐	☐	☐	
Specify locations and describe spatial relationships using coordinate geometry and other representational systems	☐	☐	☐	
Apply transformations and use symmetry to analyze mathematical situations	☐	☐	☐	
Use visualization, spatial reasoning, and geometric modeling to solve problems	☐	☐	☐	

Class:

Date:

Time:

Table 3.17   NCTM Process Standards 6–10

Activity Category	Tally	Total	Percentage
Problem solving			
Reasoning and proof			
Communication			
Connections			
Representation			

Class:

Date:

Time:

Table 3.18   Teacher Indicators of Accountable Talk—Quantitative

Teacher Indicators	Response			Observations
	Yes	*No*	*N/A*	
Engages students in talk by:				
• Providing opportunities for students to speak about content knowledge, concepts, and issues.	☐	☐	☐	
• Using wait time/allowing silence to occur	☐	☐	☐	
• Listening carefully	☐	☐	☐	
• Providing opportunities for reflection on classroom talk	☐	☐	☐	
Assists students to listen carefully to each other by:				
• Creating seating arrangements that promote discussion	☐	☐	☐	
• Providing clear expectations for how talk should occur	☐	☐	☐	
• Requiring courtesy and respect	☐	☐	☐	
• Reviewing major ideas and understandings from talk	☐	☐	☐	
Assists students to elaborate and build on others' ideas by:				
• Modeling reading processes of predicting, looking for key words, engaging prior knowledge, and so on.	☐	☐	☐	
• Facilitating rather than dominating the talk	☐	☐	☐	
• Listening carefully	☐	☐	☐	
• Asking questions about discussion ideas and issues	☐	☐	☐	
Assists in clarifying or expanding a proposition by:				
• Modeling methods of restating arguments and ideas and asking if they are expressed correctly	☐	☐	☐	
• Modeling and providing practice at responding appropriately to criticism	☐	☐	☐	
• Modeling expressing own puzzlement or confusion	☐	☐	☐	

Class:

Date:

Time:

Table 3.19   Student Indicators of Accountable Talk

Student Indicators	Response			Observations
	Yes	No	N/A	
Students are engaged in talk when they:				
• Speak appropriately in a variety of classroom situations	☐	☐	☐	
• Allow others to speak without interruption	☐	☐	☐	
• Speak directly to other students	☐	☐	☐	
Students are listening attentively to one another when they:				
• Make eye contact with speaker	☐	☐	☐	
• Refer to a previous speaker	☐	☐	☐	
• Connect comments to previous ideas	☐	☐	☐	
Students elaborate and build on others' ideas when they:				
• Make comments related to the focus of the discussion	☐	☐	☐	
• Introduce new, related issues	☐	☐	☐	
• Listen carefully	☐	☐	☐	
• Talk about issues rather than participants	☐	☐	☐	
Students work toward clarifying or expanding a proposition when they:				
• Revoice, summarize, or paraphrase another student's arguments	☐	☐	☐	
• Ask another student to repeat, restate, or elaborate on a comment.	☐	☐	☐	
• Object to another student's interpretation of their previous comment.	☐	☐	☐	
• Express puzzlement or confusion	☐	☐	☐	
• Define terms under discussion	☐	☐	☐	

Class:

Date:

Time:

References

Acheson, K. A., & Gall, M. D. (1997). *Techniques in the clinical supervision teachers.* New York: Longman.

AchieveGlobal, Inc. (1995). *Frontline leadership series.* San Jose, CA: Zenger-Miller.

Alfonso, R. J., & Firth, G. R. (1990). Supervision: Needed research. *Journal Curriculum and Supervision, 5,* 181–188.

Alfonso, R. J., Firth, G. R., & Neville, R. F. (1975). *Instructional supervision.* Boston: Allyn & Bacon.

Ambrose, D., & Cohen, L. M. (1997). The post-industrial era: Finding giftedness in all children. *Focus on Education, 41,* 20–24.

Anderson, R. H. (1993). Clinical supervision: Its history and current context. In R. H. Anderson & K. J. Snyder (Eds.), *Clinical supervision: Coaching for higher performance* (pp. 5–18). Lancaster, PA: Technomic.

Anonymous. (1929). The snoopervisor, the whoopervisor, and the super*visor. Playground and Recreation, 23,* 558.

Association for Supervision and Curriculum Development. (1990). *Another set of eyes* [Video]. Alexandria, VA: Author.

Association for Supervision and Curriculum Development. (1994). *Mentoring the new teacher* [Video series]. Alexandria, VA: Author.

Association for Supervision and Curriculum Development. (1995). *Action research: Inquiry, reflection, and decision-making* [Video series]. Alexandria, VA: Author.

Balliet, T. M. (1894). What can be done to increase the efficiency of teachers in actual service? *National Educational Association Proceedings, 32,* 365–379.

Barr, A. S. (1925). Scientific analyses of teaching procedures. *The Journal Educational Method, 4,* 361–366.

Barr, A. S. (1931). *An introduction to the scientific study of classroom supervision.* New York: Appleton.

Barth, R. S. (1990). *Improving schools from within.* San Francisco: Jossey-Bass.

Benedetti, T. (1997). Tips from the classroom. *TESOL Journal, 7*(1), 41–47.

Bobbitt, F (1913). Some general principles of management applied to the problems of city school systems. In *The twelfth yearbook of the National Society for the Study of Education, Port I, The supervision of city schools* (pp. 7–96). Chicago: University of Chicago Press.

Boehm, A. E., & Weinberg, R. A. (1997). *The classroom observer: Developing observation skills in early childhood settings.* New York: Teachers College Press.

Bolin, F. S. (1987). On defining supervision. *Journal of Curriculum and Supervision, 2,* 368–380,

Bolin, F. S., & Panaritis, P. (1992). Searching for a common purpose: A perspective on the history of supervision. In C. D. Glickman (Ed.), *Supervision in transition* (pp. 30–43). Alexandria, VA: Association for Supervision and Curriculum Development.

Bolton, R. (1979). *People skills.* New York: Simon & Schuster.

Borich, G. D. (2002). *Observation skills for effective teaching.* Columbus, OH: Merrill.

Bowers, C. A., & Flinders, D. J. (1991). *Culturally responsive teaching and supervision: A handbook for staff development.* New York: Teachers College Press.

Bridges, E. (1992). *Problem-based learning for administrators.* Eugene, OR: ERIC Clearinghouse on Educational Management, University of Oregon.

Bullough, W. A. (1974). *Cities and schools in the gilded age.* New York: Kennikat Press.

Burton, W. H. (1930). Probable next steps in the progress of supervision. *Educational Method, 9,* 401–405.

Burton, W. H., & Brueckner, L. J. (1955). *Supervision: A social process.* New York: Appleton-Century-Crofts.

Button, H. W. (1961). *A history of supervision in the public schools, 1870-1950.* Unpublished doctoral dissertation, Washington University, St. Louis, MO.

Calabrese, D., & Zepeda, S. (1997). *The reflective supervisor.* Larchmont, NY: Eye on Education.

Carnegie Forum on Education and the Economy. (1986). *A nation prepared: Teachers for the twenty-first century.* New York: Carnegie Corporation.

Chancellor, W. E. (1904). *Our schools: Their administration and supervision.* Boston: D. C. Heath.

Cienkus, R., Grant Haworth, J., & Kavanagh, J. (1996). Editors' introduction. *Peabody Journal of Education, 71*(1), 1–2.

Cogan, M. L. (1973). *Clinical supervision.* Boston: Houghton Mifflin.

Costa, A., & Garmston, R. (1997). *Cognitive coaching: A foundation for renaissance schools.* Norwood, MA: Christopher Gordon.

Cronin, J. M. (1973). *The control of urban schools.* New York: Free Press.

Danielson, C. (1996). *Enhancing professional practice: A framework for teaching.* Alexandria, VA: Association for Supervision and Curriculum Development.

Daresh, J. C., & Playko, S. (1995). *Supervision as a proactive process.* New York: Longman.

Darling-Hammond, L., & Goodwin, A. L. (1993). Progress toward professionalism in teaching. In G. Cawelti (Ed.), *Challenges and achievements of American education* (pp. 19–52). Alexandria, VA: Association for Supervision and Curriculum Development.

Dewey, J. (1929). *The sources of a science of education.* New York: Liveright.

Dunlap, D. M., & Goldman, P. (1991). Rethinking power in schools. *Educational Administration Quarterly, 27,* 5–29.

Educational Testing Service. (1992). *The second international assessment of educational progress.* Princeton, NJ: Author.

Eisner, E. W. (1994). *The educational imagination* (3rd ed.). New York: Macmillan.

Elliott, J. (1991). *Action research for educational change.* Bristol, PA: Falmer.

Field, B., & Field, T. (1994). *Teachers as mentors: A practical guide.* London: Falmer.

Firth, G. R., & Eiken, K. P (1982), Impact of the schools' bureaucratic structure on supervision. In T. J. Sergiovanni (Ed.), *Supervision of teaching* (pp. 153–169). Washington, DC: Association for Supervision and Curriculum Development.

Fitzpatrick, F. A. (1893). How to improve the work of inefficient teachers. *National Educational Association Proceedings, 31,* 71–78.

Fosnot, C. T. (1993). *In search of understanding the case for constructivist classrooms.* Alexandria, VA: Association for Supervision and Curriculum Development.

Fullan, M. (1991). *The new meaning of educational change.* New York: Teachers College Press.

Fullan, M. (1993). Coordinating school and district development in restructuring. In J. Murphy & P Hallinger (Eds.), *Restructuring schooling: Learning from ongoing efforts* (pp. 143–164). Newbury Park, CA: Corwin.

Garman, N. B. (1997). Is clinical supervision a viable model for use in the public schools? No. In J. Glanz & R. F. Neville (Eds.), *Educational supervision: Perspectives, issues, and controversies*. Norwood, MA: Christopher Gordon.

Glanz, J. (1991). *Bureaucracy and professionalism: The evolution of public school supervision*. Rutherford, NJ: Fairleigh Dickinson University Press.

Glanz, J. (1992). Curriculum development and supervision: Antecedents for collaboration and future possibilities. *Journal of Curriculum and Supervision, 7*, 226–244.

Glanz, J. (1998a). Histories, antecedents, and legacies: Constructing a history of school supervision. In G. R. Firth & E. F. Pajak (Eds.), *Handbook of research on school supervision* (pp. 39–79). New York: Macmillan.

Glanz, J. (1998b). Improvement versus evaluation as an intractable problem in school supervision: Is a reconciliation possible? *Record in Educational Leadership, 16*, 99–104.

Glanz, J. (2002). *Finding your leadership style: A guide for educators*. Alexandria, VA: Association for Supervision and Curriculum Development.

Glanz, J. (2003). *Action research: An educational leader's guide to school improvement* (2nd ed.). Norwood, MA: Christopher Gordon.

Glickman, C. D. (1981). *Developmental supervision*. Washington, DC: Association for Supervision and Curriculum Development.

Glickman, C. D. (Ed.). (1992). *Supervision in transition*. Alexandria, VA: Association for Supervision and Curriculum Development.

Glickman, C. D., Gordon, S. P., & Ross-Gordon, J. M. (1998). *Supervision of instruction: A developmental approach*. Boston: Allyn & Bacon.

Glickman, C. D., Gordon, S. P., & Ross-Gordon, J. (2004). *SuperVision and instructional leadership: A developmental approach* (6th ed.). Boston: Allyn & Bacon.

Goldhammer, R. (1969). Clinical supervision: Special methods for the supervision of teachers. New York: Holt, Rinehart, & Winston.

Goldhammer, R., Anderson, R. H., & Krajewski, R. J. (1993). *Clinical Supervision: Special methods for the supervision of teachers* (3rd ed.). Fort Worth, TX: Harcourt Brace Jovanovich.

Good, T. L., & Brophy, J. E. (2002). *Looking in classrooms* (9th ed.). New York: Longman.

Greenwood, J. M. (1888). Efficient school supervision. *National Educational Association Proceedings, 26*, 519–521.

Greenwood, J. M. (1891). Discussion of Gove's paper. *National Educational Association Proceedings, 19*, 227.

Grimmet, P. P., Rostad, O. P., & Ford, B. (1992). Linking preservice and inservice supervision through professional inquiry. In C. D, Glickman (Ed.), *Supervision in transition* (pp. 169–182). Alexandria, VA: Association for Supervision and Curriculum Development.

Grumet, M. (1979). Supervision and situation: A methodology of self-report for teacher education. *Journal of Curriculum Theorizing, 1*, 191–257.

Hammock, D. C. (1969). *The centralization of New York City's public school system, 1896: A social analysis of a decision*. Unpublished master's thesis, Columbia University.

Harris, B. M. (1969). New leadership and new responsibilities for human involvement. *Educational Leadership, 26*, 739–742.

Hazi, H. M. (1994). The teacher evaluation-supervision dilemma: A case of entanglements and irreconcilable differences. *Journal of Curriculum and Supervision, 9*, 195–216.

Hill, S. (1918). Defects of supervision and constructive suggestions thereon. *National Educational Association Proceedings, 56*, 347–350.

Hill, W. M. (1968). I-B-F supervision: A technique for changing teacher behavior. *The Clearing House, 43*, 180–183.

Hoetker, W. J., & Ahlbrand, W. P. (1969). The persistence of the recitation. *American Educational Research Journal, 6,* 152–176.

Holmes Group. (1986). *Tomorrow's teachers: A report of the Holmes Group.* East Lansing, MI: Author.

Hosic, J. F. (1920). The democratization of supervision. *School and Society, 11,* 331–336.

Hosic, J. F. (1924). The concept of the principalship-II. *The Journal of Educational Method, 3,* 282–284.

Howe, R. L. (1963). *The miracle of dialogue.* New York: Seabury.

Hubbard, R. S., & Power, B. M. (1993). *The art of classroom inquiry: A handbook for teacher-researchers.* Portsmouth, NH: Heinemann.

Hunter, M. (1983). Script-taping: An essential supervisory tool. *Educational Leadership, 41*(3), 43.

Jackson, P (1990). *Life in classrooms.* New York: Teachers College Press.

James, S., Heller, D., & Ellis, W. (1992). Peer assistance in a small district: Windham Southeast, Vermont. In C. D. Glickman (Ed.), *Supervision in transition* (pp. 97–112). Alexandria, VA: Association for Supervision and Curriculum Development.

Johnson, C. A., & Dainton, G. R. (1997). *The learning combination inventory (professional form)* Thousand Oaks, CA: Corwin Press.

Johnson, D. W., & Johnson, R. T. (1989). *Cooperation and competition: Theory and practice.* Edina, MN: Interaction.

Johnson, S. M. (1990). *Teachers at work: Achieving success in our schools.* New York: Basic Books.

Joyce, B., & Showers, B. (1980). Improving inservice training: The messages of research. *Educational Leadership, 37*(2), 379–385.

Kaestle, C. F. (1973). *The evolution of an urban school: New York City 1750-1850.* Cambridge, MA: Harvard University Press.

Kirby, P. C. (1991, April). *Shared decision making: Moving from concerns about restrooms to concerns about classrooms.* Paper presented at the meeting of the American Educational Research Association, Chicago.

Kliebard, H. M. (1987). *The struggle for the American curriculum: 1893-1958.* New York: Routledge & Kegan Paul.

Kolb, D. A. (1984). *Experiential learning: Experience as the source of learning and development.* Englewood Cliffs, NJ: Prentice Hall.

Krug, E. A. (1964). *The shaping of the American high school, 1890–1920.* New York: Harper & Row.

Lazerson, M. (1971). *Origins of the urban school: Public education in Massachusetts, 1870-1915.* Cambridge, MA: Harvard University Press.

Leeper, R. R. (Ed.). (1969). *Supervision: Emerging profession.* Washington, DC: Association for Supervision and Curriculum Development.

Leithwood, K., & Jantzi, D. (1990, April). *Transformational leadership: How principals can help reform school cultures.* Paper presented at the meeting of the American Educational Research Association, Boston.

Lieberman, A. (1995). Practices that support teacher development. *Phi Delta Kappan, 76,* 591–596.

Markowitz, S. (1976). The dilemma of authority in supervisory behavior. *Educational Leadership, 33,* 365–369.

Marshall, C. (1992). *The assistant principal: Leadership choices and challenges.* Newbury Park, CA: Corwin.

McAndrew, W. (1922). The schoolman's loins. *Educational Review, 22,* 90–99.

McBer & Company. (1994). *Inventories.* Boston: Author.

McLean, J. E. (1995). *Improving education through action research: A guide for administrators and teachers.* Thousand Oaks, CA: Corwin.

Murphy, J., & Hallinger, P. (1993). *Restructuring schooling: Learning from ongoing efforts.* Newbury Park, CA: Corwin.

Myers, I. B., & McCaulley, M. H. (1985). *Manual: A guide to the development and use of the Myers-Briggs Type Indicator.* Palo Alto, CA: Consulting Psychologists Press.

National Commission on Excellence in Education. (1983). *A nation at risk: The imperative for educational reform.* Washington, DC: U.S. Department of Education.

Newlon, J. H. (1923). Attitude of the teacher toward supervision. *National Educational Association Proceedings, 61,* 546–549.

Northern Valley Regional High School District. (1996). *Differentiated supervision.* Darnerest, NJ: Author.

Null, G. (1996). *Who are you, really? Understanding your life's energy.* New York: Carroll & Graf.

Osterman, K. E., & Kottkamp, R. B. (1993). *Reflective practice for educators: Improving schooling through professional development.* Thousand Oaks, CA: Corwin.

Osterman, K. E., & Kottkamp, R. B. (2004). *Reflective practice for educators: Improving schooling through professional development* (2nd ed.). Thousand Oaks, CA: Corwin.

Pajak, E. (1989). *The central office supervisor of curriculum and instruction: Setting the stage for success.* Needham, MA: Allyn & Bacon.

Pajak, E. (1993). *Approaches to clinical supervision: Alternatives for improving instruction.* Norwood, MA: Christopher Gordon.

Pajak, E. (2000). *Approaches to clinical supervision: Alternatives for improving instruction* (2nd ed.). Norwood, MA: Christopher Gordon.

Payne, W. H. (1875). *Chapters on school supervision: A practical treatise on superintendency grading; arranging courses of study; the preparation and use of blanks, records and reports; examination for promotion, etc.* New York: Van Antwerp Bragg.

Poole, W. (1994). Removing the "super" from supervision. *Journal of Curriculum and Supervision, 9,* 284–309.

Ravitch, D. (1995). *National standards in American education: A citizen's guide.* Washington, DC: The Brookings Institution.

Reiman, A. J., & Thies-Sprinthall, L. (1998). *Mentoring and supervision for teacher development.* New York: Longman.

Reitzug, U. C. (1997). Images of principal instructional leadership: From supervision to collaborative inquiry. *Journal of Curriculum and Supervision, 12,* 324–343.

Reports of the Record Commissions of the City of Boston. (1709). New York: Teachers College Archives.

Roberts, S. M., & Pruitt, E. Z. (2003). *Schools as professional learning communities: Collaborative activities and strategies for professional development.* Thousand Oaks, CA: Corwin.

Rousmaniere, K. (1992). *City teachers: Teaching in New York City schools in the 1920s.* Unpublished doctoral dissertation, Columbia University.

Schon, D. A. (1988). Coaching reflective teaching. In P. P. Grimmett & G. F. Erickson (Eds.), *Reflection in teacher education* (pp. 19–30). New York: Teachers College Press.

Seguel, M. L. (1966). *The curriculum field: Its formative years.* New York: Teachers College Press.

Sergiovanni, T. J. (1992). Moral authority and the regeneration of supervision. In C. D. Glickman (Ed.), *Supervision in transition* (pp. 30-43). Alexandria, VA: Association for Supervision and Curriculum Development.

Showers, B., & Joyce, B. (1996). The evolution of peer coaching. *Educational Leadership, 53*(6), 12–16.

Silberman, C. E. (1970). *Crisis in the classroom.* New York: Random House.

Smyth, J. (1991). Instructional supervision and the redefinition of who does it in schools. *Journal of Curriculum and Supervision, 7,* 90–99.

Spaulding, F. E. (1955). The application of the principles of scientific management. *National Educational Association Proceedings, 51,* 259–279.

Spears, H. *(1953). Improving the supervision of instruction.* Englewood Cliffs, NJ: Prentice Hall.

Stringer, E. T. (1999). *Action research: A handbook for practitioners* (2nd ed.). Thousand Oaks, CA: Sage.

Tanner, D., & Tanner, L. N. (1987). *Supervision in education: Problems and practices.* New York: Macmillan.

Taylor, F. W. (1911). *The principles of scientific management.* New York: Harper & Brothers.

Tsui, A. B. M. (1995). Exploring collaborative supervision in inservice teacher education. *Journal of Curriculum and Supervision, 10,* 346–371.

Tyack, D. B. (1974). *The one best system: A history of American education.* Cambridge, MA: Harvard University Press.

Tyack, D. B., & Hansot, E. (1982). *Managers of virtue: Public school leadership in America, 1820-1980.* New York: Basic Books.

Weller, R. (1971). *Verbal communication in instructional supervision.* New York: Teachers College Press.

Wilhelms, F. T. (1969). Leadership: The continuing quest. In R. R. Leeper (Ed.), *Supervision: Emerging profession.* Washington, DC: Association for Supervision and Curriculum Development.

Willerman, M., McNeely, S. L., & Koffman Cooper, E., (1991). *Teachers helping teachers: Peer observation and assistance.* New York: Praeger.

Zepeda, S. J., & Ponticell, J. A. (1998). At cross purposes: What do teachers need, want, and get from supervision? *Journal of Curriculum and Supervision, 14*(1), 68–87.

Index

**CORWIN
PRESS**

Barriers to Communication

Barrier Type	Examples
1. Judging	1. Judging
• Criticizing	• "You are lazy; your lesson plan is poor." • "You are inexperienced, an intellectual"
• Name calling and labeling	
• Diagnosing—analyzing motives instead of listening	• "You're taking out your anger on her" • "I know what you need"
• Praising evaluatively	• "You're terrific!"
2. Solutions	2. Solutions
• Ordering	• "You must . . ." "You have to . . ." "You will . . ."
• Threatening	• "If you don't . . ." "You had better or else"
• Moralizing or preaching	• "It is your duty/responsibility; you should"
• Inappropriate questioning or prying	• "Why?" "What?" "How?" "When?"
• Advising	• "What I would do is . . ." "It would be best for you"
• Lecturing	• "Here is why you are wrong . . ." "Do you realize . . ."
3. Avoiding the other's concerns	3. Avoiding the Other's Concerns
• Diverting	• "Speaking of . . ." "Apropos . . ." "You know what happened to . . ."
• Reassuring	• "It's not so bad . . ." "You're lucky . . ." "You'll feel better"
• Withdrawing	• "I'm very busy. . ." "I can't talk right now . . ." "I'll get back to you . . ."
• Sarcasm	• "I really feel sorry for you"

Communication Techniques

Listening	Nonverbal Clues	Reflecting and Clarifying
"Uh-huh"	Affirmative nods and smiles	"You're angry because . . ."
"OK"		
"I'm following you"	Open body language, e.g., arms open	"You feel . . . because . . ."
"For instance"		"You seem quite upset."
"And?"	Appropriate distance from speaker—not too close or too far	"So, you would like . . ."
"Mmm"		"I understand that you see the problem as . . ."
"I understand"		
"This is great information for me"	Eye contact	"I'm not sure, but I think you mean . . ."
	Nondistracting environment	
"Really?"	Face speaker and lean forward	"I think you're saying . . ."
"Then?"		
"So?"	Barrier-free space, e.g., desk not used as blocker	
"Tell me more"		
"Go on"		
"I see"		
"Right"		

KEY STEPS—COLLABORATIVE APPROACH

1. Identify the problem from the teacher's perspective, soliciting as much clarifying information as possible.
2. Reflect back what you've heard for accuracy.
3. Begin collaborative brainstorming, asking the teacher for his or her ideas first.
4. Problem-solve through a sharing and discussion of options.
5. Agree on a plan and follow-up meeting.

KEY STEPS—PLANNING CONFERENCE

1. Decide the focus of the observation (choose an interpersonal approach).
2. Determine the method and form of observation.
3. Set the time of the observation and the postconference.

KEY STEPS—COLLABORATIVE REFLECTION

1. What was valuable in what we have been doing?
2. What was of little value?
3. What changes would you suggest for the next cycle?

KEY STEPS—DIRECTIVE INFORMATIONAL APPROACH

1. Identify the problem or goal and solicit clarifying information.
2. Offer solutions. Ask for the teacher's input into the alternatives offered and request additional ideas.
3. Summarize chosen alternatives, ask for confirmation, and request that the teacher restate final choices.
4. Set a follow-up plan and meeting.

KEY STEPS—SELF-DIRECTED APPROACH

1. Listen carefully to the teacher's initial statement.
2. Reflect back your understanding of the problem.
3. Constantly clarify and reflect until the real problem is identified.
4. Have the teacher problem-solve and explore the consequences of various actions.
5. The teacher commits to a decision and firms up a plan.
6. The supervisor restates the teacher's plan and sets a follow-up meeting.